Music, Politics and Alternative Culture

Festivalized

Ian Abrahams

Bridget Wishart

Typeset by Jonathan Downes, Jessica Taylor
Cover by Bridget Wishart
Layout by SPiderKaT for CFZ Communications
Using Microsoft Word 2000, Microsoft Publisher 2000, Adobe Photoshop CS.

First published in Great Britain by Gonzo Multimedia

c/o Brooks City,
6th Floor New Baltic House
65 Fenchurch Street,
London EC3M 4BE
Fax: +44 (0)191 5121104
Tel: +44 (0) 191 5849144
International Numbers:
Germany: Freephone 08000 825 699
USA: Freephone 18666 747 289

ISBN: 978-1-908728-57-9

Table of Contents

Dedication

For Mum, Dad, Martin and Hannah, for making it possible
(BW)

For Keith Topping, who knew I could do this stuff long before I ever did
(IA)

DEEPLY VALE
FREE
FESTIVAL '77
JULY 22nd-24th. 3 DAZE of SUMMER FUN FOR EVERYONE. AT DEEPLY VALE. JUST OUTSIDE BURY, LANCS. ON THE A.56.
ROCK 'N' ROLL
STREET THEATRE.
POETS
FOLK
tractor, cry tough, mudanzas, gin-seng
physical wrecks, body, alchemist, S.F.W.
frogbox, starfinder, pegasus, snapper,
moonchild, bashful alley, white fire,
welcome, leviathan, sanctuary. .
trigger, movement, banned...
bring what u expect
...to find...
A FESTIVAL FOR LOVE, PEACE & FREEDOM

Acknowledgements

The authors gratefully acknowledge the time, support and encouragement of the myriad festival-goers that have generously contributed to this book; a list of contributors appears in the appendices so we'll not mention all of you by name here as well but your recollections, opinions, observations and anecdotes are very much valued and appreciated.

We are eternally grateful to Emma Wishart, whose proofreading skills have saved us from so many typographical embarrassments, and whose incisive queries and observations have benefited the whole book.

In addition, Bridget makes the following appreciations:

A big thank you here to my mum and dad (RIP Dad), who are responsible for my existence, Martin and Hannah for their unswerving support and patience, and Ian's family for being so generous with him.

A big shout out to my old band mates and festival buddies… if not for the 'legendary' Demented Stoats where would we be now? Hippy Slags, best band ever… thanks for all the good times!

Ian makes the following appreciations:

As always, primary thanks are due to Janet, Lucas, Morgan and Niall for their support throughout the writing of this book, whether I was cranky, absorbed, travelling away from home or taking phone calls at all sorts of weird times! Thanks also to Martin and Hannah, for putting up with my constant visits... and for putting me up on those occasions as well!

For my original interest in music, cheers to the assembled members of the Redruth Comprehensive School lunchtime record club, in particular: Robert Bennetts, Simon Coley, Tim Stevens, and Mark Vinson. Thanks also to my other musical comrades: Scott Abraham, Raymond Altree, Joe Beer, Martin Day, Andrew Dunn, Alan Linsley, Stuart Miller, and Richard Pascoe.

In writing this book, we solicited as good a cross-section of views and recollections as possible, and they are presented here to reflect the broad spectrum of outlooks that informed the free festival scene. The authors do not necessarily agree with or endorse the individual views expressed.

Introduction

Our journey into the history of the free festivals intended to focus on the events and back story of the festivals of the 1980s. After all, one of us experienced many of these happenings at first hand and knew many of the movers, shakers and characters from the festivals of that era.

Quickly, the project grew and refocused itself to become a survey of the free festivals from the early 1970s, taking a notional starting point of the protests outside the gates of the 1970 Isle of Wight Festival by The Pink Fairies and Hawkwind and a cut-off at the Castlemorton Common Festival in 1992. In doing so, we expanded our subject matter to the level at which a planned in-depth survey of a specific era gave way to a more impressionistic reportage of the concept and ethos of the free festivals.

As we collected research material and interviewed people across the entire involvement of festival-goers, from 'organisers' (and opinions were sharply divided amongst contributors as to whether that term was even relevant), performers, artists, attendees, and landowners, we saw our initial concept of including as wide a spectrum of voices as possible transform itself. In particular, the importance of the campfire camaraderie, juxtaposed with the multitude of opinions, whether contradictory or complementary, that emerged from our conversations with those passionate about the value and benefits of the festivals, led us eventually to take a non-linear route through the history of the festivals. Instead, we came to see it as a mosaic of those campfire conversations on different but interconnected elements.

Once we'd seen the flow of the book in those terms, we understood what we had here, and what we didn't have. So this book isn't a comprehensive record of the free festivals and you won't find here any chronological listings of those festivals and details of which bands played at which events. In any case, such information is readily to hand for those who need the 'facts and figures' and no better place exists (in our view) than to point the reader in the direction of the 'Great White Shark' and his highly-regarded Internet resource *The Archive: A History of*

UK rock festivals (ukrockfestivals.com). Likewise, both the history of the Stonehenge Festival and the subsequent chaos of the 'Battle of the Beanfield' have been set down in print by Andy Worthington, and it's difficult to envisage any accounts of these elements of the festivals being better recorded and written about.

We have, therefore, presented here an impressionistic account of the festivals, their roots, development, pinnacle and descent as told by the people who were there, who cared about these gatherings and who have taken the experiences gained from being involved and contributing to the festivals with them through the rest of their lives. A patchwork chronicle, if you like. If by doing this we've only scratched the surface of some of the issues and skimmed across others, then that's just the nature of our task in pulling together the disparate strands of our subject and attempting to provide a flavour of how these things worked and the way in which they informed the people who lived through them.

For readers who come to this book looking to relive their experiences, we hope that you find us capturing the essence of the free festival movement in the right way. Though we've written about the bad alongside the good, our intention has always been to uphold the history of the festivals in a positive way. If you've arrived at our text with little or no previous exposure to the subject, we intend that you find this book a starting point to discovering the music, politics and alternative culture of the free festivals.

Ian Abrahams
Bridget Wishart
Autumn 2015

Cast of Contributors in Order of Appearance

Nik Turner – Hawkwind, Inner City Unit, Sphynx
Peter Pracownik – Pink Fairies, Astralasia, artist
Jake Stratton-Kent – Attendee, writer
Marc Swordfish – Magic Mushroom Band, Astralasia,
Mick Farren – The Deviants, writer
Nigel Mazlyn Jones – Guitarist, Singer/Songwriter, Campaigner
Big Steve – Polytantric Stage Manager
Adrian Shaw – Magic Muscle, Hawkwind
John Perry – Magic Muscle II, The Only Ones
Michael Dog – Indoor festival organiser
Steve Lake – Zounds
Bob Whitfield – Manager of Magic Muscle, photographer
Janet Henbane – Attendee
Bill The Boat - Attendee
Keith Bailey – Here & Now
Dave Roberts – Attendee, band manager, merchandiser
Dolores Dina – Attendee
Penny Rimbaud – Crass, Dial House, musician and writer
Joie Hinton – Ozric Tentacles, Eat Static
Rory Cargill – The Invisible Band
Angel Flame – Attendee, dancer
Steve Bubble – BubbleDubble
Oz Hardwick – Attendee, photographer
Simon Williams – Mandragora
Richard Chadwick – Demented Stoats, Smartpils, Hawkwind
Jeremy Cunningham – The Levellers
Dick Lucas – Sub-humans, Culture Shock, Citizen Fish
Gary Bamford – 2000DS
Mick Moss – Attendee, writer
Bridget Wishart – Demented Stoats, Hippy Slags, Hawkwind

Steve Bemand – Demented Stoats, Smartpils
Klive Farhead – Attendee, musician
Angie Bell – Hippy Slags
Claire Grainger – Hippy Slags, Smartpils
Charlie Dancey – Sign-writer, Juggler
Chris Hewitt – Organiser of Deeply Vale festivals
Martin - Attendee
Glenda Pescado – Tibetan Ukrainian Mountain Troupe
Daryn Manchip – Attendee
Jocelyn – Attendee
Wayne Twining – Magic Mushroom Band, Astralasia
Paul Bagley – Omnia Opera
Adrian Bell – Attendee
Clint Iguana – Fanzine editor
Kevin Ellis – Dr Brown
Jerry Richards – Tubilah Dog, Hawkwind
Jah Free – DJ
Sarah Evans – Hippy Slags
David Stooke – Attendee, painter
Peter Loveday – Attendee, artist & writer of Russell the Hippie
Mark Wright – Attendee
Eleanor – Local observer
Paul Sample – Salisbury Council
Matty – Attendee
Sheila Wynter – Landowner
Craig Gregory – Attendee
Roger Neville-Neil – Attendee, writer
Boris Atha – Boris & His Bolshie Balalaika - musician
Danny – Back2Front fanzine
Hippie Van Man – Attendee
Sim Simmer – Spiral Tribe

Early Days: The Pursuit of Hedonism

Nik Turner: A festival is about everybody, it's a total thing and the focal point is as important as the peripheral things. I got involved in festivals with Hawkwind. During the Isle of Wight festival in 1970 The Pink Fairies, who were trying to put stuff together, suggested we perform in this big canvas tent there, which they said they were going to play in. In fact, they only turned up for a day, whilst Hawkwind were down there for a week playing. They instigated it but had other things to do and we played, and it was a sort of release. We were representing the spirit of freedom and enlightenment, fun and harmony with music, while this other Isle of

Stonehenge 1983 by David Stooke

Wight Festival was representing something which might have been termed a corruption of an idea of a festival. That was just a performance space for a load of bands and the people who had come to see them and not in the spirit of what a festival should be.

Peter Pracownik: In the early 60s, people really started to think a bit more; they were allowed to read more books. And by reading more you want to *know* more and you get Zen with it because no-one's listening to you. So the only way to actually converse with other people is to have a happening, in a park or out in a field. They developed that way, and then they became love-ins. I think the first Glastonbury was trying to keep that alive, just like Stonehenge would in the 80s, people of the same consciousness coming together.

Nik Turner: The festival movement really started with the Isle of Wight 1970. There had been other Isle of Wight festivals or events like The Rolling Stones in Hyde Park but there it really seemed like the festival movement was commencing. Whether that was the arrival of LSD in peoples' lives or whether it was a spin-off from the Haight-Ashbury where they had these big festivals with the Grateful Dead or Jefferson Airplane... People arriving in San Francisco all out of their heads on LSD and having sustenance provided for them by the Diggers. It was like a world movement, really!

Jake Stratton-Kent: I was a teenage runaway. My mum lived down in Cornwall so I headed down. There was a one-day festival at the Tregae Hotel [near Truro] with Hawkwind and Arthur Brown... and free apple juice went around. A couple of the older types said, 'Oh yeah, ask what's in it,' but I thought, 'Ah, they're just being generous.' Knocked it back, and by the time that Hawkwind and Arthur Brown were jamming at the end I was completely off my head, had to rush the stage and get up there with the guys! Which was all very friendly... it was understood that it would happen! I bought a copy of *Frendz* underground magazine while I was there, and it was a revelation. I started to lose interest in Trotsky and Mao Tse-tung and got interested in a more psychedelic revolution. Rebellion came with the territory. There was youth radicalisation, and *Easy Rider* had just come out... I wanted to be a revolutionary, a biker... all these sorts of things, my role models were from the counterculture. I lost interest in communism and looked to a more spiritual evolution.

Peter Pracownik: It's all pretty much about young people being angry. It's that, 'Don't do that, son,' thing ... and you go, 'Why?' And the only answer is, 'Because I said so.' It's not explained 'why'. There was lots of stuff being thrown at younger people in a sort of 'that's how it is' way. So you think, 'No, I don't agree with that,' like Vietnam... we didn't think it was right and we didn't like people dying. By having these festivals you were able to meet like-minded people into the culture and the music, people experimenting with drugs because they didn't believe their fathers. They were anti-establishment, they had to go out and find things out for themselves.

Swordfish: I look at it another way. I see it as something more primal and old, the ritual of dancing around the fire.

Peter Pracownik: It's where the rebellion comes in … 'Make Love not War' and 'Fuck the Queen'. The anti-establishment became angrier as the decades moved on. But hasn't it always been anti-establishment? It goes back to deeper roots where people wanted to separate themselves from being controlled. Now we've got the Internet and that gives us a lot more answers than we could ever have got from *Oz* or *International Times* or *Frendz*. There's more information to be had and it has become more and more complicated. But it's like music, it appeals personally and if you can send a message through that way, like-minded people will pick up on what you're trying to say.

Mick Farren: The concept of the free concert really started in city parks, in London, San Francisco and New York, and then spread overnight. You wouldn't have expected, even though it was only seven or eight years apart, to go to see Adam Faith in Hyde Park. That would have been 'What? That's weird...' Seven years later: 'Sure, Pink Floyd in the Park, great.' That was the whole breaking down of music supply providers, a whole new way of doing it. Putting a bunch of bands on for a long weekend in a farmer's field was the same kind of valuable thinking. The big problem if you were going to go down that route was feeding the people, disposing of their excrement and collecting money from them. Those were the three things that caused the most problems and what people talked about: the toilets, how much it cost and how bad the food was.

Nik Turner: The music was very important, but so was the peace-and-love ethic. Festivals should have represented freedom, and been promoted as being about natural forces. You can't quantify that by putting a fence around it and charging people to go in. Maybe the festivals became a thing about a lot of people getting out of their heads on drugs. I think of the ancient festivals and that probably happened then as well, but with a purpose to it. Sometimes people can miss the point about those things but it doesn't mean they weren't enthusiastic about its spirit. Even if they got involved in celebration through drugs... that they got involved at all was a very valid thing. The drugs might have been immaterial really, just the catalyst for people to awaken their awareness, their celebration of the festival. I suppose people got involved with the festivals almost by accident really, a gathering of like-minded people probably not realising what they were doing and all getting high together… everybody's spirits raised.

Mick Farren: There was a great wave of exploration which went in many possible directions, sometimes all at once. Particularly in your own head! All things were possible, and all things were try-able. 'Don't say it can't be done until you've tried it' became such a maxim, a lot more than one might have expected. There were a lot of landmark events that crystallised the counterculture coming together. The first I recall was Bob Dylan and The Band at The Royal Albert Hall in 1966. After the folkies had walked out there was a whole bunch of freaks left over that you'd only seen from the top of the bus before. At that point the awareness came to people like [Barry] Miles and Hoppy, John Hopkins, that there might be things to be done. They opened The UFO Club and started putting out *International Times*. There was the *International Times* launch party at The Roundhouse where people saw The Pink Floyd and Soft Machine, and there must have been seven or eight hundred people there. The UFO opened up and the first few nights there were only a couple of hundred people but that quickly outgrew the Blarney Club on Tottenham Court Road. IT got busted and Hoppy organised the Alexandra Palace '14 Hour Technicolor Dream' as a benefit and eight, nine, ten thousand people turned up. That progressed on to fifty, eighty thousand people showing up in Hyde Park until by the time the Stones played there, it was a quarter of a million, you know? The thing was snowballing and it seemed for a while there, we might have been able to take over the world, though that would have inevitably been a disappointment! But so many things were proving to be more than the sum of their parts that it was baffling. Some negative things grew out of this snowball effect, the water was so disturbed that the sharks started moving in and other people started thinking, 'Jesus, this is all too much for me, I'd better start taking heroin.' It wasn't all positives, but it wasn't all negatives either. It ballooned and the idea of getting yourself down in a field was one of the logical ways of going about it. How you survived in that field became a matter of some debate, angst and even direct action, but it was such a breaking of the rules of the way things had been done before. It was kind of a natural outcome because it just outgrew anything that could contain it.

Nik Turner: There was Sid Rawle, who ended up living in a tepee and wanting to be one of the controllers or representatives of the festival movement. He was projected as the 'King of the Hippies' by the newspapers but I don't think he saw himself like that or went around saying that, it was just a label. I knew him for a long time and he had the right sort of spirit about him, but there were conflicting ideas as to what the festivals should be about. Some people thought it should be about taking loads of drugs, or selling drugs, promoting drugs, but that wasn't my view of festivals. You can imagine that Stonehenge Festival two thousand years ago was very much like it was thirty years ago. I wrote a song about it, 'Stonehenge Who Knows' which was about the Roman army attacking the Celts and Boadicea. But it was in fact an analogy where the Romans were the police and the Celts the festival-goers. You can see how it would have been, people getting out of their heads on mead and fly agarics and transporting themselves into another place just like people in modern times with LSD and magic mushrooms.

Nigel Mazlyn Jones: You could go back to the Russian fairy stories of the 1800s and the pictorial representation that accompanied the old folktales. You'd have a fresco around a page of writing, which would, nine times out of ten, contain psilocybin and fly agarics. Some elements of a nation, the writers, the artists, the theatre people, will always explore. Street theatre has been going on forever and a day, in fact the predecessor to the newspaper was the balladeer doing theatre and song and bawdy humour on the street corner, saying 'Old King so-and-so is being cuckolded down in London.' It might have been inaccurate news reporting and embroidered by the telling and the re-telling and designed to entertain, but these people, if you think about it, started free festivals.

Mick Farren: [The counterculture] was a lot of broken up things that got conglomerated for real. There was no master plan, no linear progression. It was an organic thing with one cellular group backing into another and hooking up. For instance, the moment people needed to be fed, when they'd been at something more than five or six hours and needed to be seriously fed something more than ice-cream and hot dogs, it immediately reversed into the wholefood people and the vegans. You'd find yourselves eating tahini and rice cakes and thinking, 'Is this food?' But that was all there was. Okay, we'd go along with that, and it was a whole new perspective on, 'From each according to his ability, to each according to his needs.' That fasci-

Bread Factory Watchfield 1975 (Mick Moss)

nated me about open-air festivals. When I was at school we used to have cadets and we'd have a field day every term and there was a kind of atmosphere like that. Festivals also took on aspects of a post-apocalypse, neo-medieval, spaghetti western thing where everybody got to play out what they wanted to do. For instance, before puberty I was a pyromaniac and all that came back, especially at Glastonbury because I was quite obsessed with building the biggest fire on the field, which worked really well because if you had the biggest fire people would pass by, bringing hash and opium and bottles of Bacardi or God knows what! That was a lot of fun because it all became very tribal and atavistic, and as a science fiction writer I fucking loved it! It generated a great source of material, watching strange tribal patterns emerge.

Fireside view of Stage 2 at 88 Acktivator (Sheila Wynter)

[note they're burning a barbed wire fence!]

Politics and the 1970s

A rock 'n' roll hedonism that didn't have any political consciousness?

Big Steve: 'No Politics' was our motto, written on the door of our squat, where on the other side everything was so alternative and utopian.

Mick Farren: I see it kind of like looking in a pond; chuck a stone in a pond and the first ripples are very strong. Here, the first intense ripples were the Panthers, White or Black, which went from armed revolution to intense mysticism. The further you move from ground zero, the milder the ripples become. You had the seeds of the women's movement, the seeds of animal rights. Then you had the seeds of a very radical change in styles, of the green movement. You had the first awareness that things were environmentally amiss. Now the same ideas are incorporated into the political platform. If you go back and look at *New Statesman* or *The Times* and see what they were writing about, and you see what *Oz* and *IT* were writing about you see very crucial things kicking off. The women's movement and the environment were, I think, the two major scores that came out of the counterculture because those things were not being discussed then in the terms they are discussed now. And of course the whole question of recreational and mystical drug use, that was a complete revolution. The war on drugs was the greatest defeat the authorities ever had to stomach. It's still going on but it has been lost, and lost, and lost. All we haven't achieved is legalisation but it's really a matter of time and logistics, it has to be... anybody who wants to pop a drug these days, can. And of course the Anti-War movement reasserted itself, it didn't stop the war but it caused enough trouble when Bush and Blair wanted to go into Iraq.

Adrian Shaw: [Powys Square demonstrators] were only peripherally involved with the festival scene, I'd say. People like Mick Farren of course, had a foot in both camps. I went on the Ban the Bomb marches as a stripling, so I was politically motivated when I was a young man of sixteen, seventeen. But after that I didn't attend any rallies, certainly didn't riot, and I'm not aware of anyone that was involved in that movement being involved in the festivals, with the exception of [Mick] Farren. I'm sure there were some, but it's nothing that's sprung up in any conversation. It was more a visceral thing than a moral… for the people I was involved with there wasn't much political motivation; it was party time.

Mick Farren: Well, they *were* the same people, give or take... Grosvenor Square, I mean me and Sandy from The Deviants, we went along; we drove back from somewhere up north that night and got very seriously hauled over by the police somewhere around Watford when they started searching the vans for something other than a quick deal. They were looking for weapons, or whatever, and made no bones about it. We got back around dawn and went to bed, and about 2.30pm me and Sandy got up, because we'd shared a communal band apartment on Shaftesbury Avenue, and went and looked on the balcony and there were troops of motorcycle cops. This was where Gower Street, New Oxford Street and Shaftesbury Avenue met and it was like a fucking revolution was going on. So we went along, ran for miles along the way, joined the march to Trafalgar Square somewhere near Centre Point and followed the adventure through. We encountered Mick Jagger along the way, and also the Liverpool Anarchists which is actually where we cut ourselves in because they were a jolly bunch of crew. There were fucking insane German Maoists, and union geezers from Yorkshire who wouldn't have seen themselves as part of the counterculture, they were old-fashioned lefties, socialists and communists. Certainly Vanessa Redgrave and Tariq Ali were not terribly fond of me, because I was ideologically 'unsound.' They'd have put me up against the wall and shot me if they'd had their revolution! At that point in time there were a lot of different facets but certainly what you might call the 'Psychedelic Left' was a part of it, but not an organising part because it was Tariq and Vanessa's show. We were the manpower. The Hells Angels weren't there, so they weren't a part of the Psychedelic Left, but they were a part of the counterculture even though their 'political' responses didn't warrant much probing, in fact it didn't go much deeper than a Nazi armband, but what the fuck? As long as they didn't actually believe that shit, we were okay. They were politically unaware, and I wasn't about to start educating them.

Big Steve: I think it was totally hedonistic, very much an exploration of the senses with lots of experimentation with drugs. There was such a wide range available, hash from Lebanon, red and blonde hash, incredible hashish from Afghanistan, Honey Oil from India, Indian hash, Nepalese Temple Balls, Kashmir, Thai Stick, Durban Poison, Lambs Bread, Sensemilla, such a variety, if you were a hash smoker you could become quite a connoisseur, a delight of flavours. These countries weren't warzones then; people coming back from travelling were bringing fresh produce from those areas. There was a huge selection, like being in an Amsterdam coffee shop. But it wasn't only about drugs, there was also a raising and expansion of consciousness about important alternative movements, especially green issues and the peace movement, tribal rights, racism and feminism, and new age spiritualism. But on top of all the experience the most intoxicating thing in my mind was freedom, the awakening. The seeds of

Utopia sometimes blossomed, and were glimpsed in the seemingly chaotic state of the free festivals' strong and healthy heart.

Mick Farren: Most of its core had a line back to CND, I would think. There was also a 'Psychedelic Right', with the Church of the Final Judgement and all kinds of weirdoes like that, ultimately the Manson family. There was a whole political spectrum and lots of arguments; it was organic, nothing went according to plan, but that's what makes things interesting. One time, there was some kind of event in [Hyde] Park and people making speeches and this other bunch shouting, 'Oh, shut the fuck up, play the music.' That's all they wanted to do, a rock 'n' roll hedonism that didn't have any political consciousness.

John Perry: My friend Steve Mann was big mates with Russell, The Pink Fairies' drummer, and together with Mick Farren they set up the White Panther Party. Steve was the 'Minister for Information', though I always felt that 'Minister for Black Leather Trousers' was more like it. I think it's stretching things a bit to call the White Panther Party in England political, it was really a bunch of people out of their heads, having a laugh and trying to make themselves famous. I love Mick Farren, and his autobiography *Give the Anarchist A Cigarette* is a fine book, but I wouldn't take his politics too seriously. The Social Deviants and The Pink Fairies were more or less the same bunch of people, centred round the underground press, *IT*, *Oz*, and *Frendz* magazine which grew out of Jann Wenner's attempt to start an English edition of *Rolling Stone*.

Mick Farren: The reason why The White Panthers were instituted as a sort of holding company was for our end of the actions at the Isle of Wight. Ed Barker and Pete Cohen and some of the Phun City boys drove down there just to have a look at what was going on and were hideously appalled, so we went back to *IT* with some rapid calculations. It struck me that they'd put on The Who, The Doors, Sly & The Family Stone, such an enormous bill with such a massive security expenditure to collect the money, that most of the available capital for the entire English counterculture in the summer of 1970 was being sucked into the Isle of Wight Festival like a black hole. They owed *IT* for three back pages, they owed *Oz* the same, and that was just *underground* press advertising, they owed printers and if that thing came apart, as it clearly would, the one thing we couldn't do was have *IT* linked directly with the actions, we needed plausible deniability. We said, 'Let's have some kind of organisation that's doing this', and we put out a newsletter telling people there was this huge hill beside the site, that wasn't part of the site but from where you could actually see the bands better than if you paid. That was *White Panther Communiqué no. 5*; there wasn't 1, 2, 3 and 4, just 5, and it came out of a bit of hippie humour. It could have been The Psychedelic Rangers, could have been anything, but it was The White Panther Party. We printed up a load of badges and suddenly we were a movement. After the Isle of Wight it seemed too good to let go, there were people down the

Grove, and people in Manchester, various chapters formed up and down the country and a lot of them took their own emphasis. The boys from Ladbroke Grove were doing the free food kitchens because there were a lot of homeless hippies there, and dossers who could use a meal. Manchester did a similar thing but they were a little more artistic, so it was like a franchise and it went according to the needs and inclinations of those who were doing it in a particular area. All they had in common was the badge and rhetoric borrowed from [MC5 Manager] John Sinclair and adapted for England, because England isn't that... we don't have as many organisations as the Americans, we don't have Elks Lodges or Shiners to the same degree. It took off for a while and was useful if you needed an organisational facade to go and negotiate something. If you were going to stick Hawkwind on at Portobello Green, using the White Panthers as an intermediary meant there was someone who was speaking for Dave Brock who wasn't Dave Brock, so if something went wrong he didn't have to carry the can; it was a functional thing.

Nik Turner: The Pink Fairies were anarchistic in their way but then I think Hawkwind were as well. I don't know whether they were doing it for effect; they were quite intelligent people and were into the celebration of the festivals and quite anarchistic about the commercial festivals. They were willing to put their energies to a festival that would be a free festival as opposed to a commercial one.

Michael Dog: I grew up in London and hung out around the Portobello Road quite a lot and became aware of the tail-end of the Notting Hill squatting and hippie scene of the mid-70s. There had been a very strong freak scene in London. They put on free concerts in the summer at a place called Meanwhile Gardens in Notting Hill and another venue under the flyover at Acklam Road. Hawkwind were part of that scene and lived in that area, though by the time I became part of it they'd moved on. I was about fourteen and was really impressed with these free events where everyone was very friendly. Through that, I became aware of Here & Now who'd just begun to do their Floating Anarchy tour, so it must have been about 1977 and that led me to eventually go to Stonehenge. The festival scene went hand in hand with the alternative culture of the time. It's something that I struggle to convey to younger people when I'm talking to them about it, how different it is now to how it was then. As a teenager I came into a ready-made scene that had a regular and dedicated underground press devoted to writing *International Times* and the gamut of magazines that were printed at the time. People who were very much involved with politics and squatting and various human rights movements and a festival scene that was a manifestation or a celebration of that. In the winter these people would all go back to their squats around the country and do their political stuff, or whatever they were into, then in the summer they came out to the festivals. It was a joined-up culture; every bit of it was an essential part of all the other bits. Now people go to a festival in the summer and it's a reflection of their lifestyle and headspaces but it's almost in isolation, whereas at that time many people would spend the whole summer on the road and there were at least thirty free festivals every summer. You were spoilt for choice and it was just down to where you were in the country as to which you'd go to. So if there was one in Wales and one in Norfolk, if you lived nearer to Norfolk you went to Norfolk - but it was all connected.

Steve Lake: The thing about anarchy and Here & Now, they really were like a junior version of Gong, Daevid Allen's band, who were obviously a lot older. Daevid Allen had been around since the beginning of time, along with Burroughs and Alan Ginsberg in Paris. He was quite politically sophisticated. Through getting into Here & Now and listening to Gong and stuff, although it was hippie, trippy, weird spiritual kind of bollocks in some ways, it was also this thing about floating anarchy and finding your own way in life, finding your own ways of organising stuff with people. So I was aware of the idea of anarchy, in those terms. It was not as though I'd read any anarchist philosophers. I haven't read that many to this day. But this weird idea of freedom and doing what you want and not hurting anyone else, it was just very attractive to me. I mean the whole idea that you could have an alternative scene. Many people, including myself, just felt absolutely alienated from straight life and the world of work and all the rest of it. I know that whole hippie thing is written off as a very middle class thing but there were a lot of working class people, I came from a background of factory workers and I very quickly thought, working the rest of my life in some horrible noisy fucking factory making somebody else rich seems a pretty poor alternative to hanging out in fields, playing music and being with nice people! I very quickly raised the idea that there was this alternative culture and that between us we could work things out. As we were becoming more sophisticated you could look back on the older people, because I was at school when all that initial hippie thing was going on but you could see how all that had been packaged and sold and rather than any expression of a new alternative community actually became just a new way of marketing rock-music records to people. I was really keen on the idea of alternative things, of Free Festivals, of your own kind of networks of doing things and distributing things.

Adrian Shaw: It was very much an alternative counterculture agenda. We were a bunch of freaks. I'd hesitate to call us hippies because there was a distinction between hippies and freaks. We weren't into kaftans and bells, but we were into psychedelics and the music. I think that was a reasonable difference between the two. [Shaw was a founder-member of psychedelic rock band Magic Muscle].

Bob Whitfield: Hippies were tedious! The freaks were the kind of people who were definitely into a good time. The hippies would follow anything that happened. They would follow this kind of set, that kind of set. 'Let's form a commune,' like the Global Village Trucking Company. Nice guys, but they didn't have an edge to them, they were all privileged really. Magic Muscle were the real thing, even Hawkwind knew they were the real thing. We were living that lifestyle. It wasn't like we had any ideals at all. The people that surrounded Magic Muscle, including the Hells Angels, were heavy types, people who were going to experiment with themselves, people who had an edge to them.

Adrian Shaw: We were interested in the counterculture; we were a part of it. Once we had a band we wanted to be a greater part of it. Initially we genuinely believed in an admittedly hazily drawn-up 'better way of doing things'; in the early days of the ecological movement we realised the planet was under threat. But very quickly it turned into a hedonistic thing, and I have to say that by the time of Magic Muscle it was more about putting two fingers up to authority, rather than any expectation of changing things. We really did want to just do our thing and be left alone. It wasn't even particularly confrontational; it was simply a case of having our own lifestyle and not appreciating people trying to interfere in it. I can't claim there was any genuine desire to change things; it really was a hedonistic thing. We did like our drugs, sex and rock 'n' roll. They were the prime motivating factors in what we were doing. I've always felt if you were not harming anyone, not frightening the horses, you should be left alone to do as you choose. We did what we did and enjoyed doing it, though my habits have modified quite a bit since those days! I think I counted eleven or twelve former band mates who are no longer with us, it's a lot of people, so I'm just grateful to still be in good health and capable of picking up the bass.

Big Steve: I'd written a project at school on why we should legalise cannabis; the law was creating a lot of damage and criminalising a lot of young people. I'd gone up to Release, which was an organisation set up by Caroline Coon and Rufus Harris to deal with prisoners' rights, abortion, feminist issues, the whole range of 60s counterculture [issues]. I was in London to do some research and they had a lot of leaflets from an organisation in San Francisco called the Do It Now Foundation, one of the first alternative editorials producing drug information for young people. Not information given by the government, this was information given by drug workers or people who were actually taking the drugs and it gave a lot of information about contemporary drug use in America, but was also being used by Release as part of their library of drug information. At the time, Release had issued a book called *The Truckers' Bible*, a book that explained about English freaks who'd been busted in different parts of the world, and sentencing procedures everywhere from Morocco to Turkey, Lebanon, Afghanistan, India, and Nepal. It was the story of the people, the travellers who'd gone out and had unfortunately got busted. While I was there, I went to the Bit cafe, a forerunner of the Squatters' Advisory Service. BIT had a café underneath the Westway; this must have been about 1970 when I went down there and hung out. They had a magazine called *BIT News* which was even more alternative than *Oz*, *IT* or *Frendz* magazines. I was thrown into this world of the radical, alternative counterculture, but my motivation was to do with this school project about legalising cannabis! That was what got me interested in doing more research.

[*The Truckers' Bible* was published in 1973. Conservative MP Ronald Bell described the book as "a guide to pot smuggling" and requested the Attorney General refer the publication to the Director of Public Prosecutions. In a House of Commons debate on 23rd July, 1973 Bell thought it 'quite wrong for such seditious matters to be published without there being any question of a breach of the law.' He further went on to request an inquiry into 'the connection which appears to exist between the condoning of drug trafficking and the encouragement of drug taking and certain elements of the Liberal Party.']

Janet Henbane: I remember in the early 70s, going down to London with friends who knew people at Bit; they put out guides such as *Overland To India.* Bit was part of that 'underground' scene that was happening then, it was all new and exciting for me because I was young and finding out about life in the big wide world. I was about seventeen. I lived for a while with friends who were squatting up the road from Release, in Ashmore Road, a lively multi-cultural scene with lots of reggae music and a good buzz. It's a shame that it later on became a junkie house. I lived with friends in other squats: Burton Road in Brixton, Agnes Place, and I also knew people who lived down Grosvenor Road, another well-known squatter's paradise. *IT* - *International Times* - and *Oz* magazine also, full of alternative stuff, books, music... all part of this huge blossoming of new ideas, happenings, free festivals, squatting, and bands playing psychedelia.

Big Steve: A legalise cannabis movement was founded in the late 1960s called Sativa, one of the first British groups campaigning for a change in the law. That led me to become interested in the free festivals and the politics of the free festivals because Release and Festival Welfare Services always had a presence at them, alongside St John Ambulance, even at the early Windsor festivals. They were dealing with people who'd been busted, people who'd OD'd, dealing with the effects of the law and also seeing the problems with illegal drugs, that drugs could be contaminated, and the effects they could have on users. They would give out information at the free festivals if it came to their notice that there was a drug that was particularly bad, so that announcements could be made from the stage to tell the public to avoid it. I thought this was a responsible attitude in this situation. They weren't so much campaigning to change the law. That came later with the Legalise Cannabis Campaign. I was an original member.

Jake Stratton-Kent: A friend of mine had a card for Release and said, 'This is my passport to good tripping.' If he got busted he'd just be straight on the phone to a sympathetic solicitor. So people *were* organising the free festivals, not in an intrusive or a dictatorial sort of way, but it was being made available for us. Naïve as a lot of us were, or anarchistic as a lot of us were, we were becoming involved in something much bigger than ourselves.

Big Steve: I don't think there was a clear enough vision of the political aspects, almost situation as comedy in the Merry Pranksters tradition. I always had an interest in a political way in the sense that I wanted to see a more just, fair and better society but I think it was a very natural feast of the senses. People had a huge feeling of freedom, taking it to the edge, so it was more utopian if there was *any* political agenda to it. It was incredibly hedonistic, free drugs, free sex, people improvising and making music in ways that they couldn't have imagined before.

Jake Stratton-Kent: For me [politics and the counterculture] were identified, but when I started hanging out with younger hippies, people of my own age, they were saying, 'Oh, politics is all rubbish.' They were just about drugs and music… and clothes. That was kind of weird for me, because I was politicised; I was also a bit of a greaser, more so than a hippie in a lot of ways. When I'd first been a runaway teenager and had to leave Cornwall I'd gone to Notting Hill and hung out there. I knew Marxist organisations in London and it was through that I got into places in Notting Hill and Brick Lane. When the authorities caught up with me I ended up in a therapeutic community called Finchden Manor, which was quite a groovy place. Without the radical element, the festivals wouldn't have happened. The White Panthers, Release, they were all socialists or libertarians, highly politicised in their own way.

Mick Farren: It's my experience that very few musicians, maybe as little as five or six percent and mostly front-men, really have political awareness, they go by their gut and what seems right or good for them. I mean, a lot of musicians are stoned narcissists but the musician's brain doesn't work in a political discipline, at best you get one guy in a band who is well read and politically aware or astute. Take The Beatles, the only political figure in The Beatles was Lennon; McCartney charmed the record company, George was a Hari Krishna and Ringo got drunk and that's really how most bands function.

Jake Stratton-Kent: The Marxist types I hung out with, when I was fourteen, were going to Warwick University which was one of the most radical universities of the time, they were all into Trotsky and Marxist economics, but had huge murals of Jimi Hendrix painted on the walls. They were definitely hippies as well as Marxists. So the two things were much more fused for people who were in their twenties at the start of the 1970s than for people who were in their teens. The next generation of Afghan boutique types didn't understand where it was coming from. They got sucked into it and made up the numbers, and people were trying to radicalise them. Wally Hope in particular was trying to bring them all together and let the youngsters know they were part of something. Nowadays, we haven't got the same social impetus; it's like this idea that you can't beat them, all you can do is have fun, whereas the truth is we came very close to beating them.

The Early Glastonbury

Unless you were 'connected' you were unlikely to even know it was happening.

John Perry: Glastonbury '71 was a truly 'underground' event. Unless you were 'connected' you were unlikely to even know it was happening. The legal penalties were much heavier in those days so by definition it was a more tightly-knit scene. Information travelled down drug lines. I've thought about this a lot, the bands that were prepared to play for free and those that weren't. I suppose it was elitist to an extent, but innocently so. It wasn't elitist in the sense of *excluding* people so much as wanting to be surrounded with liked-minded people. I came from Bristol, twenty-five miles from Glastonbury, but most of the people I'd gone to school with had no idea Glastonbury was happening. The only people who knew about it were the dope-smokers and acidheads. That's a huge difference with Glastonbury today, which is a vast commercial exercise.

Adrian Shaw: Rod Goodway and I formed Magic Muscle; we'd been down at a Dorset farmhouse where Arthur Brown was based. When Arthur left the band, we formed a band down there called Rustic Hinge & The Provincial Swimmers. When that went sour, Rod and I and our respective ladies went to Bristol, with an idea of forming another band, and had a very large house at 49 Cotham Road owned by a founder member of the British Anarchist Party. We had the run of the house, and the basement downstairs for rehearsing in. Quite a few musicians came and went. Keith Christmas, the folk singer, was living there. We started gigging wherever we could. I already knew Hawkwind and their management so went up to London to see Doug Smith, their manager, and blagged us onto their *Space Ritual* tour. We did various other things with Hawkwind over a couple of years but it wound up eventually and I went back to London and joined various bands from there. There have been various reunions over the years and a couple of albums – that was Magic Muscle.

Bob Whitfield: I'd been managing Magic Muscle, getting gigs around the Student Unions. We played at Glastonbury. We didn't play on the main stage; we just played on the grass. The thing that I recall about it was that the whole thing was free, there were no fences. I lived there for three weeks and there was a whole load of us from Clifton and Cotham who went down there and camped. I slept in my car. Muscle just turned up for a bit and played and went home, but the main bulk of us lived there for at least a week. I stayed for about three weeks, doing a load of mescaline, acid and stuff. The whole thing was great. We'd just turn up. It was funny because we didn't know anybody. It wasn't until I became a photographer that I found out people actually *worked* during the 70s. I didn't know anyone who worked during the 70s at all! Everyone was just hanging out.

Magic Muscle, Early 1970s Photographer Unknown

John Perry: I discovered the scene through smoking dope, really; that was the connection. I've always thought there's a book to be written on the link between how the early bootlegs were distributed, and hash-dealing. It may have been different in London, but in the provinces the early bootlegs would turn up with hash-dealers who'd been up to London to score, and returned with a few weight of hash and a hundred copies of the Bob Dylan bootleg, *Great White Wonder*. So [the festival movement] was really a hash-smoking thing; hash and acid distinguished whether you were part of the scene or not. News travelled down drug lines. If you think about distribution lines, you had the manufacturer, or importer, then you had the wholesalers and then the retailers, the people who were bringing the hash and the acid down to

Bristol, or Wales, or Cornwall, wherever. It was a necessary secret because it was illegal, but if you drew a chart you'd find a fascinating thing. The ideology spread out down the distribution lines, and at the core were a very small number of people. Early punk was similar, people recognised one another even if they didn't know each other, they spotted fellow spirits, but the punk thing was about amphetamine sulphate. There'd been speed around the festival scene; the Fairies were big into speed, the Fairies and the Deviants. That was what the White Panther Party was all about, really. Shooting pharmaceutical methedrine and talking non-stop for three days, whereas punk was fuelled by really skanky bath-tub amphetamine sulphate – talking non-stop and puking for three days.

Bob Whitfield: We were all joined together by the fact that none of us worked, we all smoked vast amounts of dope and we were all around Clifton and news got out that there was something going on out at Glastonbury. There'd been a festival, no not a festival... Magic Muscle had played at this Downs concert. There's a film of it, I made a film of it. It's a film of a festival we got together on the Downs in Bristol by the bridge, the Clifton Suspension Bridge, just loads of faces, and the whole scene then, lots of shots of the Hells Angels. There was another band that played before Magic Muscle that I spent a lot of time filming and by the time Muscle came on I had hardly any film. There must have been about a minute's worth of Magic Muscle. Which was a shame but there is, right at the end, some great images of the Hells Angels and the way they took over the festival. Right after the Downs thing there was a lot of funny drugs going along and everything seemed to be right up in the air. I think it was about a month after that, that we heard about Glastonbury. To me, Glastonbury was mescaline, all kinds of daft stuff. I don't recall the bands that much but I do remember smoking loads of chillums, wandering around the countryside… the smell of it all, just how great it was… a really bad tooth that I had. You could walk into the farmhouse then.

Bill the Boat: The first time I ever went to Glastonbury, I can't remember the year, there was about three hundred, three hundred and fifty people there and a couple of little bands, mostly acoustic, and I wanted to use the phone because I wanted to get my friend to come. Some guy in the crowd said, 'Go up to the farmhouse.' So I went up to the farmhouse, knocked on the door and a guy said, 'I'm Mr. Eavis, can I help you?' I said I really needed to use the phone, and he said 'it's over there; mind you leave the 4p,' or whatever it was, and I used the phone and that was it. Glastonbury in the beginning, or two or three years in.

John Perry: The late 60s and the first half of the 70s were very innocent. The authorities hadn't really cottoned on to what was going on. If there were people with land, you could more or less do what you wanted and nobody interfered at all. It may be a little like the early days of the rave thing when you had secret phone numbers, people circling the M25 and you rang a number at a certain time and the venue would be announced. [In the 70s] you had people like

Arabella Churchill with social connections to the land-owners. Arabella's dad was Randolph Churchill who was supposedly a historian but he had about six personable young men at the house who actually wrote the books. Andrew Kerr was one of those guys, and it was he and Arabella who persuaded Michael Eavis to host the Glastonbury Festival in the first place. They overlapped with people like Alan Trist who was English but part of the Grateful Dead management out in San Francisco. It took people from that part of society, because they had the land. It was all very well if you were some kid from Knowle in Bristol, but you didn't have any land and you didn't know land-owners. Everything in England is to do with class.

Adrian Shaw: We were going along because word had got around; Magic Muscle, their ladies and cohorts. I think it was the second Glastonbury, but the first with the Pyramid Stage, the first recognisable Glastonbury Festival. We had an old Cadbury's lorry which was fitted out with bunks and everything, so we could get our equipment, road crew, us and anyone else in it and could sleep in it as well if needs be. We took that to Glastonbury and camped out on the hill; we had generators with us so during the day, when nothing else was going, we'd play, take copious amounts of whatever was going and then watch the main festival when the lights went down. It had been pouring with rain but the sun magically came out when we arrived and it was beautiful weather throughout. It was a very relaxed atmosphere. Once, when we were playing up on the hill, a couple came past, took their clothes off and started making love in front of us. Then someone else came and joined in… then a couple of nuns wandered past because inexplicably there was a gaggle of nuns there, genuine nuns. It was rather peculiar watching their reactions, though they were very cool, as it happens!

John Perry: I played at the first Glastonbury with the Pyramid Stage, which was 1971. There'd been one in 1970, but I think of '71 as the first. It was lovely, maybe twelve thousand people, room to move about… you compare that to Glastonbury now! It was word of mouth, tons of space, and no trouble. There was no timetable; the bands ran on until two or three in the morning. How *great* people played at that '71 festival. Traffic, I'd seen Traffic loads of times, but they were as good that night as I've ever seen them. Terry Reid was incredible; lots of people seemed to play above themselves that weekend. I've played it three times in all. In '71 with Flash Gordon, which was the brother group to Magic Muscle, '79 would have been with The Only Ones, and '81 was Decline & Fall, a short-lived group I had after The Only Ones. Glastonbury has just changed nature completely; I've done festivals this year [2008] in Norway and Sweden which reminded me what the early Glastonbury festivals were like all that time ago. Loose but so much fun. Michael [Eavis] always said he'd lost the farm over them so you'd end up doing a series of benefit gigs in his barn to help pay his debts. If you count those, I suppose I've played at Worthy Farm about six times.

Bob Whitfield: I can recall one morning after the band had played the Guru Maharaji came down, first thing, in his white Rolls. I was just wandering around and there he was on stage. It seemed to me that the whole festival was overshadowed by 'Dark Star' by The Grateful Dead. The whole thing came about because we heard that there was something going on there and then it just grew bigger and bigger and bigger and it turned out to be amazing. Afterwards, just a few people stayed on and my friend and I had this little wooden hut in the field and we stayed on for a week! It wasn't until there was a massive big thunderstorm that we thought we'd drive back into Clifton. Within a week I decided I couldn't stay around Clifton after Glastonbury and with this girlfriend of mine I sold some grass and decided to hitchhike to Kabul, which [laughing] one did in those days, and was gone for six months. I took forty quid with me! All kinds of things happened! After six months, when I came back, Magic Muscle said they'd been waiting for me and things really took off. We suddenly had all these gigs and Bickershaw festival, which was great.

WINDSOR FREE FESTIVAL

Originated for the COMMUNE by UBI, c/o Sid, 19 Vicars Road, London N.W.5
Information Centre: Magus Bookshop 314 Munster Road, London, S.W.6

STARTS 25 AUG. '73

Windsor Free Festivals: 1972 – 1974

This guy said: 'Well, we can go anywhere.'

Keith Bailey: Really, the first free festivals were the ones at Windsor Great Park. A guy called Wally Hope was involved with all that. I actually played at one of those. The music was the original focus, they'd put up a couple of stages and put the bands on; very chaotic but it was musically orientated. However, as time went on [at festivals in general] music became the excuse rather than the reason.

Nik Turner: People would get in touch with us and invite us to play. It created in me an awareness of what festivals were all about. I didn't fully understand it all, but I was keen to learn. There were the Windsor Free Festivals in the Great Park and I think by then there was a general awareness of festivals and people had a need for them. Hawkwind played one with Queen down in the West Country, there was Trentishoe, which was down by the cliffs and organised by an underground newspaper called the *North Devon Snail*. We were on a festivals circuit with Magic Muscle and The Pink Fairies. If there was a festival going on we'd be there because we supported the idea as did other Ladbroke Grove bands, such as Mighty Baby and Help Yourself. We were all mates, all into what this was about, and we weren't all totally out of our heads on drugs!

Adrian Shaw: We played the Windsor Festival in '72. Magic Muscle, The Pink Fairies and Hawkwind all had a jam together at one point. There really was camaraderie between bands, we shared equipment where necessary and bands did have a common purpose. The Pink Fairies, and Hawkwind, were very much like us in their attitudes, two fingers to authority and wanting to get on and do our thing. Muscle's music was more like The Grateful Dead than The Pink Fairies or Hawkwind, very improvised, which would sound horribly conceited, if not for the caveat that we were nowhere near as good. We would have a starting-off point and a finishing-off point of cacophonous feedback but certainly in the early days of Muscle we had no songs. We had our little ritual, Rod and I; the rest of the band were into their acid and dope, as we were, but we also looked for anything else that was going. Our gigging diet used to be a quarter of a tab of acid, and we used to carry this huge hash pipe around with us and take hits on that before going on stage. That would give us a little psychedelic tweak and we'd see what happened musically after that.

Dave Roberts: I went to the Windsor festivals in '73 and '74. I was there for the music, bands like The Pink Fairies and Hawkwind. It was unusual seeing Hawkwind in '73 because they played at midday and there wasn't a stage, just planks on the grass, and that was definitely more intimate. I remember at Windsor '74 the stages were right at the top end of the field by the gates and I recall walking back from a shopping trip into Windsor about four o'clock in the afternoon and hearing 'Echoes' by Pink Floyd blasting out of the PA, it was really haunting.

Bob Whitfield: I was at the Windsor Festival. My dad who lived in Forest Hill in South East London, was going to sell me his Ford Cortina so I dropped some acid and got the train into Vauxhall on the Saturday night, then got the bus back to Forest Hill... umm, tripping. Going from a festival which was all safe and lovely to being on the streets of South East London, got back to my mum and dad's house, sat down with an uncle and aunt from Japan who I hadn't seen for a long time who seemed to thrust their heads right into my food...because I'd dropped some acid right? All I can recall was my mum and dad and uncle all around me whilst I was eating the food. I bought the car off my dad for £30 and then drove back to Windsor. I think I must have missed the sets and stuff but to be quite frank I wasn't that into the music, I mean, I liked it, but I was much more into just the fun of it, the whole fun of just going to all these festivals.

Big Steve: I'd heard there was going to be a free festival at Windsor Great Park, so with a couple of mates I hitchhiked off there. They were building the stage when we arrived and we got ourselves volunteered into helping lift some scaffold poles to construct it. It was quite an eye-opening experience; the alternative culture with its Afghan coats and mile-wide flares. The whole flowering of the post-hippie culture was in the air, the alternative society in all its glory. Hawkwind played, The Pink Fairies played, and Steve Winwood. I remember getting very stoned on some Moroccan hash that must have cost, in those days, fourteen quid an ounce, and watching the bands. Some hippies got into an argument with a guy with a hot dog van, about him being a capitalist and exploiting the festival to make money. I think they turned his vehicle over, which was in contrast to this 'peace and love' idea I'd had of free festivals up until then. But for me, it was an amazing experience, totally anarchic, totally free, no outside control by the authorities. It was a mess: there were no toilets, the woods were full of shit, but it was still an amazing experience and ambience, difficult to describe in retrospect. As a seventeen-year-old it just seemed magic, and all of that happening in The Queen's backyard.

Dolores Dina: I was fourteen, and when I think about what I did at that age I shudder and I'm gobsmacked. My parents didn't know where I was; I'd run away from home. My background

Windsor Free Festival, 1974 (Janet Henbane collection)

Windsor Free Festival, 1974 (Janet Henbane)

was very rough, I was homeless at sixteen and I've been on my own ever since and have had no family around me. I can remember my mother saying to me, 'Your dad wants to get you married off to a man from India', because my dad was Indian. For someone who'd been brought up in this country, speaking English and doing typical teenage things, that was a real threat to me. I didn't get on with people of my own age at school and I started to hang out with older people. I was mixing with a lot of hippies, ten or twenty years older than me. That was how I found out about the festivals, and how I got into drugs. I was smoking dope at thirteen, and at fourteen I was taking acid and speed. I had a very strange, quite bizarre, life. My dad was violent, and I found sanctuary in music and dancing. I was never a groupie in a sexual sense, but I was a groupie in that I followed a lot of bands around and was very passionate about music. I was following bands like Queen, who were a hard rocking band back in 1975, Thin Lizzy, The Who, Hawkwind and lots of off-kilter bands such as Gong and Steve Hillage. I wanted to be [Hawkwind dancer] Stacia, but without having to show my boobs! Windsor Free Festival was my very first festival. I used to hitchhike on my own. In my entire life, I've never met another woman who was doing that sort of thing. On their own, at that age, hitch-hiking off around the country, off her head, taking anything that was offered to her – drugs and stuff. I'm absolutely amazed that I survived because I had a few dodgy experiences along the way. My mum couldn't control me, I went out whenever I wanted to go out, came back at four or five o'clock in the morning and was up at seven for school.

Dolores Dina: There was this guy who was a real character, he used to go to all the festivals and sometimes he'd just stand there with his arms outstretched for hours. He called himself Jesus, and because I bumped into him at a couple of things and we'd hung out, I had people calling me Mrs. Jesus, which really annoyed me. He did make a pass at me [at Windsor] after we'd been there a few days, which was acutely embarrassing. But a lot of the time I was hanging out around little campfires, talking. I met hundreds of people and remember having lots of deep conversations and then people asking me my age and where I was from and them being [startled]. I met other women, some who were fifteen or sixteen, but none would be on their own. Everyone was stoned … I can't remember a single person who wasn't stoned or drinking, everyone was off their heads. Everyone had really long hair, and everyone had Afghan coats and smelled of patchouli. The worst thing was that I couldn't wash, on site. I made the trip into Windsor to wash and to go to the toilet, because other people were doing that. If there were showers on site I didn't see them – maybe because I was too stoned! I recall not being able to get any sleep because of the noise, all night long, bands still playing or someone somewhere with a guitar.

Steve Lake: During the Windsor Free Festival in '74, the police had come in. The day before that occurred, something quite significant happened to me. I was pretty out of my brains on LSD and some guy came round with a petition saying how we were going to demand the right to have our People's Free Festival forever on Windsor Great Park. I know I said something stupid, I was just a kid. 'It *is* their land, not ours. We shouldn't be here.' And this guy said: 'Well, we can go anywhere.' And it was like some kind of weird spiritually enlightening moment and it got a lot of things working in my brain about who does exactly own the land and where can we go? I left the festival and all those feelings were compounded the next day when I started to hear about what had happened, the police going in and kicking pregnant women and beating people up. There were an awful lot of repercussions from that.

Dolores Dina: The finish at Windsor was awful. I still don't know how I got home from there, I know that I had to hitchhike back but I've no idea who gave me a lift! The reaction from my parents was very bad, my dad beat me up and apparently the police had been out looking for me. At one of these festivals there was a school friend with me a part of the time, then she buggered off with a boyfriend but I remember her saying to me, 'Yeah, the police are out looking for us,' because we were both under-age. She was with someone and wanted to be alone. I just went my own way.

Dave Roberts: I was there when all the trouble happened and got beaten up by the police. It was the Wednesday morning and we were sleeping in our tents and heard people shouting, 'Come on, pack up, you've got to go.' We shouted back, 'Go away, we're trying to sleep', and the next thing we knew we had coppers in the tent. They said we had to pack all our gear up and get off the site. It was the Thames Valley [Police]; they had a bad reputation at the time, which was definitely deserved. They were pretty heavy-handed. There was a pregnant girl who got beaten up by the police and quite a few people got badly hurt. They just came, *en-force*, and told everyone to go. We packed up and were hanging around by one of the stages, we had all our belongings stowed and when I tried to get my bag, that's when I got beaten up. In the end they let me get my wallet and stuff because that was the only means of getting home.

Steve Lake: I went to have a good time, listen to music that I liked, take drugs, chill out... but almost immediately it became apparent that doing that put you into conflict with authorities who really didn't like what you were doing.

Police Action at Windsor 1974 (Janet Henbane)

Wally Hope with friendly policeman (Public Domain)

Wally Hope and Other Organisers

At night people would be shouting 'Wally' and stuff.

Dolores Dina: There was a political consciousness about the festival, about being anti-establishment and establishing [alternative] communities. But as a fourteen-year-old girl going to a festival for the first time, the whole thing was just about freaking out and having lots of laughs, particularly at night when people would be shouting 'Wally' and stuff. I still don't know to this day who Wally is… or was! Someone would just start something from a tent and it would reverberate around the campsite, creating a really good atmosphere. I think it was the stereotypical hippy-dippy thing; we're all hanging out together. The only time it didn't feel like that was on the last day at Windsor. We'd had the police hanging around, but on the very last day there was a police invasion. I remember it clearly because there was a line of them around the field. I didn't realise the gravity of the situation at the time. Since then I've read accounts of people being beaten up very badly, though I can't remember seeing anything like that. They pushed their way into tents and were quite brutal. I remember thinking that I could be arrested at any moment, and how would I explain that to my parents, because I was already in a lot of trouble for running away.

Jake Stratton-Kent: While I was at Windsor I was on probation, but after seeing all this carnage around me I was too scared to go back and report. I went to Stonehenge and the counterculture because I felt safe there. I wasn't going back to a probation officer who might arrest me for hanging out at illegal festivals… I was scared to go back into mainstream society, and that has more or less stayed with me. There's this polarised thing behind the scenes no matter how they try and dress it up and say, 'We are friendly to the alternative type', it's not true. *The Daily Telegraph* used to say, 'These people aren't hippies, not like the loveable hippies of the 1960s.' Did you ever see any articles in the 1960s *Telegraph* saying how good the hippies were?

Steve Lake: The two people that organised the Windsor Free Festival were Sid Rawle and another guy, Bill Dwyer, who went under the name Ubi Bill Dwyer. Bill Dwyer was prosecuted after that final Windsor Festival for assaulting and obstructing the police, various kinds of charges. I think they found some dope or acid on him as well. He came to court in Reading and a girl that I was going out with at the time, who was a lot more politically aware than me in a lot of ways, asked me to go to the court case with her. We spent about two weeks in court watching Bill Dwyer, who was a very nice gentleman, possibly quite naïve, but a sincere, gentle guy, a lot older than us. He was made to seem like some sort of *monster* in court. What happened in going to these free festivals and seeing this court case was that I got a real sense of the injustice of things that were going on. We met Heathcote Williams there, who at the time was just starting editing *International Times* after it had not been running for quite a long time. He came down to the court with his followers from London, like a weird hippie elite, and we got to know them a bit and spend some time with them; they were highly politicised people.

Mick Farren: I thought most 'organisers' were fucking incompetent, they seemed to set up these things and everybody died in the first winter... well, that's a bit harsh but if you really wanted to go back to the land, be a fucking farmer! I remember talking to some German Greens once who were laying out this medieval dark-ages agricultural society and I'm saying to them, 'Yeah, but fuck it, you know that's only going to support ten thousand people in all of Germany.' That really is the point, it's the real world and if you're going back to farming you've got to learn modern agriculture. It just seems so ill-conceived, like the hippie commune in *Easy Rider* where they're broadcasting seeds by hand whereas you do actually need a combine harvester if you're going to make a capitalist profit or if you're going to feed the workers. We did once try and set up a permanent festival site, but the idea that you could live some sort of nomadic existence as hunter-gatherers in modern Europe is just unhinged.

Jake Stratton-Kent: I was at the last festival in the Windsor Great Park, when the police truncheoned the Hare Krishnas for want of anybody tougher to beat up. I must have been to the first Stonehenge Festival before that, chronologically. I heard there were people still at Stonehenge so I made my way back there, and sure enough they were all camped up. I hung around for a while and helped crack the first squats in Amesbury, because there was a force eight gale blowing and we wanted four walls. This was with the guys who were following Phil Russell, who was Wally Hope. I met him the first time I turned up at the Stonehenge Festival. I'd heard on the grapevine from some of the more middle-class hippies, 'Oh, we've always gone to Stonehenge for a bit of a gathering, but this isn't what we really want to do, he's turning it into a free festival.' but I thought, 'that sounds alright to me.' I kept bumping into Wally Hope, at Stonehenge and in London. There was the Roxy Cinema up in London which was the place for squat gigs, and he'd turn up in the squats after we'd cracked them, he was always in and out. He was very charismatic, even though he was out of his head on LSD and thought he'd met the latest incarnation of Jesus and all that. He was pretty sharp in a lot of ways, he wasn't all shot away. You hear the expression 'cultural engineer'. Well, he was a 'counterculture engineer', and he'd put some serious thought into his message. He made the 'Wallies' loveable, for the benefit of the media and tourists; the message was that we were loveable eccentrics rather than nasty, dirty, hippies and squatters. He encouraged the free festival scene, big time, getting us out of the cities, on the road, with our own calendar. We were not just weekend hippies, the way he geared it was almost like a separate society, not just an alternative one; in it but not *of* it. He promoted the idea of meeting on pagan festival dates at particular places and going from festival to festival, a separate calendar. That really takes you out of society. In society you've got this sense of time that's nine-to-five with bank holidays... but he was a counterculture engineer.

Penny Rimbaud: He was very good at PR and he had a mission; it was almost semi-religious, his worshipping of the sun. He had this determination, and he was quite disciplined in the sense of being able to create an idea and follow it through and recruit people – I mean, he recruited us, at Dial House, a pretty hard-working group of people to engage in that project. I don't think Phil was political, I think he was missionary but he had inflated ideas about a guru-type role; I'm not saying 'inflated' in a negative sense, but in an observational sense. He'd leave people to do stuff, and in my opinion he wasn't careful enough who he was leaving it to... in my view. So you could suddenly find you were working alongside people with attitudes you certainly didn't share, so a group of hedonists – and I haven't a lot of time for hedonism – could be allotted jobs or tasks with no one keeping any eye or saying 'hang on, this could get out of control and go the wrong way.'

Jake Stratton-Kent: I think he *was* political, though not in a cut-and-dried anarchist type of way because he had a strong spiritual element. I saw him talking to the press at Windsor Great Park and he was really trying to downplay the idea that we were all unemployed dropouts. He'd emphasise that festival-goers were still doing part-time work; he was trying to give a positive image. Tony Blackburn would say on the radio, 'Now, Wally doesn't mean stupid person, it's the Wallies of Wessex.' You'd hear this on Radio One around the summer solstice. Tony Blackburn would stick his neck out. The media liked the Wallies, and that was generally down to the words that Wally Hope, Phil Russell, had put in our mouths. He was able to manipulate the media so we had a positive press. I was quite young and naïve at the time, but had some political awareness and found there was something very charismatic about Wally Hope compared to some of the other festival organisers.

Penny Rimbaud: We set up Dial House in '68 as a sort of open house, drop in place. 'Don't drop out...drop in here and we'll create something.' We became a place where local kids visited and got into film-making, music, all sorts of projects quite apart from looking after the place, all very small scale. There was a particular group of kids from Ongar, the local village, who came here regularly, still as school kids and they knew Phil Russell from Ongar because his guardians lived locally – he was in guardianship because his father had died – and he'd heard about us and turned up. He went off to Cyprus and then came back in the year before the first Stonehenge festival, saying that he'd had this vision of putting on Stonehenge. He'd become very unhappy with what he saw as the political nature of the Windsor Free Festival, he very much preferred the idea of people being able to enjoy themselves without the possible, and in fact inevitable, intervention. I knew Sid Rawle. I think he was an egotist; I didn't have a great deal of respect for him. He was unrealistic. I didn't like his attitude, he was almost reactionary.

Jake Stratton-Kent: Sid Rawle, I thought, just saw people heading in one direction and ran to the front shouting, 'Follow me.' Phil Russell [Wally Hope] had ideas of his own. Rawle liked to call himself the King of the Hippies, but he wasn't at the first Stonehenge Festival, he just wasn't there. I don't remember seeing him at Windsor Great Park either. I remember seeing Bill Dwyer and Phil Russell there, present and correct. Sid Rawle had become a bandwagon jumper… what he'd been earlier, I don't know… in the 60s maybe he'd been a bit more genuine. Bill Dwyer was okay, and Philip Russell had definitely… whatever the 1960s message had been, had reinterpreted it and brought in into the 70s a bit more forward looking. It took me a while to really appreciate what Philip Russell was up to, apart from seeing syringes in the grass at Windsor, a tree getting burnt, and realising that some of these hippies really weren't that together at all and that they didn't represent my values. But at that time I did feel part of it all.

Joie Hinton: Sid Rawle, he was a funny character, he *was* the King of the Hippies, really; he couldn't deny it, he *was*. He was probably almost the most hated person there – but I always got on really well with him. He lived it.

Rory Cargill: What I saw of Sid Rawle was a sort of 'Fat Freddy' type guy who took great fun in sticking it to the man very much in the way that Fat Freddy is sticking it to Norbert. In spite of Sid's tendency to be a bit pompous, by blowing his own trumpet he could actually get results. In terms of getting things organised at a festival, he pulled it all out of the hat. Stonehenge Festival... who was it that organised the sanitation? All the rubbish clearing, or setting up where everything went? He did it perfectly, can't argue with that. I think back to the man on the flatbed truck at the start and end of so many festivals, going round with the crew. Handing out bin-liners, marking out posts, 'Put your rubbish here.' Rubbish collection points, organising stand-pipes or piles of wood for people. I never really got to know the guy, but from what I saw he was a man who filled a gap and a role that was definitely needed in that environment. There were people who were in competition [with him], and little cliques that wanted to be in charge of this and that, as you always do. Part of life, isn't it? He and the people around him got results. It had to be him, or one of these groups of people, or everything would have disintegrated and there would have been no Convoy, no touring community going round festivals. There would have been no continuity. Sid Rawle was pivotal in bringing together many strands.

Angel: Possibly the most poignant festival that I went to, in terms of teaching me very important lessons in life, was Molesworth Festival. I remember arriving and there was Sid Rawle. He had all the Tepee Valley people with him. One of his kids had just been born and he stepped outside of his tepee and he held his baby up to the sky. How could you not be affected by the realisation of life being born there? That was the beginning of a very incredible place. You know they had oxen that ploughed the land. Everybody built this temple; it was going be a place of prayer and worship. They put crystals in it, and they built it all up. There were the Tepee People, the Rainbow Tribe. A lot of them had chosen that way of life, which was born out of festival life really, offering an alternative way of living and being.

Jake Stratton-Kent: The Home Office hated us. That's the other side of the coin. I don't think it was just a conspiracy theory that they were out to get [Philip Russell]. They realised this wasn't some bunch of dropouts, there was something going on that they didn't like. The directive to smash Windsor Great Park festival definitely came straight from the Home Office and the police were told 'gloves off.' I take the point about Edward Heath and Harold Wilson not being anything like Thatcher, but there were elements of the establishment that knew just what was going on.

Penny Rimbaud: I think it's possible to look back on Heath and Wilson as being more benign, but the undercurrent of control… the simple fact is that back in the 60s there was a lot of shouting and screaming but generally speaking if it was happening in a university you could just change the curriculum, which is exactly what happened as they institutionalised, particularly the art schools, and got them back under control. I actually think that things like the hippie movement… I mean, in America, I went there in 1972 to visit my parents who were in Washington, my dad was with the World Bank and was very well connected in Washington and knew what was going on and the big fears at that time were the Black Panthers, which I could completely understand, and the hippies, which I just didn't understand at all. These were people the State were concerned about and were going to do everything they could to squash. There's no reason [not] to suppose that the same thinking was going on here, I mean MI5 and MI6 have a far longer tradition… the CIA are brash, vulgar and obvious whereas MI5 and MI6 are truly undercover. Wilson was totally paranoid about them. I think that's relevant when you look at the fates of people.

Jake Stratton-Kent: It was class war. There weren't any Communist flags or anything with the Wallies, it was a completely different movement, but it wasn't a direction the establishment wanted the youth of the country to be going in. With people like Wally Hope involved, it wasn't just about drugs and music any more. You've heard the expression, 'Turn on, tune in, drop out'; well there was also 'Turn on, tune in, *take over*.' We weren't into *just* being separate from society; we wanted to have an influence on it. I thought society was likely to disintegrate, and I was probably not alone… and probably not wrong, it's just that the timetable was a bit different from what we imagined. David Bowie saying, '*five years*', well society takes a lot longer to disintegrate. It's a big pyramid construction; it's not going to just fall over. It's not like a tower. It has got to crumble. Back then it looked like it was crumbling fast, revolution looked very likely, and in fact I don't think it was as unlikely as we were told. Heath and Wilson might not have wanted to do us down, but there were elements just as powerful that did. These were the days of 'D-Notices' in the newspapers, you couldn't publish certain things… where did that come from? It was a strange society back in those days, and quite capable of falling.

Penny Rimbaud: Wally was a visionary; he had a picture, he had a dream, and without the vision… that's where I have an argument with hard-line leftist thinking, it's not visionary, it's organisational.

Drugs and the 70s

One Person's Story

My first festival was Windsor Free, 1974. I wasn't bothered about taking any substances, such as LSD, or even alcohol. The people I was there with, however, were consuming all the usual stuff: acid, alcohol and, of course, dope or blow. They were the main drugs of the time in the scene I hung out in. Because of the drug laws, people were being stopped and searched going into and leaving festival sites so you had to be very careful and stash stuff. Even a small amount could get you arrested and banged-up. I've always been cautious about drugs. When I was fifteen or so I borrowed a library book about drugs and decided it's best to be happy and high on life without having to resort to drugs, especially alcohol which seems to be the drug of choice for many. However, I think I was in a tiny minority back then. All the people I knew and hung out with took drugs. People dealt this and that... that was the norm. I occasionally used blow or weed. I hated tobacco so usually had pipes or chillums and preferred sun-grown grass or weed. Stuff that makes you laugh your socks off! I knew quite a lot of folk who'd been out to India on the 'Hippie Trail' and brought back good dope and the chillum ritual. Chillums really knock your socks off, I remember the first one I ever smoked, back in 1975; I was nineteen. I blacked out briefly after smoking it and silver stars were flowing out of the top of my head – very cosmic!

I went to Stonehenge for the first time in 1976. I'd gone on my own, didn't know anyone when I arrived. I ended up going with some people to London, someone gave me a package to take back into the festival site – I never knew what was in it. I was a bit gullible. Blow and acid were a huge part of the free festival scene, speed to a lesser degree and taken as a treat by some at festivals. I didn't like being around 'speed freaks', didn't like what speed did to people; made them nasty and paranoid with rotten teeth. I knew people who got into 'fixing it' and some of them moved on to smack. Smack in the 1970s was frowned upon on free festival sites. I remember one year at Stonehenge some smack heads being chased off site. Fortunately, because of the chaotic lifestyle of a smack head, life on site was a bit much for them to hack. Coke was hardly seen back in the 70s but that changed slowly and in the 80s you could see 'Coke' signs up outside people's gaffs on sites. I remember at the Silver Moon, Nenthead,

Cumbria in 1984, the 'Peace Convoy' had made it up there and 'Drugs for Sale' signs were everywhere. A friend of mine who was quite straight went into a bender to buy a *can* of Coke – he'd seen the 'Coke' sign! Some stories of the drug scene on festival sites from the Peace Convoy days are legendary. Dealers and suitcases full of cash being a common one.

Occasionally on site, opium would appear – usually someone back from out East with some. Festival sites were known to have good gear and I think people went to them specially to score: good black, Temple Ball, Nepalese, Afghan black, Paki black etc; a cornucopia of wondrous hashish all with different highs. Lots of grass too: Thai, South American, and Californian. It's all different now because of different wars, usually involving the USA. The supply routes have either stopped or changed. I was quite into hash cakes, but if you didn't know how strong they were you could end up being comatose for hours. At the Magic Mushroom Festival, Pontrhydygroes, 1976, I was so stoned I couldn't move for hours and missed a band I wanted to watch! I was interested in more natural substances for tripping and mystical experiences; I had read some of the Carlos Castaneda books about the Mexican shaman Don Juan and the different plants and cacti used for 'journeys.' I *never* took a tab or blotter or microdot of acid, it scared the shit out of me, and by the time I had no fear, I'd kind of missed the boat! I did feel a bit pissed-off about my LSD fear but I more than made up for its absence by taking Magic Mushrooms, aka Liberty Caps. Magic Mushrooms were always in demand on festival sites but quite rare. Wales was a good place to pick them, hence the Mushroom Fayre in 1976 which continued for a few years afterwards.

Around 1977/78 I made friends with some people from Nottingham; lovely people whom I subsequently travelled with. They always had good dope and we had lots of chillums. One of them sold blow, though I don't know how he kept it all together because of all the chillums! One of this group was selling acid and he asked me if I fancied selling some so I thought I'd give it a go as it would be good to make a few quid to support 'life on the road.' He must have had a good supply. I went around the camping areas shouting 'Acid, acid for sale.' Plenty of people wanted acid – it was door-to-door delivery! At one festival, this guy approached me, he was Dutch and wanted to score thousands of tabs of acid to take back, I just handed him to my mate to sort out. It was too much for me, that amount and all that dosh to count! I later discovered that this LSD was part of the 'Operation Julie' acid bust. The LSD had been made in a Welsh farmhouse. I had visited another farmhouse not far from where the first Mushroom festival was held and this was part of a connection to a connection of the LSD supply route. The people living at the farmhouse were 'rich hippies' and were connected to a well-known actress. 'Operation Julie' was quite a big acid bust. A few years later we went back there with some of the Nottingham friends but the farmhouse was empty and abandoned. However, I have a memento: a heavy cast-iron frying-pan that had been left in a kitchen bin! I remember at free festivals in the 70s, and possibly the early 80s, it was common for plain-clothes Drug

Squad to be on site done up to look like ‘hippies’ and festival-goers. They were usually sussed out and chased off site. I did hear back then of one officer who left the Force to join the ‘hippies’, he hadn’t enjoyed working as a DS officer.

Smack was another drug that wasn’t my cup of tea. When we parked up on buses back in ‘83/’84 a few people started dabbling in smack and when word got around what was going on, people weren’t happy and made a move to do something to stop it. One guy wrote in bright red paint in huge letters ‘SMACK KILLS’ on a bus, which happened to be white so it was really obvious, but it did put a stop to it all. The problem with smack and the people who take it is that you start dabbling now and again and you’re ‘in control’ of it, then that gets more regular and you still think you’re in control but it’s got you and you have a habit. Loads of people I knew got into smack and a lot are now dead or became alcoholics.

When you look back to the 70s, early 80s, the drug scene appears almost ‘quaint.’ There are lots of powders around now, and God knows what is in them. Back in the 70s with the ‘heads’, smoking hashish seemed much nicer and more chilled out.

STONEHENGE
FREE FESTIVAL
SUMMER SOLSTICE CELEBRATION
STARTS 19 TH JUNE · STONEHENGE, WILTS.
HARMONY · MUSIC · FREEDOM · SUNRISES + SUNSETS

Early Stonehenge Festivals

Phil Russell was the single reason for Stonehenge, there's no question.

Steve Lake: There were a lot of festivals going on. The big one was Stonehenge, which I started going to and playing at. The thing about the Windsor, Watchfield and Stonehenge festivals was that an awful lot of people used to go to them. There was your kind of hard-core free festival elite and followers, but you'd also get quite a lot of casual people going to them. You got thousands of people at Stonehenge and it was pretty anarchic, not always in a good or sensible way, though generally they turned out okay. I latched on to Here & Now a bit. They were living over in West London, so they were also in that anarchistic tradition of Hawkwind and The Pink Fairies. They became the people that were the organising force. The more you went to these things, the more you would come into conflict with the police and the authorities and that shaped your world view. There was the Meigan Fayre in the Preseli Hills and Severn Vale down in Dursley, in Gloucestershire. A lot of these would happen because Here & Now would turn up with a generator and they were mates with these people of the Polytantric Circle, which I think at the time was based down in Brighton.

Penny Rimbaud: Phil Russell was the single reason for Stonehenge, there's no question. I know that, I was there when he came up with the idea.

Rory Cargill: Stonehenge Festival was just in a little triangle field, where the A303 splits, then in subsequent years it was over in the field by the car park, and it grew there. It was like watching a little town grow. In '76 and '77, when I was travelling around with the festival people in the big yellow tepee, it was like this floating village. Later, it became like a visit to an alternative Brighton, I suppose. A pleasant away-day experience, an away-week so to speak, and then back to the smoke!

Penny Rimbaud: Stonehenge, in those days, was just a bunch of stones in the middle of nowhere; people did stop to look at them but it wasn't any big deal; it's *become* a big deal, with

English Heritage and all that stuff since. Partly [for Phil] it was to do with the sun as well; we know its history as a place of sun worship and its lineage with the sun gave it a significance to him because he was a sun worshipper. His whole mythology, his religion, was based around the ideas of the sun, so Stonehenge was a great choice, and we all felt that it was a place we could go and have fun and not be buggered about. We wouldn't get into trouble or have what was happening at Windsor, which he was really badly shocked by and was badly beaten up himself there by the police, as were a lot of people. Initially I thought he was crazy; I was into trying to build communities such as Dial House and become operative as a community and not particularly look out beyond, whereas Phil was much more about the 'grand picture', he felt that was a better way, or another way, of expressing similar ideas. Eventually, and on his insistence really, I thought, 'okay, let's do it, we'll help', so from the winter he got back from Cyprus, probably the January, we set about deciding what we should do, and that was creating posters, flyers, stuff to advertise it and everything was bits of paper and word of mouth. But he had crazy ideas. His guest list included everyone from the Dalia Lama to Prince Philip, and the one that always amused me, 'the Air Hostess of British Airways', or BOAC as they were in those days, because he always had this penchant for uniforms. It was light-hearted and happy, sort of fun but hard work at times because he was quite insistent. He would have been in his mid-twenties. So that happened; the posters went around and he used to go up with flyers to London, to places like Notting Hill Gate where the hipsters and the hippies would hang out, to Petticoat Lane and Brick Lane, any of those sorts of places where he could hang out, handing stuff out. We tended to do little more than stuff that was necessary here, but it was an awful lot of work; we had silk-screen printing facilities and an old Gestetner stencil machine which was just fantastic. The net result of that was that a very small band of, maybe, thirty people at any one time would turn up, pretty close to the stones. The one thing he hadn't realised, and neither had I at the time, was that the Military installation, the chemical warfare installation that is just to the back of Stonehenge, Porton Down, the land there is all Ministry of Defence. Phil, initially, was on MOD land, which wasn't a good idea. I could never really understand why it was that the authorities objected so much, there wasn't many people there and they weren't doing any harm. There weren't really even any bands or music; there wasn't any facility to do that. I think people did turn up and do some acoustic-y things but there was no organisation. One or two fires, one or two tents. We did the bread run, so I never even stayed the night there; we used to do baking [at Dial House] and take a big sack of stuff down there once a week, or supply stuff if it was needed. We did some banners and that sort of thing. But it wasn't something that particularly interested me; I've never been a festival guy, I don't like festivals. I've appeared at one or two, but I don't really enjoy them and don't like the 'play' element of them. I'd have probably been happier with something like Windsor, which was more politically motivated.

The story of the Stonehenge Festival was brought to a full-stop – more or less – in 1985 in such a violent manner, with it having grown from those early days and the handfuls of festival-goers to a sprawling festival rivalling the resurgent Glastonbury's mid-80s attendance numbers, that it has often been lost sight of just how anti-Stonehenge the government and the MOD were, essentially from the start.

Penny Rimbaud: They were taken through the courts to get them evicted off the land [Stonehenge] and they lost the case, of course, but Phil felt he'd won the case in the sense that morally he was on the high ground and it didn't really matter what judgement was made and they just moved over the fence, off the MOD land and I think they hung out there for a while and then budged off somewhere else. Come winter, Phil was back again saying 'well, that was great; we'll do the next one soon.' Well, again, we helped with the posters, and this time more contacts had been made because he'd created a certain amount of interest and we could tell that it was going to be something in the coming year. Same process, same invites – perhaps slightly more sensible – and now one or two bands were expressing an interest; I'm not sure if Hawkwind had at this point but they might very well have done. So there was this sense of 'this time it's actually going to happen.' I've always tried to look back and understand why there was such an extreme reaction to something that was actually so un-intrusive, a few hippies hundreds of miles from anywhere just having fun. Phil met up in Portobello Road with the Scottish group; I think they called themselves the Tartan Army. He never checked anything, and it was round about the time when the oil pipeline was blown-up in Scotland. When I was investigating Phil's death a year or so later, I made the connection that these people could have potentially been people who were a part of the liberation movement, if you like, in Scotland, who had done a bombing, or a piece of arson, because there was always that undercurrent of everything being 'under control' and may be it was not 'under control' any more. One of the fliers we did had 'People Involved' and that included the Tartan Army. It was probably little things like that, that weren't sending out the right message to General Headquarters [GCHQ in Cheltenham, the government's 'listening station'.]

Angel: My first recollection of what a festival was, I was in Selsey Bill, it was in the 60s and I knew that Hendrix was playing on the Isle of Wight. I was only a child, asking my dad if he'd please, *please...* I was begging him to take me and he thought it was hilarious that he had a little kid who was a Hendrix fan. I didn't get to go to the Isle of Wight Festival, but my older brother used to go to all the Windsor Festivals. I remember crying my eyes out because my mum wouldn't let me go with my brother and I was probably thirteen, fourteen. I had to leave home at fifteen. The good side was it meant that the festival porthole for me was well and truly open. My first festival experience that I can remember clearly was Glastonbury, 1977, with my son Jack, who was then six weeks old. Apart from the fact that it was one field, it was a very different affair because it was a unique experience, very elitist in a way and, you know, a place where you could experience things that you'd never ever experienced before. They were places where people could express themselves. It didn't matter what you wore, you could walk around, and you could be who you were. It was a secure environment where everything was allowed and no harm was done. Stonehenge holds the most sentimental and deep experience for me, and I've been going there since the 70s and I've seen the changes. My children have memories of me actually waking them up when it was still dark and wrapping them in blankets and taking them to the Stones for the dawn. That was a really magical time, and it was lovely that they grew up and told me how it was for them. I actually christened my children there. I always felt the healing power of Stonehenge and saw what it did to people.

Joie Hinton: The first I went to was Windsor in 1973, and then continued on through the mid-70s. The next ones I remember after those were the Severn Valley and Priddy… there were lots of little free festivals. I went to some at Worthy Farm in Pilton, two or three festivals there. This was 1978, something like that; there'd been the big one there in 1971 after which Michael [Eavis] didn't do any more for a while, then he only did free ones where travellers would just turn up. I was with a motley crew of types, who were my mates at the time. We eventually became a band called the O'Roonies; we had a little green tepee and stuff like that, we were like the outcast tepee bunch – really out there. It was just a fun thing to do throughout the summer. A friend of ours had a van and we built a tepee and off we went, months and months of that, staying in farmers' fields. We were the sort of people that used to follow Here & Now around and it was just a good laugh, great days. I remember seeing Nik Turner there a lot; he was doing *Xitintoday* [album], his Egyptian stuff with Harry Williamson from Gong. We were just following everyone about and learning to play instruments and would occasionally try and join-in on jams.

Nik Turner: I did the album about my 'take' on Egyptian mythology [*Xitintoday*] and had this pyramid constructed, a scaled-down version of the Great Pyramid made of aluminium and canvas and took that to Stonehenge every year. I saw that as my contribution to the Stonehenge Festival, putting up my Pyramid Stage and letting people perform in it. Then I gave it to the people that were going around the free festivals to erect at their festivals. So what became the Convoy would take my stage around the festivals in the summer and bring it back in the winter to keep it dry and make sure it was maintained in serviceable condition. Then they'd come and pick it up from me the following spring. It was a useful piece of equipment. I started off with it at Stonehenge and took it to Deeply Vale and Inglestone Common and up to Scotland. I used it at Observatory Hill as part of the Edinburgh Fringe Festival and then took it on to Findhorn, which I found quite an interesting place. We had this big crew of people who were travelling around in a big furniture lorry with the Pyramid Stage in tow and all the scaffolding on top – fifteen of us all living in this Pantechnicon lorry and going to festivals in it! We had a kitchen in the back, which we'd try and make some money with – a vain hope! At

Findhorn we parked up in the [Findhorn Foundation] car park and in the morning there was a knock on the door, I opened it and there was this guy standing there who I hadn't seen since he was a drug-dealer in Brixton! 'What are you doing here?' he asked. 'Well, we've come for a visit.' He said, 'I'm the director of entertainment here and you're very welcome to come in and perform a show, and live here for a week or so', which was very nice. They usually don't want anyone who hasn't paid their hundred pounds to live in the hotel... rich Americans looking for enlightenment. So it was nice to be welcomed in and fed and watered! But we'd started out in the West Country, in Clovelly, with some guys from the Liverpool scene like Adrian Henry. Then this guy, Jeremy Sandford, who'd written *Cathy Come Home*, attached himself and his two girlfriends to us and became part of our group as well.

The Convoy used the Pyramid stage as a rave tent at Birkenhead (Mark Wright)

Trentishoe (Janet Henbane)

Trentishoe - 1973

John Perry: There was a great, but less well-known, festival at Trentishoe in 1973; a beautiful location, up on the cliffs in North Devon on the edge of Exmoor, overlooking the Bristol Channel. There was a massive PA, about twenty thousand watts, loaned to the organisers by Joe Cocker. My sense of time isn't *that* reliable, but the festival seemed at least a day late starting because nobody knew how to wire the thing up! When they eventually got it going, there were ships about twelve miles out in the Channel that could hear it – you played something and they'd honk their horns back at you. I remember the Fairies turning up, pitching their tent and running a casino at that one! They'd gone into some cash-and-carry joint, bought up all the beer, and were selling it at inflated prices. Once they'd run out of beer they decided to open a casino! There'd be all these people, tripping, wandering into the Fairies' tent and getting all their money taken off them, rings and watches… the Fairies were always funny but less idealistic, shall we say? Different forms of chaos. Boss Goodman, who I suppose you'd call the Fairies' tour manager, though that doesn't begin to cover his many roles, was usually at the root of Pink Fairies scams. Boss's thing was food, he loved his food. I remember him at Trentishoe, when provisions started to run low [laughs], proposing to kill a few people and eat them! Wandering around the festival site at 2am, and suddenly, looming out of the fog, there's the ghastly form of Boss Goodman, muttering 'Kill 'em and eat 'em … kill 'em and eat 'em.' I don't think he actually had a carving knife or a chef's hat but he certainly looked hungry…

Bob Whitfield: Magic Muscle played at Trentishoe, which was a fantastic place but it was cold. It was right on the cliff edge. We set the stage up and then I didn't normally have the pipe before they went on but I thought I'd have it this time. It really threw me right out and just as the band went on I had to go and lie down in the tent. When I woke up it was the morning and the tent had fallen down on me. I was just lying there wondering what the hell had happened! But it was very misty and there were all kinds of things going on. There was this guy called Paul Davis, who was like the MC. He had a tent and he set himself up as 'Norbert.' He had this kind of little plastic dummy that he would sit on a table and people would go into the tent and they would ask Norbert, as if he was some kind of a God, for advice. Paul would be hidden and be talking through this dummy and it was the funniest thing ever!

Big Steve: I helped a little bit with the construction of the site, various large amazing geodesic domes were constructed and incredible organic bread ovens were built. There was a free food kitchen there that maybe was heavily spiked with acid. I think the whole site, everyone, was tripping. One of the best, most hilarious bands I thought, was the Hare Krishna band, who played all night, jamming, 'Hare Rama Hare Krishna', while we were underneath all this polythene on Alpha Centauri listening to them play. There was an astonishing dancer making mudras and twists and turns, dancing as Hawkwind played, and also a brilliant set by The Pink Fairies. It was so incredible, the way that people came and worked together spontaneously. There was a guy with an ice-cream van and he'd go, 'What do you want? Normal or special?' So you'd say, 'What do you mean? What's the special?' The normal was a '99', an ice-cream with a chocolate flake in it. The special? He'd dip the ice-cream into a huge tub of marijuana. That was really bizarre because there'd be all these straight tourists who´d come across from Minehead for the festival and they were queuing up going, 'Oh, I'll have a special, please.'

Watchfield 1975

The Government said, 'You can have this site.'

In amongst the mass of ad-hoc or regular free festivals came Watchfield, remembered as the only festival actually sanctioned by the government.

Jake Stratton-Kent: The Government said, 'You can have this site, we'll let you have a festival.' I think this was to take some of the militancy out; we would have taken an alternative site anyway. They'd taken Windsor off us and were trying to take Stonehenge too. What they didn't tell us was that we could only have it for one year.

John Perry: The whole free festival thing had fragmented by 1975. I don't know if that was a universal thing or just my own experience, because I moved to London that year and started working on The Only Ones with Peter Perrett – and punk was starting too.

Steve Lake: What's weird to consider now is this rag-bag remnant of the hippie movement was limping on and still had enough clout for the Government to say, 'Well, you can't have a festival there, that's the Queen's land, but we will find you an alternative site.' 1975 comes along and I went along. Again it was about listening to music and taking a lot of drugs… everything was really chilled out.

Jake Stratton-Kent: We turned up at Watchfield thinking, 'Isn't it nice of them... somewhere to go,' but it wasn't the same, it was like a halfway house between a free festival and a commercial festival. You could have music, big stages and so on, but the atmosphere was different. There was a much bigger biker presence than I'd seen at any festival, before or since. I think the government was trying to undermine the free festival thing by semi-legitimising it. If they could stop the festivals for one year by appearing to give in, by the next year some of the militancy and fire might have vanished. The hard-core knew that Wally Hope had been busted but there were a lot of people who used to come to the festivals who weren't that radicalised, didn't know what was going on and just turned up on site.

Dave Roberts: We went down to Watchfield about a week before the festival started, about fifteen of us, and it was great, just living off the land. We went into Swindon, bought a brand new aluminium dustbin and were cooking in that! One guy had an air rifle and shot some rabbits, we got some vegetables, and we'd be having rabbit stew. We thought when we got there we'd be dossing in tents but we actually had the old barrack buildings, a room each! It was brilliant! I think they'd tried a few places but this was the best possible site, pretty deserted and away from houses. I helped build and maintain the stage. When we'd built it someone came up and said, 'Do you realise this is right in the middle of a ley line?' The atmosphere was great – until the Hells Angels turned up. They came in, took over one of the hangars for themselves, kicked out anyone who was sleeping in there.

Dolores Dina: Watchfield seemed massive in comparison to Windsor. I distinctly remember people talking about the Hells Angels, that they were trying to take over the festival and whilst I was there I was nervous about that. I didn't see them at Windsor, wasn't aware of them hassling people, but when I went to Watchfield the following year I do remember people talking about them and saying 'Don't go there' or to avoid certain places. I was one of the people who

Watchfield 1975 (Mick Moss)

Watchfield 1975 (Mick Moss)

slept in the hangar where the aircraft used to be. I didn't have a tent and some guy found out about that and said, 'Come and sleep in the hangar with us' and that it should be okay because the Hells Angels had left.

Dave Roberts: On the whole, the festival was fantastic. We saw Traffic's last ever gig there. There were all the usual rumours, such as that Pink Floyd were going to turn up. It was pretty easy to get bands to play though; most bands were well into playing the festivals. A band that were local to me, Strife, played and went down a storm. Hawkwind played, Arthur Brown played, and I think he jammed with Traffic and with Vivian Stanshall as well. When Hawkwind played on the main stage on the Saturday, there was a Liverpool band called Warrior playing at the same time on the 'B' stage and they were doing Hawkwind covers!

Dolores Dina: At [Windsor and Watchfield] all the stages were very ramshackle, things were organised okay, but there were no real set times and people just ambled on and ambled off. I went to Reading [in 1975] and there you really got the feeling that they were the artists and you were the audience. Never the twain should meet.

Swordfish: All that stuff disappears [at free festivals], all those barriers come down. In heavy rock, and in pop music, it's a lot more cut-throat and ego-based whereas in the festival situation egos get dispersed. Now we have a more homogenised festival scene that has been allowed by the government and is very controlled. I know that some of the nastier elements that were happening in some of the festivals needed tidying up but I don't think it has been gone about in the right way. I don't like the way Glastonbury has gone and it's not what it should be… it's a sad reflection when you look at what it was and where it came from and now where it's ended up. I suppose commerce has had to make it go that way, but I don't think it's particularly good. The only nice ones now are the little ones dotted around the country that keep themselves to themselves and don't preach what they're doing too much and are therefore allowed to get away with certain things.

Steve Lake: One of the significant events there, in legend if not in fact, was the first gig by Here & Now who became stalwarts of the free festival scene. For a while they more or less *were* the scene, to be honest. Ever the hippie hustlers, they had a synthesiser player called Twink and they kind of let people think it was Twink from The Pink Fairies.

Jake Stratton-Kent: There were some funny incidents. A bishop turned up and apparently was going to do a big mass on stage… this weird looking drongo sidled over to him and said, 'I have reason to believe you are head of Thames Valley Drugs Squad.' He so obviously *wasn't* but it was hilarious, so ironic and satirical. They did a mass on stage, and that was all very odd. A few years before, Mary Whitehouse and Co tried to organise the 'Festival of Light', Cliff Richard was there and so, strangely enough, were the Hells Angels but it was like this big Jesus Festival, a counter to the counterculture with all its free love and drugs. 'Let's have a festival for Jesus.' Quite what the Hells Angels were doing there I've no idea, but the National Front was also there. The people who were mainly militating against that were the gay community, who at that time were fairly well integrated with the counterculture in Notting Hill. Gay Liberation was putting up posters about the 'Festival of Shite' and was really against it. I think there was an element of that opposition to the free festivals represented by Whitehouse that went into the thinking about Watchfield, 'Let's have a festival that accommodates the less militant types.' Actually it was trying to take it in another direction, having a big mass on stage, trying to say, 'No, look, we love you, come back into the fold of mainstream society.' After they'd beat the *fuck* out of us the previous year! The irony was all too obvious.

Of the key 'organisers' that were integral to the early days of the free festivals, many are now gone. Sid Rawle passed away of a heart attack in 2010, Arabella Churchill succumbed to pancreatic cancer in 2007, 'Ubi' Bill Dwyer died in 2001… but of all of these movers and shakers, it's the tragedy of Wally Hope, Phil Russell, surrounded still in controversy and mystery and possessed of both myth and conspiracy that is a sobering part of the festivals' stories.

Steve Bubble: The first that I'd ever heard about free festivals was via anarcho punks Crass and their LP *Christ - The Album*. There was a booklet inside called '*A Series of Shock Slogans and Mindless Token Tantrums*' which included the story of Wally Hope, the organiser of the first Stonehenge Free Festival, written by one of his friends, Penny Rimbaud, who was then in Crass. Wally was, so the story goes, murdered by the State by being incarcerated in a mental institution and fed high levels of drugs which killed him...

Penny Rimbaud: He was the person who instigated Stonehenge. Certainly from that point on, Dial House was, not targeted, but it was certainly under constant surveillance. I don't know whether Phil was more or less targeted [than others]. Ultimately it's almost like what people bring to themselves. He played the wrong game. He believed that his truth was his truth and it would carry him. He had a sort of Gethsemane complex; there was the choice at Gethsemane of saying 'fuck that' and doing a runner; you see them appearing over the hump in the hill and you know what your fate is. That's the choice. We could have got him out, but he would have had to have been in agreement, we couldn't have kidnapped him against his will, and we couldn't get his agreement. On the two occasions he was visited, once by Gee Vaucher, and once by Gee and myself, he was under constant surveillance with a guard never very far away. At the same time we'd employed a very good lawyer who actually found it almost impossible to carry through the lines of contact, almost impossible to find information; he very much felt he was being hampered at all points.

Jake Stratton-Kent: I was at the Wally squats the day that Wally Hope got arrested. He wasn't living there all the time. He would come and go. A young lad from Glasgow, another teenage runaway who was only fourteen, got busted for acid and Wally Hope took the rap for it. He thought he could do some great speech in court saying acid is a spiritual sacrament, so as well as doing the right thing and getting this fourteen-year-old out of trouble, he was wanting to use it as a platform. There was no sign on that day that he was in any kind of decline. He was *himself*; he was charismatic, just as I'd always seen him, a natural leader. They took him away and, as the story goes, gave him more Largactil than they were giving the Kray Twins between them.

Penny Rimbaud: He headed off [to the second Stonehenge festival], stopped over at Aylesbury and while he was there the Military Police turned up looking for someone who'd gone AWOL. They discovered some acid tabs in Phil's coat and he was arrested. Well, the Ministry of Defence don't arrest civilians... but anyway he was arrested and that's all hazy but the net result of all of that was that he was taken in to Aylesbury clink, held on remand and while he was on remand, he found that he was unable to get in touch with anyone, and we didn't know where the hell he was. Nobody from the squat attempted to help or to get in touch, so we were completely in the unknown, we didn't know anything. Then his guardian received a letter from the authorities and he came over immediately, saying 'look, I've got this…' and then we knew what had happened to him. By that time he'd been sectioned. Phil claimed that he was never given any opportunity to get in touch and I'm inclined to believe that story. The authorities could get away with more in those days, because there wasn't the media focus and communications were just by letter or telephone. By now he was in Salisbury, at a mental hospital there. I felt strongly that he was getting comeuppance for the embarrassment he'd caused in the high courts the year before, when they were trying to get an eviction, and it had become the 'joke' story of that summer in the papers, the 'silly season'. It was a perfect story for that and got a lot of coverage. We started to plan a way of getting to see him, which we couldn't because we weren't family, but Gee posed as his sister and we created this plot to get him out and get him over to Spain because we found that in sectioning, you had to be re-sectioned at the end of each 28 days and if you're not re-sectioned then you are actually free. So we'd set up this boat at Malden to get him over to Holland but we failed to do that, partly because he wasn't interested in being liberated, he was going to fight his battle, which was a serious and silly mistake on his behalf but he believed he could pull it through. He'd been diagnosed as schizophrenic, which he certainly was not. He was certainly a free-thinker, but he was a very gentle person, a very kind person, and had some pretty wild thoughts.

Jake Stratton-Kent: He was released after the Stonehenge festival, turned up at Watchfield, and he was broken. He was pissed off… but he was also broken. I think *that* was done to him… that's not just what I've read, it's what I *saw*. I think the drugs they gave him, and whatever else they did to him, broke him. They were force-feeding him a downer, and it didn't suit him one little bit. I don't know what else they might have done to him but they'd certainly given him drugs and he was a different person. They'd broken his spirit, but not entirely, he wasn't craven and cringing. As the saying goes, 'I might be paranoid, but that doesn't mean they're not out to get me.' They *were* out to get him; they'd done it deliberately.

Penny Rimbaud: The [Stonehenge] festival went down well that year; I went down to it, mainly to see if I could persuade people at the festival to get together to march down to the mental institute where he was being held to do some sort of protest but I'm afraid to say there was no interest, which was quite extraordinary. We went from person to person, saying 'look, do you know what happened to Phil…' and people just were not interested. At one point there was an announcement from the stage saying 'you'll notice two people…' which was a description of myself and the person I was with, 'please don't talk to them, they're police officers.' You know, it was really fucking weird. But the festival was good, bands turned up, great food, great stages, over the road from the actual stones, very nice venue actually with thousands of people. Not tens of thousands or hundreds of thousands, but certainly thousands. So it was lovely, apart from the fact that nobody seemed to care too much [about Phil]. Eventually he was freed, one day after the last person left from the festival, as being cured, and put out on the road again. He got back to Dial House, eventually; it took him two days because he'd lost his coordination and we could see that he was seriously fucked up because he'd been massively overdosed on various psychotropic drugs and his brain was frazzled. For some reason the state had offered Watchfield and he wanted to go – we did everything to try and prevent him from going because he wasn't physically in a good enough state to cope with anything, but he did go and we never saw him again. It got to about seven days and we hadn't seen him, having been looking after him, trying to heal him, giving him lots of ginseng and different herbs, but he really was in an appalling state, he couldn't even walk properly, and the next thing we knew a friend turned up saying 'did you know Wally is dead?' It had been in the local paper, he'd been found dead at his guardian's in Ongar. But the festival just grew and grew, it had its impetus, and there were enough people to grow it.

Jake Stratton-Kent: After he died, a couple of police turned up at the Wally squats to make sure we knew. 'Your glorious leader choked on his vomit after an overdose of barbiturates.' Barbiturates were nothing to do with Wally Hope, nothing at all. He would not have taken them voluntarily, not even recreationally.

Penny Rimbaud: I met [Sid Rawle] when I took Phil's ashes down to Stonehenge and he immediately took control; I didn't mind… I might appear to be a public figure in some respects, but it's not a role I enjoy. It's a role I'll play in something that's valuable or meaningful but I wasn't interested in being the person who did the ceremony or anything like that. I'd made this beautiful box, which still exists. I didn't really know Sid before that, but he took over and did all the ceremony but there was something about his attitude. In the evening, I hadn't got a tent with me but I thought I'd stay overnight and ended up sleeping in the hedgerow because no-one was offering me somewhere to sleep. One of my attempts to get somewhere to sleep was Sid's tepee; two young kids from Liverpool were there, scruffy, poor, working-class kids who'd made the effort to get down there with their little cotton tent which wouldn't have lasted half a minute of dew let alone rain, and Sid was saying how *easy* it was 'Oh, you know, man' and I thought 'what are you talking about?' This was someone privileged, who was using his privilege, had a beautiful tepee, telling these really under-privileged kids about how easy it is to drop out. Well, fuck off, you know? I really felt upset about that; that was an aspect of that moment, the well-to-dos being well-not-to-do. That was an element; Heathcote [Williams] had this privileged background. Wally – Phil - had nothing to worry about; he had a massive inheritance in line. He'd fucked up at his public school. I'm not putting him down for that but it was an aspect that I was uncomfortable about. It wasn't classist but he had no understanding of class. It's like the Tories aren't necessarily classist, they've just never had an opportunity to see what's happening because they're not there being a part of it.

Rory Cargill: Festivals themselves were very much an eye-opening experience; just the sheer fact of this magical environment was created and sustained. One can look back on it with very jaundiced and cynical eyes and say it was just the garden party of the well-to-do but there were other levels to it as well. With any experience you can deconstruct it one way or another. It depends on your bias and prejudice or what you're looking for. I try to remember it with a positive view. On some levels, it's a private garden party. On a very cynical level you could say it was like a Victorian costume drama party where the factory workers are dressed up and they're allowed to do this. Madam and Lord Blah-blah-blah, they can cavort and pretend to be artists and be fauns and the magical people, the rest of us are filling up the gaps in their little fantasy role-play drama. Very picturesque but then you try moving from one level to another, because you look at these people and think, I can do that, I can do it a damn sight better than any of them. Then when you try moving you find suddenly doors closed, you're back in the machine grind city.

Richard Chadwick: In retrospect, the festivals movement when they started were very elitist, all hippies and 'astral alignments', cosmic this, that, and the other. Glastonbury and all that stuff. But the transmogrification into something where we had more festivals than anywhere else in the world, you know? It became a really popular pastime, for young people to go out camping and listen to bands, on a scale in this country that's never been seen before.

Penny Rimbaud: I'd become disconnected with it... or in many respects I was never connected with it in the practice. In the ideology, then I *was* or at least in some of the ideology. I'd been disgusted when we'd gone down and tried to recruit support for Phil. Maybe it wasn't that I was disillusioned, maybe it was that my doubts were confirmed because I wasn't part of that culture, and the drug element of that culture pissed me off. I always kept my ear to the ground... my role in it was very significant but unlike the people that are always mentioned when festivals come up, I'm not included because I didn't use it as a platform in my life and if it hadn't been for Phil's fate I'd have just gone on with what I was doing. I chose to write about Phil's fate because I was so shocked, disgusted, and unhappy about the treatment of a friend, who I genuinely did not believe committed suicide. I set out to prove that point, and to myself I satisfactorily did.

The Hells Angels

'Silk and leather got to come together.'

Jake Stratton-Kent: The old hippies had a love–hate relationship with the bikers, it was like Jack Kerouac, who tried to absorb them into the alternative society but it never really worked. They liked the adulation, but most of them had a completely different political ethos. But there were hippie bikers as well and the lines blurred on occasions. I have seen bikers turn up on site and suddenly there are more drugs on site. Inglestone Common, a fairly good festival site for a few years, big chopper suddenly arrived one night and suddenly there was loads of LSD, loads of acid, it was obvious he was a courier. The last big amount of bikers I saw was at Watchfield; I know for a fact they came in ones and twos without wearing their colours until they got quite close to the site and then they all joined up as though they'd ridden like an army across the country, which they certainly hadn't. But they were there, and though they used to throw their weight around a bit, it was usually fairly good-natured. It never really worked, never really gelled, though we wanted it to, like that Pink Fairies track, '*Silk and leather got to come together.*' We tried to romanticise the bikers, but they weren't having it!

Mick Farren: The Angels were a part of the counterculture. They were there; they had their problems and their advantages as much as anybody else. We didn't make the mistake that others did, of thinking they could be shaped into some kind of private army. They had their own mythology, and ways of doing things. Some of it needed questioning and sometimes that *was* questioned, but there was a lot of holier-than-thou crap going on.

Big Steve: When you talk about the Angels, you've got to be very careful about this. Maybe it was the Windsor Chapter, but maybe they were outlaw gangs of bikers; I don't know what the politics were at that time. But, I was something of a biker myself; I had a bike when I was sixteen. I was involved with a campaign to change the law to give people of a certain age who'd bought motorbikes, before the licensing law came in, the ability to keep their motorbike. I'd always had this relationship with the bikers and related to them as well, it wasn't like I was in a counterculture that was totally disconnected with them, but I didn't understand the violence in the bikers.

Adrian Shaw: We were initially involved with the Hells Angels because when we formed Magic Muscle, the West Coast chapter of the Angels were based in Bristol. There were various charter chapters of the Angels in England, but they were constantly at war with the London chapter who claimed they had the only genuine charter. The local Angels befriended us, which was something of a double-edged sword. It's better to have them on your side than against you on the one hand, on the other we got banned from every venue in the West Country because they'd turn up and, not exactly cause trouble, but they intimidated people. There was nothing we could do about it because when the Angels are your friends you can hardly say to them, 'Don't come to gigs', because then they'd be your enemies. They were organising the 'All England Run', at Worthy Farm; they invited us to play, so we did. The West Coast [chapter] came to escort us there and I remember we had to stop for petrol on the way there and this Special Patrol Group, which was keeping an eye on them, was trailing us. As we were filling up, two vanloads of SPG cops came and were trying to move us on and a guy called Denny the Pervert, who had a penchant for shagging sheep, if you asked him what it was like he'd say, 'All right, but a bit smelly', was face-to-face with the head of the SPG. He fronted him down. I'd never seen anything like it. The copper would say, 'Right, get going', and he'd say, 'We're filling up. *When* we've filled up we'll get going but we don't want any hassle.' He actually said to him, 'If you want any hassle, get your boys and we'll have it out.' And the cop realised he was serious and just said, 'Okay, fill up and then get out...' which is what we did. We got to Worthy Farm and it really was extraordinary, hundreds of Angels, initiation ceremonies, us playing, mayhem going on. They were doing things like... the trick was if you were a 'prospect', someone who was waiting to earn their colours, you'd get thrown on the bonfire and the way to demonstrate your class was in the length of time you'd stay on the bonfire. Motorbikes roaring all over the place and us bunch of freaks playing, which was okay, they liked and looked after us so we weren't in any particular danger. I think they genuinely saw us as some kind of kindred spirits, if only because we could take more drugs than they could!

Bob Whitfield: I recall a wedding at which Magic Muscle played, which I didn't go to as I was away at the time. They were playing in a field, and I heard that after these two people got married, the rites were that the Hells Angels pissed on the bride and then set fire to the groom. Magic Muscle were thinking, 'God, this is heavy stuff...'

Mick Farren: At some festivals there was a kind of 'attitude squad' that would go around putting heavy manners on people's behaviour they didn't like. Probably why we got along with the Hells Angels so well was that there were plenty of people who disapproved of me and Lemmy! You had to kind of go with the flow; when you're breaking things down, certain things still have to function. In the festival context the stage has to be put up, holes have to be dug and if somebody has a tribal culture that you can actually get them to dig holes or put up scaffolding [that's fine]. If you didn't hire the local contractors you could get this weird mix of Trotskyite radicals, Hells Angels, and out of work roadies all working together on the same project.

Adrian Shaw: They were the 'muscle' of the freak movement. Rather than get a couple of professional gorillas in it was considered cool to have the Angels doing it. But whatever their good points might be, they are uncontrollable and not the kind of people to be entrusted with security. If ever there was any trouble, they would come down very hard indeed. You had your weekend freaks who thought it was cool to have Angels about, but of course they're the ones that hadn't actually seen them in action. By and large, good guys though. My wife always remembers a guy called Tank sat in Bristol drinking a cup of tea and stroking the cat the wrong way – going *up* the cat's fur!

Stonehenge 1984 by David Stooke

Nik Turner

Nik is Mr. Festival; that's his charisma

Simon Williams: Nik Turner is one of the coolest people I ever met, just a *dude*, and I love him to bits. One minute he'd be doing his Hawkwind thing, then he'd be doing Inner City Unit or his Sphynx project, or his All-Stars, but whatever music he's doing, he's doing it with a lot of fun and passion. And he had his Pyramid Stage, which was *everywhere*. Nik was a pioneer. The amount of people I've seen him jam with, or that he's allowed to jam with him, is just part of that whole free festival ethos, he was made for it. And he's always moving with the times so he's always got a new angle.

Angel: He wasn't just about the music; it wasn't just his music, or Hawkwind's music. It wasn't *just* that that brought people together. I'm talking about who he was as a person. Nik Turner put a lot of energy and thought into what was happening at the time and he *was* influential. He was influential over the right kind of people, and over the masses of people that were there who came on almost a pilgrimage. The great pilgrimage [laughs] to listen to Hawkwind! And I was one of them. I grew up on all his music and we had a mutual friend who owned a café in the back streets of Peckham whose name was Stuart… Stuart and Linda ran this café called Just In Time. Nik was always there and [Hawkwind singer/poet] Bob Calvert often came there. It was very intimate. They used to play music, and we all used to eat together and had incredible conversations into the early hours, go home in the morning. That's how I got to know him on a personal basis and then again at festivals, sitting with him and talking to him. He invited me to his home and I met all his family. I did the festival there with him and his partner, Marguerite. I actually named it. She said, 'I've got African stuff, I've got Celtic stuff going on,' and so I named it The Afro Celtic Experience. It became The ACE Festival. I was there at the very first, getting the signs ready and doing the advertising. I think later it changed it to Explosion or something, but it was the same festival.

Big Steve: I liked what Nik was doing as a project with Inner City Unit, the gigs were hilarious. They used to have a vaulting horse put in front of the stage when they played and it was like something out of a drama, *Escape from Colditz*, like they were digging a tunnel under the vaulting horse, planning to escape. The group were very surreal, very funny, and *very* psychedelic. Nik was a huge inspiration for the free festivals, probably the *most* influential figure. He designed his Pyramid Stage after he'd been to Egypt and played and recorded his flute in the King's Chamber at Giza. I've got some of his designs and they're quite amazing, like architect's drawings. He gave them to me and said, 'Right, this is how you erect the stage.' These hieroglyphs came in very handy in 1982, putting up the stage solo at Stonehenge.

Oz Hardwick: It was always worth seeing who Nik Turner was jamming with – whether a bunch of freaks hitting scrap metal, a Klezmer band, or the orchestra at Gerry Cottle's Circus. There was always a performance element and an edge of the unpredictable. The only downside was the proliferation of jugglers… I mean: why?

Angel: Nik is Mr. Festival; that's his charisma, that's his persona, his nature, that's what people want; he is a man of the people and he embraces it all. He's a bit of a guru, that guy!

Seasalter – 1976

It was one of the most desolate places you could hold a festival

Steve Lake: After Watchfield the authorities decided they weren't going to tolerate the festival scene. I didn't go to Seasalter for a number of reasons, but everything I heard about it was pretty grim. Certainly that was the word on the streets. Everyone I know who went there got busted or taken into the [police] station and strip-searched. It seemed to be a dour sort of event.

Dave Roberts: I got involved with the Seasalter festival, which was originally going to be at a place called Broad Oak, in Kent. I got there about a week before. We were shacked up in this cottage, about twelve of us, with the police surrounding us. The festival organiser was trying to keep the location a secret until the last minute and then it was moved to Seasalter... so we had to sneak out in the middle of the night and get down there without the police knowing. It was one of the most desolate places you could hold a festival, right down on the coast, windswept, raining. I was working on the main stage again; we saw Tim Blake playing two nights in a row doing his Crystal Machine set. He turned up in a battered old ambulance with all his gear and played at 2am with a fantastic light show. Seasalter was a successor to Watchfield, we couldn't get that site again, but it wasn't as successful because of the location. The police were really heavy-handed, they were searching everyone. Some people got strip-searched four or five times during the week, belongings were being searched and then thrown into the mud... it was really bad. There was definitely a reaction from the authorities. They were really clamping down on the festivals [by then]. There were a lot fewer people than Watchfield, we were down to two or three thousand but that was partly due to the police stopping people coming in.

"If anyone has got a Polaroid camera, can they please lend it to the BIT, as we've been told there are DS [Drug Squad] on site, and we want to photo [sic] them."

"Bob Chapman and Mr. Warren, you might as well use your uniforms you are so obvious. For those who haven't seen them yet, Mr. Chapman is wearing a kaftan and looks much too old to be dressed as a hippie (even older than Sid). Mr. Warren looks like a squaddie trying to be a hippie in T-Shirt and jeans. There's a guy wearing an 'Ohio State University T Shirt', be warned, he's DS. That's a red T-Shirt."
Stonehenge Free Festival Newsletters, 1977

Richard Chadwick: Heavily beset by rain and *really* heavily policed with everybody being searched coming in and out… it was that simple thing of one road, a coastal road, the festival on one side and the sea on the other with police on either end of the road but they'd ignored all the inland areas so people were just walking across the fields. Tim Blake played a really good gig there, fantastic.

Mick Farren: Usually festivals were enclosed in a fancy police cordon, particularly in regard to drugs. At the Isle of Wight they were searching everybody coming off the fucking ferries. Phun City, they sent in a load of narks on the Sunday afternoon, and they just got followed around and laughed at because they were so Keystone Cops about it. They would try and infiltrate, 'Excuse me son, do you know where I could buy a quick deal?' Guys in paisley jeans and big hobnailed boots; they were very gauche about it, but essentially the cops realised that what they didn't want to do was to upset ninety thousand people because then you get a soccer riot. If they didn't do it, it was reasonably peaceful and that was a kind of blackmail which sort of worked for a while. Heaven help those who lingered behind and were going to set up a commune. Heaven help those who strayed beyond the unspoken boundaries. But in many respects the sites themselves, with the exception of some pretty incongruous drug squads, were pretty much no-go areas [for the police]. They smashed up Phun City in the end. They'd wade in... if it had been a bank holiday weekend they'd steam in on the Tuesday morning, break up everything, arrest everybody who was left over because they didn't want them setting up some kind of Diggers' Commune on the land. But then, neither did the landowner. After that it was pretty much free game, which started to linearly lead to the travelling crusties who, in the summer, would go from festival to festival, when there were enough of them. However, when the festival was going, you could pretty much get away with anything – and did.

Big Steve: There were always searches going in and out of the Seasalter site. Through my work with Release, and Festival Welfare Services, I was always aware that on the edge there was this dark side. You could get lost in the hedonistic side in the midst of a festival, float on your bubble and think everything was marvellous and really get into the music, dancing, chatting, and working for the ethos. On the fringes, getting in and getting out of sites, it seemed that you could flow in and out, go from one world to another, but there was a police presence doing stop and search. If you were involved with the welfare scene, or with Release, you were aware that people were getting busted. Or you could see in the newspapers that there were court cases and people were getting fined or even sent to jail or deported if they were caught for a more serious offence. We manned a stall for the Legalise Cannabis Campaign and put up a graffiti sign, '34 people busted Friday', to warn people to be careful and tell them what was happening. So I *was* aware, but I can't say everybody was, because if you were a young person going to a festival you're probably not aware of all the things that are going on, on and off site.

Dave Roberts: Watchfield got a bad reputation because the police were sending in plain-clothes to try and bust people, whereas at Seasalter the police never came on site, possibly because they were so successful stopping people attending. You see, there was only one road in because it was on the coast, on a headland.

Jake Stratton-Kent: After Wally Hope was gone, the festival scene kind of lost its way. Bill Dwyer had taken refuge in Ireland, he was that worried. 'The Home Office are out to get me. I can't stay in the country.' So it had fewer and fewer organisers. Sid Rawle got more and more prominent but he didn't actually do anything. He was just always there saying, 'I'm the leader, I'm the spokesman.' But the festivals did lose their way without Wally Hope. We still had the ethos for a while but things like the Brew Crew intruded.

Tibetan Ukrainian Mountain Troupe, Hackney 1983 (Janet Henbane)

Action at the Argyle St squats (Janet Henbane)

Squatting

You had the whole squatting movement beginning to evolve and that was a political statement as much as anything else

Simon Williams: The Free Festival scene at its best was always an alternative society, whether for the summer or just for a few weeks, and it overlapped into the squat scene so you'd have squat parties.

Keith Bailey: It was incredibly productive, because it allowed all these people to come together without any obligations. Yes, it was a political thing, because at that time, you had the whole squatting movement beginning to evolve and that was a political statement as much as anything else. Councils at that time were leaving thousands of properties rotting away. I thought the two things were intertwined and that the free festival movement was an extension of the squatting movement. But it was also part of the right of people to congregate where and when they wished. That made it a threat to the authorities because there was stuff going on that they weren't in control of… that they had no way of controlling, in fact.

Big Steve: Working with the Legalise Cannabis campaign from the 1970s, I was aware of the changing drug scene and though to me it had nothing to do with the free festivals, certainly there were people who went on, mainly in our big cities, to get into heavier drugs and some got addicted to heroin. But I never gave much credence to the progression theory. I was more aware in the 80s that people living in some squats, particularly in the squatting scene in London towards the East End, were junkies who were fixing up and taking smack. I've never had much contact with that world of people who were heroin users, but I was aware that there were people in the squatting scene using heroin. I knew one tenement squat in London, between Islington and Clerkenwell, around that area. I think nearly every day someone there was OD'ing. It was *sad* seeing people getting their dole cheques and forming long queues outside a squat to score their fix... the poverty and the struggle to survive. It makes you wonder how these people managed to keep it all together. I'd organised squat gigs. I was a member of the

Islington Squatters Group and we'd squatted the St. James Church, which was between Kings Cross and the Angel; this was a Clown's Church that was built, or dedicated, to [Joseph] Grimaldi who was a famous Italian clown and we squatted that and did a few gigs and benefits there.

Jake Stratton-Kent: Wally Squats were great, anybody could turn up there; we'd meet people up at Stonehenge, hippies who'd turn up there, and we'd say, 'Come back to the squats if you like.' Anyone could turn up on the doorstep, we had one chap there who was sixty-five, full of conspiracy theories, UFOs and stuff; we made sure he had a room. But if someone came who was causing trouble with the locals, we'd throw them out. Anybody was welcome in, but it didn't mean we couldn't throw them out again. You had to be tough to do that. Tough love, if you like.

Keith Bailey: Misty In Roots used to come and rehearse at our place when we were living in 'short-life' housing out near Iver in Buckinghamshire – the M25 was going to go through this place which was a millionaire's house. We had a little bungalow, like an outhouse, turned into a recording and rehearsal studio. 'Short-life' housing was an extension of the squatting movement; we got it through an organisation called Patchwork which was born out of the squatting of Centre Point in London in 1971 by a bunch of early radicals, who made front-page news for quite a long time. So the government said, 'Okay, what do you want?' Well, these guys said, 'Look at all these houses that you've got that are rotting. We want you to set us up with a grant to take them over, do them up and rent them out to people who are squatting and can't afford commercial rents.' The government agreed to this and gave them these houses that they'd compulsorily purchased for the route of the M25. Of course, it took them years to get the planning permission for the M25 so all that time we were living in a millionaire's house, miles from anywhere and perfect for rehearsals, which worked wonders for the Here & Now band. We got probably our best album of the time, *Fantasy Shift*, as a direct result of that.

Jeremy Cunningham: 2000DS used to put on squat gigs at one of the big colleges in London, them and a band called Conflict used to do cheap punk rock nights and we used to go and play that. 2000DS would always do a slot with all their hangers-on, who were called the Crow Force. Their call to arms was '*The Weigh-in*', because in those days we used to weigh-in scrap for money. They've changed the law now, you can't do it any more, but we used to make enough to live on. You have to have a licence now, but you didn't then and some of us would go around trying to find old breweries, places like that, where there were loads of old copper pipes, hammer the pipes out and have the roof off... not anywhere that was lived in, obviously! Old breweries were the main [targets].

Dick Lucas: [2000DS] had a bad reputation for blagging everything, doing everything for as much money as possible without giving anything away and never having any equipment that worked and generally being rude and catastrophic. But on the other hand Gary [Bamford, 2000DS] was very self-organised and whipped up a lot of other people to get things happening.

Gary Bamford: We were part of the Hackney squatting scene. After the mid-80s, when we'd got thrashed by the cops, I shot off to Europe and lived in France and Spain for a good while. Came back in '87 and went to Hackney to start a new band, because after being in Europe for a year you missed that heavy-duty, trashy, metal music, full-on stuff. It seemed a good time to try and do something a bit like that in our country. At the time there was still a free festival scene; lots of musicians wanting to play anywhere and anyhow. So a squat in Hackney was a good place to put a band together to be able to hit the travellers' scene again in the summer. There was a squat in Hackney that was an old bus station, and when they got evicted from there, there was a street being closed down called Brougham Road. Lots of squatters went out of the bus station and took the whole street. The whole street was squatted. When we got there, we just hung around in the street in our vehicles and ended up getting one of the houses. We used that as a practice room but got a bit loud for that place. Then there was a British Telecom building that we moved into. It was huge, a whole block just behind Holloway Road where it meets the Seven Sisters. It was the perfect place for practising and we'd put on a gig every Friday.

Steve Lake: Zounds lived in Brougham Road. We were based there for most of the time, certainly while we were making records and were most active. It had been a street of squats for years before Zounds moved in and brought all their rock 'n' roll punks with them. Before that it had quite a serious kind of Squatter/Anarchist scene and a lot of separatist lesbians, feminist households. Dave Morris, the guy who was sued in the McLibel case, had previously lived in the house we moved into. All the older, more serious activists moved out and hippie punk squatters took over. There was a big bus garage just in the next street to us which had been abandoned and a couple of [squatters] had buses there. Some people broke into the bus garage and started to squat that, this was 1980 or '81, and suddenly there were buses turning up. There was a beautiful irony to this old Hackney bus garage suddenly becoming home to a whole convoy of buses and trucks.

[McDonald's Restaurants v Morris & Steel was a libel case brought by the McDonald's corporation against two environmental activists, Dave Morris and Helen Steel. Running for many years, it had been instigated by McDonald's following the publication of a pamphlet (*What's Wrong with McDonald's: Everything they don't want you to know*) which made a large number of serious allegations regarding the company's involvement with deforestation, Third World famine, and the nature of the food sold by the chain. The original judgement found in favour of McDonald's and awarded the business libel damages of £40,000 though there were subsequent appeals, and litigation by Morris and Steel against the British government.]

Janet Henbane: 'My Man' was telling me about when they 'took' Hackney Bus Garage in 1982. The TUMT buses and people [Tibetan Ukrainian Mountain Troupe – see separate section], and various other people with buses, met up in the early hours of the morning having been parked up near Roehampton, at 'Robin Hood's Roundabout'. They drove over to Hackney and squatted the abandoned bus garage. It still had all the offices there, and all the crockery and cutlery was still in the canteen. There were three toilets, two with smashed basins and one that 'Pete the Bus' plumbed in and fettled up. For baths, some people went to the bath house, 50p for a bath with towel! At some point someone hot-wired the electricity to the outside supply; there was a line of bright neon lights running the length of the garage, on all the time. The fuses kept blowing and bigger fuses would be put in. At first the electricity was connected up to a house down on Brougham Road, just round the corner; one cable supplying all of the people squatting there! HBG was raided a few times by the Old Bill. The first time was when someone was stopped and searched after leaving the garage on a motorbike with £2,000. They raided and found nothing, because the person on the motorbike had been on his way to buy supplies of blow. The garage still had large derv tanks with grungy stuff in the bottom, this was filtered and used. It's rumoured that that is how the TUMT drove up to the Blue Moon festival in Nenthead, Cumbria at the end of May 1982, and indeed how other people got there too. Later on in the summer, when people went back after the festivals, the garage had filled with more people and vehicles. People were even living in the offices. The only problem with the bus garage was it was on hard-standing so could be very messy. There were people fitting up vehicles all the time and dogs wandering about. Nevertheless HBG is legendary in the new age travellers' tales of the old days; they have fond memories of the place and atmosphere. The energy was fuelled by the events of the time. The Punk scene and its off-shoots were all part of that energy. The authorities were in the process of clamping down on the travellers and the free festivals, but without the aid of all the computer data that is held now on people and vehicles it was a case of immense 'freedom' and getting away with all sorts of shenanigans.

Gary Bamford: In those days there were more empty buildings, and you could get quite central, whereas nowadays everything is jumped on and you don't get squatted streets any more. Some of these buildings were huge and as long as you kept the door locked and didn't let [the local authorities] in, you were okay. You didn't take any notice of them, you had your rights, and it was a good place to make a noise. You've got to live whichever way you can and whichever way you feel comfortable. Lots of people wouldn't feel comfortable living in a squat but we found it a lot freer and easier and you could put your music equipment in and make a noise and do lots of other creative things as well. But most people abuse situations and just get pissed or off their heads on drugs. Squats are no different, if you want to respect your space then respect it – if you want to go smash your room up, smash it up but don't smash mine up. I think it's the only way, especially if you don't want to work with the system. But we were living in vehicles most of the time; the only reason we went into the big squats in London was to have rehearsal rooms. The minute the weather was any good we were off, going to festivals and living in vehicles. If it's a nice day, you sit outside your vehicle, if it's raining you go under a marquee and watch a band, whatever, but everybody needs that space.

Bridget Wishart: I first met Gary from 2000DS when I was at Art College in Wales. I became mates with a friend of his, a Welsh punk girl called Nyx from his home-town of Cwmbran. Sometimes I'd get back to our flat and Gary would be there having climbed up the fire escape and come in through the window. We all went to gigs in Cardiff together, we saw The Damned one time. It was always crazy; people getting out of it, spiked drinks, police, chases, losing friends or clothes and inevitably missing trains. Gary got bored with England and moved to Berlin. When I went to there for an art school video project in 1982, I stayed with him and his girlfriend, Kath, for a week. I slept under the kitchen table, the other room was their bed-sitting-room and the toilet was outside the flat, on the stairs. The area where they lived was the old Nazi headquarters; there were still bullet holes in the walls. Faded wartime décor lingered in the entrance hall and on the stairs of their building. He showed us the Berlin Wall at 4am, said it was 'the best time to see it', as the tube trains started again at that time. We looked across at the guards watching us through binoculars, their weapons ominous and obvious. Copious billows of smoke enveloped the guard towers, smoke from the East German factories that powered up at night to get around pollution restrictions. Around 6am we went on to a nightclub, which at that time of day was free to get in. It was quite hard to tell who was male and who was female; it seemed transvestism was big in Berlin. Later in the week I went to a squat party with him, from which my abiding memory is arriving and seeing guys peeing out of all the windows. When we arrived the music was really quiet, until Gary found the sound system and cranked it up. None of us had money so we kicked all the empty cans piled up around the walls until we found full ones. We'd run out of money because we'd been caught jumping the trains and fined. The next day we went to the hospital and sold our blood as they paid around a tenner for about a pint of blood which gave us enough to go out for the night with a couple of American transvestites who were living in Berlin to avoid the draft. In the 90s I saw Gary occasionally at free festivals when he played in 2000DS and I was in the Hippy Slags. Gary lived and breathed punk and had little time for people who in his eyes just *played* at being punk. He later went back to Berlin when the wall came down and lived in a vehicle on the old no-man's-land, which was just a vicious piece of ground that had been poisoned by weed killer for so many years.

Joie Hinton: I remember one festival down in Penzance with 2000DS, who were fucking amazing, absolutely mental, *the* festival punk band of the mid-80s, they were *it*, no doubt about it and I had a lot of respect for them. *The Travellers Aid Trust* album that Hawkwind released... their track on that, '*More BASS in the mon-it-tarrrr...*' I remember that actual show, that was Penzance and they were absolutely awesome.

"Squatting's a good idea. But you can't really enjoy living in squats. It's just a place to put your head down."
Paul Simonon, interviewed by Chris Salewicz. *The Face*, February 1981

Mick Moss: Everyone had the *Squatters Handbook*. I've still got a copy somewhere. You just sussed out an empty house, usually popped into the library or the town hall to check out the ratepayer or owner; council owned was best or large property owner. You got in, secured the door, put up a curtain and made a fire, and that was it. Home, while it lasted. Electricity was usually connected via a six-inch nail for a mains fuse! And water was connected using plastic hoses, if it was off. I squatted in various places in London and more when I moved to Bath in the early 70s. In Bath you had to squat. There were so many empty places and no one could afford to rent, but it was also a political act. I shared with lots of people, some nice, some not so nice – such as a motorbike thief who used one house to store nicked bikes. Most were run communally but not in any sort of structured way. Rules were developed as you went along. People came and went. Most food, cooking was shared. As with shopping, cleaning, repairs etc. - but, as always, some did more than others.

Squatting – Stoat Hall, Bath

Life was very unregimented and free in a way that many other young people never experienced

Bridget Wishart: There was Stoat Hall, in Bath. Steve Bemand, Richard Chadwick, Will (what *was* his surname?), and Rob Grainger, who were The Demented Stoats, came from Newport, started a squat at Anglo Terrace and ended up squatting 6 Cleveland Row. 'Stoat Hall'… they were collectively known as 'The Stoats', though when I joined them I wasn't called Stoat… for some reason I was called 'Bridget Noise'.

Richard Chadwick: We'd all met up in Newport. I was there as a student, and Rob and Steve had come up to visit and we'd hang out and brave the pubs together. Rob, who was six feet tall and very striking looking, used to wear mirror-shades to avoid any potential eye contact at all - it was that volatile an atmosphere. We were hanging around, taking mushrooms and playing music together and it sounded really quite good and that's a definitive thing from my point of view where I thought I could be a musician. I only had bongos, well, not even bongos really, just a drum sawn in half! But we decided, 'Okay let's go and live somewhere, and Rob suggested Bath as a laid-back sort of town. He told us all about the scene and we thought, 'Yeah, let's try it.' Rob Stoat had lived in Bath as a hippie in the 1960s and when I talked to him I realised that he'd lived in the centre of Bath… in the park, under a tree! But he had a record player, the whole scene, life going on in there… and nobody nicked anything, which tells you something of the sensibility of the times. He lived there a few weeks in the summer before someone who was moving let him have their flat. This entranced us because Newport was a hard town. Steve came down as a scout and sent us a letter back, that was how primitive it was, saying, 'I've found this house called Merlin.' By the time we'd got there, the house wasn't an option any more so we moved into an existing squat, Number One, Anglo Terrace. That was a rough squat. It was started off, like most squats, by highly organised and motivated people, then more people move in who've got issues and that fucks the whole thing up.

Steve Bemand: Dereliction moved in from the bottom and each floor got more and more tramp-y with meths and cider and we eventually retreated up to the top floor.

Richard Chadwick: Rob scouted out this place, which turned out to be a dump but we turned up anyway and from there we found Stoat Hall at the end of that first winter. My parents came to visit me, for them it was a significant thing. I'd moved out of the college town I'd been living in for the last three or four years and they came over to see where I was. They had to come up through what we called the basement, the bit we called Doom Valley with the alcoholic living at the bottom of it, a lovely man but absolutely hopeless. I was with this woman at the time and we'd taken acid and were sitting on a bridge and I heard my Mum saying 'Oh look, there's Richard', and they'd seen us. We took them back and gave them some tea and they were making allusions to drug culture. I said 'Oh, yeah, I'm on acid at the moment.' And they were very much, 'Call the police right now', and I had to talk them down from that! 'Don't do that, it's a very irresponsible thing to do... you need to realise the ramifications.' Dad was driving along in his car and I'm running along the side shouting, 'Don't do this!'

Bridget Wishart: There wasn't a bathroom at Stoat Hall, there was a bath in the kitchen but it had a wooden board covering it and that was always covered in dirty crockery. I think I only had one bath there in all the time I lived there. Cleanliness wasn't highly prized. The electric meter was drilled and a joss stick placed in it to stop the wheel turning. We did try to remember when the guy would be likely come to read the metre and take it out a week or so before, but sometimes whoever showed the guy where it was would have to pull the joss stick out and rub dust in the hole… in was in a grim and dark passage so it was easy enough to do. The band used a lot of electricity practising, and we didn't have had the cash to pay the bills.

Richard Chadwick: We had to use a public toilet, an underground toilet buried in the middle of the road, because none of the water in the house worked at all, apart from on the ground floor. It was very primitive and we wanted a better standard of living than that. We were all hunting for somewhere else and I remember walking along the canal and seeing this house that was empty and a friend of ours moved us there. We'd been in Bath for a while and knew people from hanging around the pubs. The Department of Transport intended a change in the road system and had bought the properties in the street up as blighted, then the scheme was given up and the houses came up for sale. Immediately more organised people than us jumped in, people like self-help housing associations and Bath Housing Association, government-funded bodies, who went straight to the owners and said, 'These houses are empty, we'd like to take them on.' The D.O.T told them there were squatters and they'd evict them, but that was a bit embarrassing for the Associations, given they were supposed to be *housing* people. 'Well, they can join your organisation and if not, then we'll evict them.'

Mick Moss: Evictions were common, but mostly we left without too much fuss or agro. I do remember a bunch of people from Oxford who had squatted a whole area of streets called Jericho which was due to be demolished - it was much more of a communal or political thing for them. Protests against letting good housing go empty, when there were families in need of housing!

Klive Farhead: The really important thing [about Stoat Hall] was that bands could practice there every day of the week and if you've got somewhere bands can practice then a scene develops. So when Richard went to America [in 1989 as drummer with Hawkwind] and met Jello Biafra, Jello thought that the Bath scene was as big as the Seattle scene because he'd heard of lots of bands and things like that. So you've free housing, free electricity, plenty of rehearsal space and that creates myriad bands. Every summer, bands from these houses would go out to all the festivals; a melting pot of all sorts of people. There are people who are really successful musicians now, who used to go down to Stoat Hall to buy their dope and said, 'I really want to do this.'

Steve Bemand: People we'd met from the festivals would just turn up. Hampton Row/ Cleveland Row was very much a free festival outpost. In 1986/87 the Smartpils bus was parked up in the street with a cafe on it with parties going on, bands played in the houses and

Waiting for a ride - Smartpils on the London Rd, Bath (Chris Abell)

down in the land below the street where there was a bender site.

Angie Bell: Convoy people used to park up there so it was a quite a hub of the street, really.

Claire Grainger: When I was young it was a good way of life, it was quite easy to squat in this country in those days. There was a shortage of places to play gigs so people would squat warehouses or churches or wherever, play a gig for the night and then leave it. Unfortunately some vandalism would occur but we'd try and hire generators and just plug in and play. Or there'd be traveller sites and we'd turn up and play there, like the bender site at the bottom of Cleveland Row in Bath.

Bridget Wishart: Living at Stoat Hall meant that life was very unregimented and free in a way that many other young people never experienced, those who either had to live at home because they couldn't afford rent, or had to work five days a week to cover their living expenses. The Natural Theatre Co had the house next door and they were brilliant neighbours because we really were very noisy and had many odd folk passing through who quite often ended up living on the street and on the railway land by the river at the end of the rank, though that was a miserable site to occupy in winter, subject to flooding and damp.

Richard Chadwick: It's having the time and the space to do things. Lots of people on the dole had the time, but you also needed the space. Accommodation away from your parents when you are young is fundamental. Living in your own space and controlling your own destiny. That, in essence, was the idea of squatting. Our lifestyle evolved around our accommodation because as soon as we had established something that was cool enough and big enough to live our lives the way we wanted to, a whole house that we had control over, we could integrate and mingle and get to know people. The intrinsic thing about Stoat Hall was that it was just a good place to hang out. A lot of people who came to visit us were local people who lived with their parents and they liked smoking dope and listening to music, but they couldn't do it in their own home so they'd hang around the streets or the park and then they'd meet up with us and 'oh, there's this place we can go', so we'd have this thriving community coming around to visit just because it was fun. We had a load of bikers who squatted a house next door to us and they'd come around at weekends with a load of dope, and get us stoned, and lay around in our living room because they knew as soon as we were stoned we'd start playing our music, this hippie, spacey stuff – drone rock instrumental stuff. Once we had Stoat Hall, the world started coming to us.

Friends at Vinegar Hill:
Bridget Wishart, Claire Grainger, Spider, Richard Chadwick (Chris Abell)

Culture Shock at Treworgey - Photographer unknown (Jasper Pattison collection)

Cartoon by Charlie Dancey

Charlie's Story

The vagaries of being involved with the festivals and travelling scene are well-documented, but this charming story from Charlie Dancey, who describes himself as a 'disillusioned and bomb-traumatised middle-class hippie in 1977,' roughly when this story takes place, neatly sums up its whole air of unpredictability.

Charlie Dancey: I can't remember what year it was, but it was certainly the mid-70s. I'd been to Ashton Court Festival previously, and that's really where my journey began. That year I was travelling about in my old school bus, 'Max', with my partner, Lynne, and the kids who variously belonged to Lynne and me. The year before, we'd managed to make enough petrol money to stay on the road for most of the summer by selling coffee to the festival-goers. Our trick was to sell decent coffee in real china cups, which, amazingly, never seemed to get broken or lost. We had a small fleet of percolators, about forty cups, and a nice big urn to help us keep plenty of water nearly boiling. We also had a nice sign, since I made my living in those days, when not on the road, as a sign-writer and would-be show painter. That year had been good, and we'd shared our adventures with Diddicoy Paul, Pirate Paul as some knew him, who was a good-looking, cheeky, general dealer who will be well-remembered by those that knew him in Bath before he passed away some years back. Paul's addition to our fare was bacon sandwiches, which despite the fashion for vegetarianism in those days, proved a sure-seller.

During the previous winter I'd loaned my bus to a friend who totally failed to listen to my warning that he absolutely *must* return it by nightfall. I hadn't told him why. In any case, and as things went in those days, he failed to bring it back. Since the bus had a slowly leaking radiator there was no anti-freeze in the system and it had to be drained every night to prevent it from freezing. It duly froze and when I picked it up in the morning things were not looking good. I thawed it out, but a couple of days later the engine seized and more or less exploded on the side of the M4. I dragged Max home behind 'Gus', the Walcot Village Hall lorry, lifted the engine out and scrapped it. We were always short of money, so the replacement I found was a cheap diesel engine that had, apparently, been put together by a one-armed mechanic named Dave. Instead of being impressed, as I childishly was, I should have taken that as a warning because the engine was a pile of poo.

One afternoon the unwilling engine dragged us all up the hill to Ashton Court where the story really begins. On arriving, I noticed a beautiful, unrestored, 1955 Ford Thames radio truck parked alongside an impressive looking tepee. I took one look into the cab and, noticing the elegant tulip-shaped gearstick and the incredibly low mileage (1,500 miles from new!), I just knew that this had to be my new truck. I made my way into the tepee and sat down quietly in the dark, as people passed joints around, and tried to figure out who the truck belonged to. Somehow one guy caught my eye. The briefest of smiles told me I'd found the right person. 'I was just wondering,' I asked timidly, 'if it might be for sale?' Another twinkle. 'I'll buy it!'

'Don't you want to know how much it is?'

'Not really, I just sort of figure that it will cost me five hundred pounds.'

Turned out I had that bit right as well. Mike explained that he was an epileptic, so, despite owning the truck, he couldn't drive it. The people with him were using it as a tepee transporter and not really looking after it. I explained that I didn't have the money right now, but maybe after the festival was finished I'd get it to him and pick up the truck. Mike said that would be fine. After Ashton Court the truck would go back to Talley Valley with the tepee and then Ned, the driver, would run it up to London to Mike's place, to drop off Mike's big flight case of musical kit at his studio and then I could have the truck. The deal was done.

God knows how I managed to sell Max the Bus with that awful engine, but I did, and less than a week later I phoned Mike to say I had the money and could I come and pick up the truck? 'Well you could, except that it hasn't made it back from Talley. The last I heard was that Ned was going to take it to Glastonbury Festival before coming back here.' I didn't suppose that Ned had a phone number, and I was right not to.

So I grabbed Pirate Paul, and loaded Lynne, several percolators, an urn, about forty cups and the usual complement of children onto the back of his flatbed truck and we set off for Glastonbury Festival sitting on boxes of bacon and rolls. We arrived at Glastonbury to check out the scene and discovered that there was, in fact, no festival that year. Where, I wondered, would people in trucks heading for the festival have ended up? We found them in a line of about thirty vehicles parked up on the road just behind the Tor, but noticeably missing was the 1955 Ford Thames that I had come to find. I had five hundred pounds in my pocket, my family, a lot of coffee and bacon and cups, but no truck. There were now thirty one trucks stopped on the road and the cops showed up, keen to move us all on. I was desperate to locate that

Thames so I had an idea.

Paul, who was always a canny chap, knew just the place. 'It's OK!' I said to the cops. 'We're going to escort this entire convoy to some private land!' That wasn't strictly true, but Paul had suggested an amazing spot for an impromptu festival just a few miles away, at the old Roman lead-mine workings near Priddy, a place that has forever been a favourite travellers' haunt. With much cajoling we managed to get all but two of the trucks to start their engines, and tied those to better vehicles with tow ropes. Of course hardly any of the trucks had any fuel. Those that were lowest on juice were piloted, as you might imagine, by people who didn't bother much about money, and hardly any of them could manage more than twenty miles an hour. Everybody needed a pee and all the dogs escaped. It took about an hour to drag the entire grunting, wheezing convoy as far as the garage in Wells to top them up with fuel for the gruelling hill climb and another forty-five minutes to process them all though the pumps. Two more vehicles had broken down by now, one we fixed and another was tied to the back of Paul's truck. I had shelled out about twenty-five pounds of my own money on other people's fuel.

Barely half a day later the entire convoy, except for one truck whose wheel had terminally fallen off, made the last of the epic ten miles and rumbled onto the grass at Red Quarry. Paul lit a fire; we made bacon sandwiches and put the coffee on. If the Thames did actually make it from Talley, there was no doubt that it would eventually find its way to the new festival we'd created (which, incidentally, ran for years afterwards).

Paul decided that business wasn't brisk enough, so resolved to go back to Bath and pick up enough scaffolding to make a stage and try to locate a couple of bands. I decided to go back with him, because it was obvious that the Thames had never left Talley at all. The next morning, at the crack of dawn, I 'borrowed' a 1960s Wolsey (from the very man that had caused Max to blow up by not bringing it back) and my mate 'Coke' as a spare driver, stuck some petrol in the tank and hightailed it to Talley. I gave Coke some money for helping me out. My cash was dwindling. We arrived a few hours later at the field above the tepees and there was the Thames, parked with its doors wide open, the ground around it littered with festival junk. I sent Coke home in the car and made my way down the hill looking for Ned.

Ned, it turned out, was in love and not minded to do anything in a hurry, so it was after an agonising night in the tepee with him and his girlfriend, who made extremely noisy love for more than six hours, that I finally got him to come back up the hill and sort though the gear. I packed Mike's stuff in his big flight case, offloaded the tepee junk, bolted the steering box back on and set off down the track to civilisation.

Later that day I arrived back in Bath with a hitchhiker I'd picked up. I dropped him at the train station with the flight case, drove the truck home, whizzed back down the hill on a bike, locked it to the railings and bought two London tickets. My rider needed to get to London and I needed help with the enormous flight case full of musical kit. Fortunately Mike's place in London was only a couple of miles from Paddington, but we were shattered after pushing all the kit over the big flyover and down cobbled streets. I said goodbye to my hitchhiker and handed him a fiver for his trouble and then, finally, I rang on Mike's doorbell.

He let me in and made me tea. He was impressed that I'd managed to get everything sorted out. 'Everything except one thing,' I said. 'I did have five hundred, but with one thing and another...'

'You got four still?'

'I do.'

Mike smiled. 'Then we have a deal.'

That night, at about one in the morning, I arrived at Priddy Festival in 'Trigger', the truck. The place was kicking; Paul had got stage lights and two bands together. People were buying coffee and our secret sideline 'Special Coffee.' It was a fine night and I felt very pleased with myself. Little did I realise that in just ten short years from then, I'd have to buy Trigger all over again.

Good for the Soul...

There was a massively educational element to all of the free festivals

Angel: Places like Rougham, and Deeply Vale, offered an alternative way of life, of sustaining life independently. They showed you how that could be achieved. They were incredible festivals. Rougham was a very special place. You couldn't get that education anywhere else, and not only to be told about it, but shown! Now they've got a whole field dedicated to similar stuff at Glastonbury, the Green Futures Field, but it all originated from Rougham Tree Fayre. I wouldn't be surprised if some of the people at Glastonbury aren't the same.

Nigel Mazlyn Jones: Rougham Tree Fayre had a total mix across the board, it wasn't a free festival but one based on traditional fairs. It was set under a parallel set of very old lime trees and they had one or two Romany gypsy people there every year, with their horses, living in caravans with beautiful cut-glass.

Big Steve: The East Anglian fairs up at Rougham were on-going fairs that the travellers would go to, then end up, in September, at the Mushroom Fayres, in Wales. The East Anglian fairs seemed to take on the characteristics of traditional fairs that had been established for a long period of time. It was almost like the free festivals were adding to what was already there, maybe traditional crafts, and artisan peoples. At the beginning of the summer, the first festival was normally the Strawberry Fayre in Cambridge and that was a long-established tradition that went back to medieval times. Rougham was very important; they were involved in many alternative things, such as collecting money on the festival sites in the 1980s to raise funds to send water pumps to Ethiopia for famine relief. They were a precursor to, and had an influence on, Bob Geldof and Midge Ure when they did *Live Aid* in 1985.

Nigel Mazlyn Jones: The people who organised the festival aimed to do charity work overseas, and Green Deserts, who were the first people to use the term 'Green', started it. An award winning ex-BBC cameraman, Harry Hart, was behind this; it was his vision. He'd been filming for the BBC and recognised ecological problems when he was flying across an island

Rougham, Late 1970s (Janet Henbane)

and saw the deforestation. He could see in the bay how the orange-brown silt washed down from the small island out under the azure ocean. It inspired him and he became a macrobiotic who advocated an idea, that the world could house itself from old western coaches, coaches like the thirty or forty seaters that the army and the public use. You could insulate the glass with bubble-wrap. He lived in two of these coaches – one was his living module and one his work module for his graphics. He started up Green Deserts, Green Deserts then started up the Rougham Tree Fayre, which ran for quite a few years and raised twenty to thirty thousand pounds a year. With the money, they subsequently sent out two coaches to Ethiopia. One had environmentalists, biologists and educationalists on board, all qualified, and the other coach had a theatre puppetry team. The whole ethos of the thing was about desertification of the planet. When I found out about that, it was a hugely educational thing. So I think there was a massively educational element to all of the free festivals and to the low-cost gatherings across the social board, across the economic earning board. This particular one, in my case, was the first time I'd learned that two-thirds of the deserts were man-made. That was because the tribes out there, who were the nomads, counted their finance in their herds; and as they moved their bigger herds across, if they ate the bark from one of the trees, you lost six square metres to desert. I didn't know that. They were teaching the locals how to reclaim the deserts. The coaches worked like this. The puppetry people would do shows for the children, entertaining without language but using puppetry. The parents would see that these people could be trusted, gained their confidence and they would then describe how they were there to help them reclaim the desert. The biologists would come in and say, 'You plant one small sapling and put a wicker cage over it which, in the sunlight creates a condensation trap. You nurture *that* for a year or two, increasing the size of the wicker basket until it can nurture itself.' Create a whole group of them and you could widen the oasis back out into the desert very quickly.

Big Steve: I went to the Mushroom Fayre in 1981, which was held beside a river in a beautiful Welsh valley. People were living in tepees; they were the original travellers, maybe a thousand people. It was at the end of the summer and people were going out on blackberry hunts, somebody would organise a bus or a van and take people up to the top of the mountains. They'd be wandering around the fields, amongst the sheep, looking for psilocybin mushrooms which they'd been collecting, bring back to the site and make up huge pots of tea. People would sit there drinking mushroom tea and smoking a chillum, eating blackberries, enjoying the music… a much more low-key scale than the big festivals but probably more authentic to the hippie ethic. If you were an anthropologist going back in time and studying this particular culture, you'd probably see the real hippie culture back in festivals like the Mushroom festivals in Wales. It goes back to that Epicurean idea of the hippies, this idea of foraging, collecting the fruits that were in season, living off the land, living with an organic perspective. There's always been that thing in Shamanistic cultures across the world, the Shaman was always seen as the outsider but he knew the way, he was the road man. He knew the best way to use things like the magic mushrooms, the right way to take them in the right setting and context in order to communicate with the ancestors, or with spirits. Or to be able to tell stories that were part of the tribal folklore, a way of communicating to the future generations. Maybe he'd go into a trance, start dancing and take on the form of animal spirits of the forest. Communication with God, an almost divine or spiritual aspect to shamanism, it goes back to a very old tradition, that connection between the profane and the sacred.

Angel: You had healers at festivals all those years ago, those with the ability to affect people in certain ways, to help them. These people came with their gifts and their knowledge and they gave it freely. It was an experience and the only reason you had it was because you were there! It wasn't anywhere else, and spiritual healing people were very much a part of that. Now you've got healers and you've got crystal shops everywhere, but in those days to go to a festival and have someone lay their hands on you, or to hand you a crystal, was a unique experience. It didn't happen anywhere else, it was so important. It is sad the way it has become, and that's not because of the Government or the police. Unfortunately a certain element of people realised they could make an awful lot of money and probably did! It has turned into this entire thing that they now call 'New Age.'

Nik Turner: The Tepee Village is all part of the same Free Festival celebration of natural forces and native spirits and so on, they aligned themselves with the Native Americans and spent time with them and their culture and were very in-tune with that sort of thing. They were part and parcel of the festival scene because they were all pushing in the same direction and were at the heart of some of the festivals, instigators really. Not a huge amount of people, probably a hundred or so – maybe twenty-five tepees with three or four living in each.

Jeremy Cunningham: I was a part of the later days of the Peace Convoy, which was what it was called… which was a bit strange. We were into peace and all that, but we were punk rockers, we hated any hippie connotations. That used to really wind us up. We didn't have anything to do with the tepee thing and all that; I parked in the wrong field once on a festival site by mistake in the dark and when I woke up I was surrounded by tepees and people doing Red Indian dances around fires and I was, 'What are all these white people doing pretending to be Indians?' They were all having a go at me about being a diesel-spewing monster, raping the planet!

Deeply Vale 1976 – 1980

There was a real 'all help together' hippie vibe

While a lot of the annual summer free festivals occurred in Southern England or in Wales, the descent into free festival chaos of the Northern 'pay' festival, Bickershaw, had its own legacy in the Deeply Vale festivals that ran from an initial low-key gathering in 1976 through to its own collapse into hard drugs and anti-social behaviour in the early 1980s. What set Deeply Vale apart from the Southern festivals, however, and why it is considered so influential today, is that the merging of cultural scenes typified by the spacerock / punk / reggae hybrid that has become colloquially known as the crustie was accentuated by Deeply Vale's embracing of the rapidly developing punk scene. The Fall played at Deeply Vale in 1978 and 1979, introduced to the festival scene by Here & Now, who themselves successfully straddled the 'old regime' and the new; The Ruts also represented the punk ethos whilst Misty in Roots brought their multi-cultural vibe to the Vale. This cross-fertilisation of genres didn't come together completely smoothly – in one notable instance that veteran of the hippie movement, Sid Rawle, became involved in an altercation on stage with punk band Wilful Damage after being offended by the band's haranguing of his followers that led to their singer sustaining a broken arm after being forcibly ejected from the stage. Nevertheless, Deeply Vale (in recent years the subject of an ITV documentary) is a key link to the festivals of the 1980s in its wide ranging artists and its cross-cultural acceptance.

Keith Bailey: Deeply Vale I remember with great fondness. It was a Northern thing, up near Bolton and supposed to have been in the valley where the first factory was ever built, the birthplace of the industrial revolution. It was a beautiful setting, and just about the right size – there was always about twenty, twenty-five thousand people there and such a nice vibe. The last one moved to a different location, but one equally as beautiful.

Chris Hewitt: A lot of people from the North Manchester area went to Bickershaw in '72. There was quite a good counterculture scene in the whole of Manchester and its satellite towns. At that point, there was a venue called Stoneground which was run by the guy who used to be the manager of Manchester's Virgin Record store, and that tended to put on all the weird and wonderful bands:

Hatfield and the North, Gong, and Kevin Coyne. I was, and still am, production manager for Tractor, and we played there. There were a few 'head' shops in Manchester; one in particular, On The Eighth Day, used to sell incense and copies of *IT*, *Frendz* and *Oz* and had lots of flyers for gigs and happenings. There was quite a healthy, burgeoning counterculture scene. The idea of festivals appealed to quite a lot of people and by the time we actually got it together to do something we'd been to the Rivington Pike Free Festival which was on a hill between Bolton, Horwich and Chorley, a beautiful area of countryside belonging to the Water Board. Nearby was Lord Leverhulme's Chinese bungalow, a wooden building that he'd built on top of a hill, with some walled Chinese gardens. I think eventually it was the subject of an arson attack, and he moved away, but the gardens were left. They did go a little bit to rack and ruin, but it became a park area and someone managed to get permission in the summer of 1976, which was a nice long hot one, to hold a small free festival there. It was just a beautiful setting, not many name bands; the Hare Krishna people and Tractor performed on the stage, and Liverpool's spacerockers Body appeared.

"In a funny, raggedy, dope-and-cider befuddled way, Deeply Vale was the North West's Glastonbury... the crucible of North Lancashire's gently anarchistic counterculture."

Stuart Maconie, *Q Magazine*

Tractor Music Shop, 1970s (Chris Hewitt)

Chris Hewitt: We'd opened a music equipment and hire shop in Rochdale with rehearsal rooms, called Tractor Music, which had become a bit of a focal point for people to hang around. There was a commune about half a mile up the road where a lot of friends of mine lived as well. It just got into a bit of a buzz. September 1976, we decided we'd hold a quick festival at Deeply Vale. So we approached the landowner, told him it was a birthday party for about thirty friends and could we rent the valley off him. He agreed, so we started the publicity. We got about three or four hundred people there the first year.

Janet Henbane: Being from Yorkshire it was brilliant to have a northern gathering to attend. I was there with the Hull posse, one of the Hull folk had a bus - this was in 1977 - so that was our base at Deeply Vale. In the 70s I'd camped up with the Hull crowd at various festivals, starting off with Windsor 1974. There were some right characters and always good fun and banter. We always had a campfire, kettle, tea-making equipment, and pans, veggie stews, and plenty of entertainment and music. It was at Deeply Vale that I decided I had to have a bus; I was getting a bit fed up of my leaky little 'handkerchief slung over two matchsticks' tent and I had seen the Thandoy bus and this had inspired me. I was very much into the festival scene and travelling around them all summer, meeting wonderful people with different ways of doing things and making use of whatever was available and improvising. I loved it, good fun, adventures and mucking in, very hands on! It would be another four or five years until I eventually acquired a bus and by some fluke it *was* the Thandoy bus, purchased in 1982 right after the Blue Moon festival; I still have it now and it's still a runner.

Chris Hewitt: The great thing was about the first one was it was Friday, Saturday, and Sunday. I think we arrived there on the Thursday and threw the stage up. A friend of mine, Trevor Hyett, was a presenter at Granada TV; he was actually on the same programme as Tony Wilson and Anna Ford; they were all local presenters. Trevor was a bit of a folkie, as was Anna Ford back then, and Tony Wilson was just a news reporter with a little bit of an interest in music. On the Friday, as we were building up the festival, I think it must have been a quiet news day because they sent Trevor off to film people erecting scaffolding for the stage. We were fortunate enough that Body saw the news report and decided to get their bus and come down with all their lights and projectors and perform one of their great spacerock sets. Tractor were billed to play, lots of local bands; I think The Drones came, the following year they were a punk band, but in '76 they were actually a glam rock band called Rockslide. The next year things grew, about three thousand people. We moved it from September into July because it used to get very cold at night.

Janet Henbane: The Hull camp at Deeply Vale always had some money making scam or other, the older guys had decided they would be running a beer tent near the bus and Bones had made a pub sign for it. Unfortunately the name he had given it didn't go down too well, especially with women, and after a few complaints came in 'The Jolly Rapist' was changed to 'The Merry Pervert.'

Deeply Vale (Janet Henbane)

Chris Hewitt: We didn't have a scaffolding mixing tower the first year, we'd mixed out of the back of a transit and it was that cold that we went back and got a fan heater and plugged it into the generator with a cable running down to the back of the van to try and keep warm! Moving the festival to July gave us slightly more time to do posters, and we did a poster with the names of the bands. That year we had a band called Pegasus, who, within about twelve months, became Orchestral Manoeuvres in the Dark.

Deeply Vale Tepees and Stage 1978 (Chris Hewitt)

"The OMD connection with Rochdale firstly comes via Deeply Vale Festival where I performed with my early band, Pegasus in 1977. It was the first time I had ever performed at a festival, indeed really the first gig for me beyond a youth club in a church hall. That was an experience that certainly helped me get my head around what was eventually to come.

We were so unprepared that we had no money and no food. There seemed to be a charity soup kitchen going on and we begged a few bowls of what appeared to be cabbage (and nothing else) soup. There was a real 'all help together' hippie vibe, which was wonderful."

Andy McCluskey of OMD, interviewed about Deeply Vale (source Chris Hewitt)

Chris Hewitt: I think we got a write-up in the *NME* as well that year. Tractor put out a single called 'No More Rock 'n' Roll' which we actually released on the day of the festival and that made it into the *NME*'s Indie Charts, even though there were quite a lot of punk bands in there. Attendance? There was quite a growth from three hundred to three thousand, but nowhere near the growth of the next year when we extended it to six days and it suddenly became twenty thousand! It was quite a breakthrough to get a write-up in the *NME*, and it was also quite a breakthrough to start to get the Nik Turners, the Here & Nows, and the ATVs of this world to actually travel north! If you'd have said, 'There's going to be a Stonehenge or Glastonbury type festival in the north of England' to a lot of the hippie bands down south in '75, '76, they probably would've said, 'Oh, you're joking, aren't you? Who'd want to go north? Does life exist beyond Watford?' We broke through that, but there was still the old guard/new guard situation. When Here & Now came, and when Nik Turner came, they camped further up the valley from the main site. Nik Turner set up his own little Pyramid Stage. It wasn't like the modern festivals where there are stages all over the place. The way that we designed Deeply Vale was that there was one stage and that was the focal point and whether you were Steve Hillage or a punk band from Whitworth who'd only formed the afternoon before, you all got to play on that stage. That was the whole idea, one focal point. When Here & Now and Nik Turner's Sphynx turned up, and Sid Rawle with the tepees, they almost felt that they were the experienced 'Southern festival, we've been doing this for a few years', sort of thing. And there was a certain amount of... they went away and did their own thing. Nik had his Pyramid Stage and Here & Now played on that as well as playing on the main stage. It all evened out in the end. The turning point was really when Sid Rawle threw a member of Wilful Damage off the stage because then there was this almost backlash against the old hippie mentality. You can't have this new Aquarian lifestyle and also be intolerant to other people's ideas.

Penny Rimbaud: When the punks started turning up at Stonehenge, Sid Rawle really didn't like that, the 'these people aren't us' sort of thing. I was actually much more comfortable moving around in the punk thing, which was much more acknowledging of working-class issues and standards than the hippie movement which was always floating up there somewhere [in social class], certainly its leaders… as one has to admit most of the leaders of punk were fairly comfortable. [IA: Joe Strummer for example]. Myself for example… Malcolm McLaren, for example. But it was taken over by a predominately working-class youth in the way that I would say hippie was predominately middle-class. Hippie and punk were totally intertwined; I mean, there was conflict on the journey there, but the fundamental attitude… I mean one of the key things about punk, which probably came more from the anarcho-punk, although Strummer said 'do it yourself', DIY, well DIY was an entirely hippie thing, it's just that one was DIY-ing with nature rather than with urban things but even that's a media perceived difference. Haight Ashbury is hardly a rural area and Kings Road, where the hippies hung out, certainly is not

"Take a look at the free festivals. They're like cinemas with no films."
Mark E. Smith – The Fall

Keith Bailey: Here & Now gave The Fall their first ever tour, and we persuaded them to do the free festivals; Mark E Smith is no idiot, he can see the publicity opportunity when it presents itself and he went along with it, supported by his record label.

Chris Hewitt: The person that helped bridge the divide was Grant Showbiz from Here & Now, their sound man. He was the one who picked up on the whole new wave thing, he was the one who invited The Fall and Danny and the Dressmakers and Wilful Damage to go on tour with Here & Now and ATV. In 1977 we'd had a religious band, The Movement Band, who did rock songs but were fronted by a vicar. They did a spot on the Sunday afternoon. But at the same time we also had The Drones, who'd just had a single out called 'Temptations Of A White Collar Worker.' The Drones were a bit of a happening band in the same upcoming punk circuit as Buzzcocks and Slaughter and the Dogs. The Drones were the festival's first punk band, but by '78 we had a new wave afternoon, though over the six days it was probably sixty/forty in favour of prog over punk. We'd also had a band called Hit and Run, who were like a jazz/rock band. They played in '76 and '77, but had mutated into The Ruts by '78. We also had Misty in Roots because the week before Deeply Vale '78 we'd also done a stage in Manchester for a multi-day Rock Against Racism event and we had a Rock Against Racism day at Deeply Vale as well.

"The staging, by the Deeply Vale Free Festival people... [was] excellent."
Paul Morley, *NME* July 1978,
on Manchester's Rock Against Racism concerts.

Chris Hewitt: Rock Against Racism was very strong in Manchester; there was a very big free RAR/Anti-Nazi League concert in Manchester. I think we had about forty thousand people there the Saturday before Deeply Vale started, and that was a cross-section of punk bands and reggae bands, and Graham Parker and the Rumour. It was a real mix of cultures and that was one of the things that we tried to encourage at Deeply Vale, so we had a Christian rock band and we opened the stage to Rock Against Racism. We tried to be slightly non-political but in a sense… the politics of it was that if we felt it was good for the community then we would let people come and put their views across. But it was getting to a situation where you couldn't have twenty thousand people on a bit of land without someone being accountable for things like first aid, making sure ambulances can get to the hospital, that people aren't shitting in the stream and the drinking water supplies are clean, and that people leave the festival site after the festival's finished and the place is left tidy. Smack started to appear, as well as the development of what later became the Brew Crew. We had problems from '79 onwards with people who stayed in the valley in tepees for quite a lot of the winter, people stealing cars, taking them up to the valley and then scrapping them and taking the bits down to the scrapyard to get money. It's not what an alternative culture should be about. So we had the politics of, 'Is Deeply Vale really a festival aimed at providing music for people or is it a statement about an alternative lifestyle? If it is about an alternative lifestyle, does that revolve around people ripping off the existing lifestyle?'

Janet Henbane: I attended Deeply Vale for two or three years and then the site was lost; in that year a gathering was held on the moors near Blackburn, it took me a while to find the site as I

The crowd at Deeply Vale, 1978 (Chris Hewitt collection)

hitchhiked to nearly all the festivals I went to, usually on my own. The site was rough moorland and I met friends there and we camped together. I think I saw The Ruts play at this gathering. I lost my tent at this festival - a windy day up on fell tops and I had leant in the tent doorway to light a spliff, threw the match down onto the grass outside and because of the dry windy conditions the grass caught fire right next to my tent and the whole lot went up: my tent, wellies, sleeping bag, blanket and some clothes, and a hole burnt in my rucksack, what a shock but big lesson learned! Someone had a spare tent and bedding they loaned me!

Chris Hewitt: The other problem we had later on was that the farmer had a sub-lease to a Mr. Neave, who was actually a relative of Airey Neave, the Tory politician. Mr. Neave was an extremely right-wing farmer who'd got a lease on the land, and in later years he did become a thorn in the side of the festival. He had to take his cattle off the land for several weeks whilst we rented it for the festival, and it was something that he didn't like. He also didn't like all the festival-goers being in that area, which is always a problem with festivals. I phased out my involvement in '79 because of the fact that the authorities were saying that we needed an address for someone to be responsible, and we need certain provisions, and there were two schools of thought about that. One was that we should have a responsible committee, and the other was, 'Fuck 'em, we're going to have it anyway.' 1979 was the last year in the valley and then it moved to a place called Pickup Bank near Darwen, where there were all sorts of problems. There were signs advertising 'Chase the Dragon Here' and bad cases of parvo virus and hepatitis, all sorts of stuff. Although people still call it Deeply Vale, in our eyes it wasn't really because it wasn't in the beautiful valley where we had Deeply Vale originally. It was more like the Convoy arriving at a particular place on the weeks that Deeply Vale had become established in the calendar and saying, 'We're going to have Deeply Vale here.' There was no major structure to it. Because I used to go around the country doing musical events indoors and outdoors for various councils, companies, bands and people, we did have a great structure to the stage. Although it was chaotic it was much more organised than, say, Glastonbury was. Bands actually knew *when* they were going to play. You didn't really *hear* back then of a free festival where people actually knew at what time, on what day, they were going to play - and yet we *did* have a timetable. For '78 we had a six-day timetable which we pretty much stuck to. We might run late, but it wasn't just a question of, 'Oh, someone's turned up in a van, they're going to play.' We'd try and accommodate those as well, but we did actually have a preconceived structure which I think a lot of the free festivals didn't have then. That's why it was slightly different and was, for a few years, successful.

LOOK OUT THERE'S A FESTIVAL ABOUT

SITE WITHIN 10 MILES OF BRISTOL PHONE BRISTOL 519491 ON MAY 27th FOR SITE DETAILS......

THE AVON FREE FESTIVAL...

MAY 27-31st

TRAVELLERS SKOOL BUS

GATHERING ON SITE (28th-30th)...

INVITED BANDS: HAWKWIND, NIK TURNERS ALL ✧'S RING, HERB GARDEN, KARMA SUTRA, OMNIA OPERA...

plus many more.... STALLS, CIRCUS SKILLS. FULL MOON 31st MAY

THE FESTIVAL IS A CELEBRATION OF LIFE
ANYONE CAUGHT DAMAGING LIFE ON THE SITE
WILL BE REMOVED........

FOR MORE INFO
- BOX FIN,
37 STOKES CROFT,
BRISTOL

BRING - LOADS'A WOOD, FOOD, WATER AND BENDER POLES

AVO

CASH FROM CHAOS

Merging of Music Scenes

One month they were real hippies, the next they'd become punky

Steve Lake: The amount of time between the Watchfield Free Festival and the birth of punk rock, it's only a year! But it seemed to go on forever! Joe Strummer lived next door to Here & Now. He was in this band that played in The Elgin, a pub in Ladbroke Grove; Joe lived next door in 101, Latimer Road which was why his band were called the 101ers. I saw them at a few festivals. Certainly I saw them at Stonehenge a couple of times, I'm pretty sure I saw them at Watchfield, possibly in Wales. Sometimes they'd have Tymon Dogg, the hippie fiddle player playing with them. They were doing an R&B thing, a not very good version of Dr Feelgood to be honest. Strummer was going to all those things and for all his anti-hippie rhetoric he was absolutely embroiled in that whole West London squatter scene, playing at squatters' pubs and free festivals. That was really where he was at. Johnny Rotten was selling acid down the Roundhouse, and a few years later The Damned do their favourite tunes and they're all like bloody Jefferson Airplane!

Joie Hinton: I noticed it amongst friends, the Here & Now band for example. One month they were real hippies, the next they'd become punky, wearing torn-up clothes where before they'd been in sort of Aladdin suits! Loads of bands were turning up that were punky. My first outdoor gig was with a punk band called Idiots International, basically people from a band called the Mercy Federation, a Hammersmith based punk outfit. There was a band, Zounds, who were hippies at first and then went really punky, it became the in-thing to do. I think [the hippies] had become a bit fluffy really and punk was the antidote.

Steve Lake: There were loads of people at that time, I suppose people of my generation who missed out on the hippie thing altogether, totally alienated from everything but who still wanted to do things. When the punk thing happened, there were a number of different elements to that, it seemed to me. One of those was the very glitzy Malcolm McLaren, Bernie Rhodes, metropolitan showbiz end of punk rock; in the daily papers *every day* and all part of the media circus situation. Then of course there was the whole other thing of the *Sniffin' Glue* scene, of Xerox-ing your own fanzines, or when the Desperate Bicycles and the Scritti Politti records came out and they explained on them how you made your own records. Although the aesthetic was different, what you were wearing and the sounds you were making, I thought part of it absolutely fitted with the idea that we were involved with in the free festival scene. Don't wait for some big capitalist daddy to come and provide things for you. Get it together and do it yourself. I saw the two things as being very compatible. Zounds really transformed as a band because of line-up changes and our whole thing got more… aggressive is the wrong word, but a lot harder, a lot grittier. I took over the writing and the things I was writing about were the situations I was living in. I wasn't writing political manifestos, just songs on how I felt about the life I was living. To me, there was no kind of difference in content between that do-it-yourself side of punk rock, the fanzines, the small pressings of records, organizing your own gigs… and the free festivals. Zounds had met The Mob at a festival. We'd gone down to play at this festival and Here & Now was there and The Mob was this punk band from Yeovil. Somehow they'd stumbled onto Here & Now and were travelling and going to gigs; we met The Mob and along with them and The Astronauts, from Welwyn Garden City, we decided to do this kind of free tour ourselves. We toured twice, playing the normal rock venues of the time; free gigs with the ethics that we'd taken from that free festival scene, that hippie alternative thing. We just transplanted it into a more modern musical setting and we continued to play the free festivals.

Simon Williams: The Sex Pistols said, 'Never trust a hippie' and were anti long-hair, but there was a great blurring of those labels and great crossovers between the two. There was a big punk ethic in the festivals of the 1980s. There was even the biker element, the Hells Angels, and the Tibetan-Ukrainian people who were putting on more than just music, putting on stage shows and that sort of stuff.

Steve Lake: Malcolm McLaren might not even have known that there had been a free festival movement. That's highly likely. That's not the aspect he was involved in; he was doing the showbiz and big spectaculars. The rest of it was irrelevant to him because it was outside his career ambitions. Of course, whilst there's those big spectacular things going on, there's kids up and down the country putting on gigs in youth clubs, community centres and the back rooms of pubs and that to me was the aspect of punk that I was into. I enjoyed all that Sex Pistols and Clash stuff, but to me that wasn't really the essence of it. It was what was building up in communities around the country. We saw a lot of that, we used to play a lot, but we never denied that thing about where we came from. We spread the word, all of them did, all of those bands in the anarcho-punk scene were very open people and quite willing to chat and, like anybody in a band, fairly egotistical as well, you know, happy to hear the sound of their own voice!

Mick Farren: The counterculture, I'd draw a line into punk. The festival scene, no I wouldn't, actually. When I wrote the thing in the *NME*, 'Titanic Sails At Dawn', that was a response to what a fucking mess these stadium shows were. Punk was spawned out of that but I wouldn't put a load of punks down in a field and expect them to live. Wrong drugs, wrong attitude... the wrong shoes! Totally fucking urban! The crusties had really taken over the festival thing by the mid-70s it seemed to me. A lot of us had kind of given up on it because after debacles like Bickershaw, where it rained for three days straight and it was like World War I... we sat in a tent being profoundly miserable and said, 'I'm not going to another of these', and it had stopped being fun. It seemed to have served its usefulness. A lot of the ideas were being directly funnelled into punk, McLaren being completely obsessed with the Situationists, different haircuts but the same sort of ideas but the rural open-air festival wasn't really for the punk palette. And they had enough on their plate anyway so it took them a while to come round to it. You've got to remember, for us the free festival scene took several years to evolve.

Poison Girls (Daryn Manchip)

Steve Lake: Zounds, The Mob and The Astronauts were kind of doing this free gig scene, as were Here & Now. Here & Now would get other current bands; The Fall played with them a few times at free gigs. They didn't really like it: I remember Mark E. Smith saying they only did it because they wanted to tour Scotland and it was a way of doing it. But then Mark Perry, who started *Sniffin' Glue*, and who was really instrumental in kicking off the whole punk thing, he really embraced the whole scene and did a lot of free gigs; [Perry's band] Alternative TV came and played at a lot of festivals. He saw those connections between punk rock and that kind of free festival, free gig mentality. That happened quite quickly. By the early 80s, Zounds' records were going out and we finished playing in '82. I'd become very disillusioned with a lot of that kind of thing, the free festival scene, the rock and roll thing, the kind of things that happen around groups. I removed myself from it all and what happened after that I would hardly hear about. Obviously when things would happen like the Battle of the Beanfield, those things were really significant events. That whole anarcho-punk scene, Crass, Zounds, The Mob and Poison Girls, they took on board a lot of those ideas that had gestated in the free festival scene.

Penny Rimbaud: Phil Russell used to talk about guitars being machine guns and cymbals being bombs. And that was fucking right, that's what they were for us. Out of that grew a very real social movement. It certainly wasn't the one that Phil would have designed, but it was partly out of honour to him that it occurred. So many people over the years have asked me, 'how did you set up Crass'? I didn't set up Crass, it was the result of a series of different interactions, meanderings… there was never any sense of 'well, we ought to…' and I don't think in things that work there ever is. You can always tell the consensual; you can tell it by the work. I didn't feel any different, I didn't feel like [part of] a movement. In the hippie era I was part of a band called EXIT which was a much more radical band than Crass was. Not in the direct political sense but certainly in a cultural sense but there was no point at which I could define a difference in my life, just as now – nothing's changed, one is the person one is.

Gary Bamford: I don't think you could put Crass into the travellers' scene, they were a heavily punk band but they never really hung out in the festival scene, though they played at Stonehenge. If you want to make a name, you want to be 'in', you go to certain places. If you want to be the real deal you go to places nobody knows or nobody's bothered about too much, to contribute to the real underground. Some bands would only go to places where they knew there was going to be crowds, knew there were going to be photographers and it's going to be written down in a bit of history. That's what they do. Your name will crop up because you were there, but there's probably lots of other festivals going on at the same time which were just kids playing in a field having a laugh and that side of it I respected even more. I don't know about Here & Now because none of those bands would really come and do a gig in the squats in the winter. Though, saying that, we put Hawkwind on in a squat we had in London, at Waterloo Fire Station.

Simon Williams: One of my memories of the Free Festivals, we were on the White Horse at Uffington, the one that's on the XTC *English Settlement* album cover. We were playing up there, playing some really trance-y head music, and there was a strobe going and I looked around and there was an archetypal 60s hippie in an Afghan coat making shapes and then there was some hip London black dude with all the 80s get-up but they were getting down to the same music. And I thought: 'This crosses cultures.' Also, all my travels in Africa and India made me realise that the whole thing that was going on there was a hark-back to our old tribal beginnings, which sounds a bit sort of *anthropology* but I really believe that. It's a kind of natural gene in us all that makes us want to get out and dance and celebrate the sunrise and express our freedom and music is the thing that goes along with that.

Not all cultures crossed over so successfully...

Martin: My first experience of a festival was in about 1979. My brother was living near the Downs in Bristol at the time. Growing up together, he had lots of biker mates turning up at the house. They were older style bikers in jeans and leathers with cut-offs; they all owned old British bikes. We were due to meet them at Ashton Court for what was then a free festival. Latterly it became a big council funded event but in the 70s it was on the free festival circuit, a festival on the way from somewhere to somewhere, from a festival in Wales to Stonehenge, most likely. We headed off over the Suspension Bridge and it was a beautiful summer afternoon and evening. It wasn't a big festival and it was the first time I'd seen hippie buses; there were tepees and benders. It was a very relaxed atmosphere with people openly smoking dope, and drugs on sale. There was a bender with 'SPEED and TEA' painted in big white letters down the side. At the time I was about 15 and had started smoking dope, so thought all of this was pretty cool. We stayed into the evening. I don't remember any organised stages for music but we sat and watched a guy jamming at the back of a van that I remember as being full of electronics with coloured lights. He was playing spacey Steve Hillage type music. Later on we headed back across the Suspension Bridge and there was a bunch of skinheads coming the other way chanting 'Bristol City'. They spilled over the barriers, ran across the road and started chasing us. They wanted to have some fun giving the hippies a kicking. That's how it seemed to be in Bristol in those days, quite tribal and risky out late at night. We managed to run away, just getting punched a couple of times. We went back to my brother's bedsit and were really shaken up. Later that night there was ringing on the doorbell, we just didn't want to open the door but when we did it was my brother's mate Kev. He'd followed us on his bike and had been caught by the same bunch of skinheads while he was waiting to pay at the barrier to cross the bridge. They'd given him a beating and then laid into him and the bike with metal posts grabbed from some roadworks. His helmet had probably saved him and he was more gutted about his bike, a Norton Interstate Commando which he'd just bought on hire purchase. The festival seemed a lot more civilised than the streets of Bristol outside and I didn't want to go out for a few weeks afterwards.

Nik Turner at Smokey Bear's Picnic (Charles Herwin collection)

(Charles Herwin collection)

Smokey Bear's Picnic - 1981

Big Steve: We organised the Smokey Bear's 'Legalise It Picnic' in Hyde Park with the Tibetans, stuck posters up all over London, fly-posted overnight around Brixton, Hackney, Islington, as much as we could. We got on this psychedelic bus that one of the Tibetans had, drove onto Hyde Park and immediately proceeded to establish a stage. The police rapidly arrived, 'Who's organising this? What's going on?' And we said, 'It's HIM… OH! Where's he gone? He was here a minute ago!' So we carried on like that, built the stage and set up the PA and the generators. There were about seven thousand people who turned up, all quite peaceful, and I was MC'ing it. Here & Now played, and Inner City Unit, Black Slate, Androids of Mu, speakers, poets and it was very good. Unfortunately the police started to wade in towards late afternoon after some freaks tried to free a guy who the police were trying to arrest for smoking a joint and a huge barney started underneath the stage; it had been quite peaceful until that. At that same time, a woman came backstage and said, 'I've found this baby and don't know where his mum is, his mum must be somewhere in the crowd, can you make an announcement?' So I went out onto the stage waving one hand with a baby in the other, police helmets flying through the air in front of me, and said, 'There's a little baby here who is lost, can we please stop the violence and the fighting? There are young children in the audience.' We'd been reading out notes that had been passed backstage, which was a typical free festival thing. People would send their messages, 'Trying to meet Todd from Southampton, backstage', and so forth. Fortunately things calmed down after that and we had a big party back at the clown's church in the evening with Misty in Roots and ICU, and me dressed up as the Vic...

Bridget Wishart: We went up to London and drove round the park until we saw the crowd and the stage, drove up to the site in our van and parked up to one side. Androids of Mu played, an all-girl space punk band… they were so cool! Inner City Unit were there too. I sat on top of the van and had such a great view of the whole thing, a huge party of hippies in the middle of London… all smoking dope like they were invulnerable, an amazing scene. But as I looked around I saw coaches and more coaches appearing at the edge and loads of police getting off. They held truncheons, police on horseback appeared… I watched and wondered what they were going to do. Then they charged. They had certain targets in the crowd; Red Ice

Brian (RIP) was one of them. A line of police ran in, separated him from the rest of the crowd while three or four grabbed him, rendered him incapable of defending himself, and dragged him off. Other people were arrested in this way, and what happened next was truly horrific. The police went out of control. They started fighting and hitting hippies, I saw a policeman hit a woman on the side of her head with a truncheon. Mind you, I also saw policeman getting punched back. The MC on the stage was asking people to sit down and telling them it was all right. It WASN'T all right! I could see a lot of people getting badly hurt! Dodging fights and flying helmets, I scooted through the crowds to the stage; I needed to tell the guy on stage what was really happening. I got there, jumped up and shouted in his ear, 'THEY ARE BEATING UP WOMEN!' I didn't listen to what he said into the mic but it wasn't 'Sit down', because everyone jumped up to help their companions who were being beaten up. No one published the truth about that afternoon; even the music papers portrayed it as hippies beating up on coppers. It wasn't like that. It was the police getting their own back for the beatings they'd taken during the riots but they were taking it out on the wrong people. They were hurting and arresting peace-loving hippies, not political insurrectionists and violent, mob-crazed rioters.

Red Ice at Stonehenge 1983 (Boris Atha)

The Tibetan Ukrainian Mountain Troupe

It was such a totally romantic image...

Angel: I started to go to Glastonbury on a regular basis because of a really important group of people, The Tibetan Ukrainian Mountain Troupe. They grew out of the festivals; then the Peace Convoy grew from them. I used to run to find them as soon as I arrived at a festival, whatever festival I was at, because I loved what they'd created. They made any festival a good

TUMT on Stage (Janet Henbane)

Wystic Mankers (Charles Herwin)

place to be. They had an offering of circus-based entertainment but with a unique edge, kind of resembling something like Papa Lazarou. If you think Papa Lazarou then you're almost there. It was bizarre and exciting. They were wonderful, funny, comical entertainers. It was always a sensory experience: lights and sound. They really lived the life. They went from festival to festival, and they took it abroad.

Glenda Pescado: When the troupe first formed in the late 70s the driving force was undoubtedly a couple of London-based clowns who, with a few of their mates, got the ball rolling. They bought some old buses and managed to get hold of a marquee, and all the stuff to go with it, and their dream of an 'on the road' travelling show became a reality. It started well but eventually came up against the distractions of a lifestyle already involving various substances that had a definite influence on how things progressed. They weren't entirely happy with this situation, so in early '81 they split and decamped to the Pyrenees to form a more traditional style of circus. This left the original troupe with all the sub-structure of a travelling show, the marquee, generator, PA, lights and all that sort of stuff, but no show! We had a bunch of musicians who weren't particularly a band, but we needed to put a show together pretty quick, so we decided to improvise and see what happened. As the two original clowns left, one of them actually called the rest of us a bunch of Wystical Mankers, an accidental spoonerism directed at our use, or possible overuse at the time, of the ancient Chinese oracle the I Ching. I thought this was a great name for a band and so, along with the basic idea that anybody could do whatever they wanted, the Wystic Mankers was formed. As it happened we had some pretty good musicians amongst our ranks and the band took off straight away. We had no problem improvising music and playing all night, with a little bit of chemical stimulation to keep us in the zone! Because of the general 'anything goes' approach we also had a lot of fun. We'd do these elemental-type sets where we wouldn't even use regular instruments, instead we'd make use of acanthine pipes and scaffold tubes as wind and percussion instruments and various wood and metal items like gas bottles and metal water tanks and anything that could be used as a bell or a gong. These sets would usually start off quite subdued and end up as a wonderful cacophony. These were also, by design, very visual performances with dancers, acrobats, fire-eaters and jugglers. We had a trapeze in the tent in '84! We managed to get some pretty trippy visuals going on by using black light and UV sensitive paint and body paint. We introduced pyrotechnics into the shows to give a bit more impact as well; we actually blew up a gas cooker during one performance. We only wanted it to go bang, but overestimated the amount of explosives needed and totally wrote the thing off!

Angel: Tony Cordy from the Tibetan Troupe, his children were born on his bus. He truly lived the life and he was one of the most inspiring people to meet when I was growing up. Tony Cordy's mother, Dot Clancy, has gone on to that great festival in the sky, but she was the all-time diva queen of festivals and was still going to festivals in her eighties. She was a wonderful woman and an incredible poet. I really miss her. Tony and Dot were major influences over the whole festival way of life because of who they touched along the way.

Glenda Pescado: My first free festival was Stonehenge in 1977 and I just couldn't believe it, it was like coming home. I was sixteen at the time. I grew up as a kid in the 60s and what I wanted to *be* was a hippie. Stonehenge was everything I'd ever aspired to. After that I went to a few of the Psilocybin Fairs, Caesar's Camp and Priddy Pools, and some much smaller ones as well. I'd seen the Tibetan Ukrainian Mountain Troupe at Stonehenge in 1980 with their colourful buses with these posters in the windows, *Festival of Fools* – Amsterdam, and it was such a totally romantic image that I just thought, 'Wow, that's what I want to do.' That year a little bit of a convoy left Stonehenge and went to a squat in Bristol; from there we went to the first Inglestone Common and the Tibetans were there with their blue and white marquee and their circle of buses.

Big Steve: Inglestone Common Festival seemed to be next to an antique junkyard. People

Tibetan Ukrainian Mountain Troupe, Fire Stunt (Charles Herwin)

from the festival site used to wander around it. I met a guy there who claimed he was the Greek god Pan, living in a tent… God only knows, but you met some strange, wild and wonderful characters. He did look a bit like Pan, I must admit.

Glenda Pescado: The Troupe had been going for a little while when I first met them. They were going to one of the Albion Fairs in East Bergholt, which is where I originally came from, so I was just hitching a lift and that's how I started travelling with them. I got on a bus, and didn't get off for the next six years. They'd come out of London, a bunch of people who'd become disillusioned with the kind of society they were living in and felt there was another way. I think they were socially disillusioned to an extent and of course there was also a kind of open-mindedness that came about with the use of certain substances in those days. A lot of people were having their eyes opened to the possibilities of other ways of living. The whole ethos of the Tibetan Ukrainian Mountain Troupe was based around communal living. It was, in fact, a mobile commune and we did live communally. We had a central pot which all the money went into, everything that we made, and everything we needed was bought out of it. It worked because we all had the same dream, we weren't just living together and on the road for the sake of it; we felt that we were pioneering something different. Living on the road and getting back to a travelling lifestyle that we felt was rooted inside us and could be achieved again in some sort of modern way. I think a lot of people were feeling that at the time. Of course, practically, it was also a cheaper way of living; once you'd bought a bus, which again was pretty cheap to buy in those days, it was a lot better than having to pay rent on a flat or house. We had to make a living and we made that living at the festivals. We'd set up a whole scene, we had our marquee and a generator, we had a stage, lights, and we put bands on; while they were there we'd do food and refreshments.

We did occasionally get paid, there were things like the Albion Fairs in East Anglia and they would pay us to hire the marquee, or as a venue with the stage and lights. We'd have a few paying gigs like that. The Wystic Mankers became the house band; we never played songs, particularly, it was kind of jamming but a little more intricate than that. Because we played together a lot we were able to do things spontaneously. As well as the Wystic Mankers, we also performed as The Rainbow Warriors, fronted by the enigmatic Rainbow Ron. We developed a set of fairly traditional folk tunes, played on penny-whistles, accordion, mandolin and that type of thing, which we had developed for our busking shows in Europe. We also had Jolly Jay, the Hippy Chippy, travelling with us and we'd do a set of his minstrel-type songs… actually the boundaries between these various bands often blurred and a set might start out as a Jolly Jay set, morph into a diddley-diddley folk set and end up as the Wystic Mankers! Sometimes we would deliberately start off with a nice gentle diddley, folk set and then, just as the audience were settling down with their cups of mushroom tea, start warping the music and lights into something very much more 'out there'! We've been described as 'The Surreal

Pranksters of the Festival Scene.' The whole time we were at festivals, in the tent or around the buses, we felt very much that we were 'on show.' We'd get up in the morning, dress as colourfully as we could – and that worked for us as well when we were travelling around. I don't think we looked very threatening when we were on the road, even though we were a convoy of six buses and twenty-three people; we were very conscious of how we might look to people and tried to be as friendly and as open as we could. We played on being a travelling circus or theatre and I suppose that's actually what we did become. I think people [in the communities we passed through] would look at us, not with horror but not knowing what we were or what to make of us. Being quite open, friendly, colourful, and smiling, did help. I mean, we'd park up in a motorway service area and people would give us a wide berth, but they'd look with interest. Because of that persona we put out, people felt they could look from a distance; it wasn't like people were looking away and not wanting to make eye contact. We were quite open to that; we liked people looking at us, there was never any kind of, 'What are you looking at?'

Tibetan Ukranian Mountain Troupe keeping the site tidy (Janet Henbane)

The Convoy

We all sprayed 'Peace Convoy' on our vehicles.

Jake Stratton-Kent: I don't know if anyone really knows where the Convoy came from. It was connected to the earliest festivals at Stonehenge and to Tepee Valley. You also had eco-warriors who refused to drive trucks and used handcarts and horse-drawn carriages.

Nik Turner: People were more enthusiastic about festivals in the 80s. In the 70s it had started to become a movement and towards the end of the 70s you had this whole itinerant crowd developing who were living in run-down vehicles and having trouble getting around and that's what became termed the Convoy. Now, a lot of people that I knew on the Convoy had previously lived at Talley, so the Convoy absorbed the festival movement which was, to a large degree, perpetuated by people who lived at Talley and were pyramid dwellers.

Rory Cargill: You had this village that floated from festival to festival. This is what the Convoy was. You would have a group of people; Sid Rawle, John Pendragon, Phil the Biker, and a few others. They were like a core and you'd get to a festival and they would organise things. The Tepee Circle goes here, the shit pits go there, the stage is going to go here. The Babylon marquee with all the little traders is going to go there. You build it up and you mark it out and shepherd people in and out of the place. It was quite organised in that sense. The Convoy as such was the equivalent of a travelling circus. The people who were travelling were sometimes the bands, in other words the circus acts. Most of the time it was just the worker crew who were setting it up, organizing it, putting in the groundwork, the spade work at the actual site. Then the punters would arrive. In come the campers and bands and whatever, and it was a pretty stable routine. So the Convoy already existed. When I joined the festivals in '76 it was largely made up from expatriates from the Tepee colony near Lampeter which had just closed that spring. The guy who owned the land had decided he was going to sell up, so everyone had to hit the road. That caused a big migration from there, before they ended up where they are now at Cwmdu near Llandeilo; Tepee Valley. That, essentially, became the Convoy and was the only convoy that existed in '76/'77, that crowd of people, led by Sid Rawle who, shall we say, had been evicted from Lampeter and were on their way to find a new home. The migra-

Stonehenge 1982 (Boris Atha)

tion of the Jews led by Moses, going around the country partaking in many drugs and festivals on the way, as you do! That kicked open a door, the idea that you could have this alternate circus of sorts travelling around, setting up festivals.

Keith Bailey: The first time that Here & Now turned up at Stonehenge with a bus, it was amazing. A queue of people right around the festival wanted to come on board and have a look and understand how you did this thing. Lo and behold, by '77 there'd be a couple of dozen buses appearing at Stonehenge and it really caught on. All those people began interrelating and building up this thing that became 'The Convoy.' That was kind of weird. By the time it'd got to the mid-80s, to 1984 and the last Stonehenge you had a few smack dealers and those sorts of people involved with the Convoy and the whole influence wasn't good, I felt.

Glenda Pescado: It started out as the Peace Convoy and it was, in 1982, that huge Convoy from Stonehenge to Greenham Common. We all sprayed 'Peace Convoy' on our vehicles. I mean, it was very definite who the Peace Convoy was at the time. Having said that, some people weren't happy about having 'Peace Convoy' stencilled on their vehicles so they had it sprayed on to bin liners and taped them on the side of their vehicles. That got a lot of press and it changed the scene. People in the cities, disillusioned people, were reading about that stuff and thinking, 'Hang on, that sounds great.' The Convoy, and the free festival circuit, started attracting all those people who hadn't really come into it with the ideology that had started the whole scene in the first place. They were coming at it from somewhere else and that changed things.

Martin: It seemed like the Convoy became an entity. I remember in 1984 being on the London Road in Bath when the Convoy started coming through, and it came and came and came and there were loads of people. There was a sort of excitement about it. There was a guy jumping out and shouting 'Come on, come with us,' this raggle-taggle band of buses and trucks and all sorts of different vehicles. One guy was parked up in the middle of Bath in a truck, broken down. But there were a lot of vehicles moving together. Before that, up to the early 80s, there were disparate bands of travellers, but then it conglomerated into a whole. I worked with a guy more recently, who used to be a traveller, and he kept away from the main Convoy because he didn't want to be a part of it, it wasn't what he was in it for. For a lot of people it was the start of the big, greedy, 80s. There was a lot of money around for some people but others, many others, were disenfranchised. So it was an opportunity for a lot of people to buy a vehicle, not necessarily taxed and insured, and get out on the road with a group of like-minded people. One time, I heard the Convoy was going to be at Bannerdown, which is just outside Bath on the way to Stonehenge. This was at the time that there were big conflicts at Stonehenge and [the authorities] were going to clamp down on it. It was about '83 and the traveller thing was building up and they were on the move and might say they were going

Convoy to Glastonbury reaches Street (Mark Wright)

somewhere but they'd go somewhere else. I went from Fishponds in Bristol to Bannerdown and there was nobody to be seen. Perhaps I had in the back of my mind that it was going to be free and easy and have some mushrooms under the stars and it would all be great. But there was nobody there and I cycled back to Fishponds again!

Jake Stratton-Kent: From fairly early on, people at festivals had trucks; the Tibetan Ukrainian Mountain Troupe, the cooler, more together types. After a while they'd travel together in convoys; safety in numbers when you were up against the police. Initially a lot of it wasn't *hard*, they weren't bad people; they were the more together, more pleasant types from the scene. But they were totally demonised by the press. There was this guy in *The Daily Mail*, 'The Convoy has been totally smashed by the police, well done to the boys in blue.' This was from up North, and I was living in the South West at the time and there was a lot of sympathy for the festival movement down there, a lot of the people who'd grown up down there, the

Warminster punk musicians, were very into Stonehenge and we organised our own Convoy. Just after the Convoy had supposedly been beaten, they had to announce that it had come back and labelled it the 'Convoy of Doom' to make us sinister and demonic from the very beginning, like an even nastier Convoy had appeared. Sid Rawle appeared in the woods where we were camped up and congratulated us on starting a new Convoy and getting into the media. Not my favourite character, but it was good to be appreciated.

Glenda Pescado: In 1982 *The Sun* had the headline 'Gun Convoy Hippies Attack Police.' That kind of opened our eyes a bit and we thought, 'Hang on, we don't want to be tarred with this brush.' It started to drive the Tibetans abroad, because it was in 1982 that we first started travelling around Europe. So whilst we did come back in the summer to do a few festivals, it was a big push on us going abroad.

Jeremy Cunningham: I just ended up on the road… it was like the last refuge of scoundrels, really [Laughs]. I didn't have any money so I was living in a squat, I'd done the squatting thing for a long time and I was just, 'Jeez, it would be great to get on the road because then I'll own my own house and can take it anywhere I want to go.' As soon as I managed to scratch together four hundred quid, I bought my first truck and that was it, really. I got another one after that, about four years later… a Dodge 450 Crew Carrier, which they used to use on the railways, a big Renault chassis with a cab at the front and then a big box on the back with windows… that was really nice to live in. It had a Perkins diesel engine, which is the best engine in the world, never goes wrong. The electrics used to fall apart all the time, but the engine… you'd put a blowtorch in it in the winter to start it, you could take the air filter off and put the blowtorch straight into the engine and it'd go bang, start first time. I loved that lifestyle, I couldn't do it now but in my late teens, early twenties, it was fucking great!

Daryn Manchip: In the early 80s I hung around with bikers. This form of transport was the cheapest means of getting around, and coming from a rural area of West Devon you needed transport. I knew and formed strong friendships with people and family groups who lived in buses and trucks in the lanes and byways of the West Devon district. At that time, family groups could park up with little disturbance from the police. That said it was usually local people who caused problems for my friends. It wasn't unusual to hear that friends' buses and trucks had been vandalised with windows broken by local rednecks. Our group in the summer months held parties at remote spots on the western fringes of Dartmoor such as Blackrock, Belston Common, Spitwich. Many of our traveller friends would attend and it was always fun.

Jake Stratton-Kent: There was a young girl getting into one of the trucks when we first set out. She was a bit nervous about it all but she had been reassured by the fact that Jake and Kinger were in the lead vehicle. I was really flattered by this because Kinger was this huge monster of a guy and I was a tiny little bloke but had a reputation for being militant and standing up for what I believed in. This Convoy was a good thing, a real buzz moving from one festival to another. Stonehenge had started off with quite a lot of goodwill from Joe Public and really did involve quite pleasant people... besides which Philip Russell had presented them quite well. The Miners' Strike was at its height and they weren't going to dislike the Convoy just because the Tory media told them to. And there was this nice edge to the Convoy, somewhat romantic, new age gypsies and all that. The lead vehicle, for a lot of the Convoys, was called the Unicorn because it had this sign above the cabin... *Unicorn.* A guy called Spider used to drive that and he was definitely *The Man.* But there was this thing about having to be rough and tough to survive in those days, there was a lot of unemployed youth who'd decided they'd rather be unemployed in the countryside than in the cities and they joined the Convoy. Some of the hippie bikers had also graduated to the Convoy; you had motorcycle outriders going ahead seeing if there were police roadblocks, and also letting us know if anyone had broken down and been left behind.

Nik Turner: I don't think the Convoy was inherently negative. I think it became rather negative because of the drugs, through being exploited by drug-dealers who saw it as a means to make money and who got a lot of the people on the Convoy working for them. Possibly people started to see it as a way of making a living or something to identify with that they didn't previously have, and it became corrupted by the drugs, a bit of a low-life thing. The essence of it, the positive side of it became [swamped] by the negative, though I'm not saying that all the people who were involved with it were drug-dealers or negative people. A lot were very good people.

Martin: I was on the fringes of the festival scene with my brother and mates going off to Stonehenge. A friend of mine at Sixth Form told me how he went off to Inglestone Common to score and was met by a guy as he arrived simply asking him 'Hard drugs or soft drugs?' The festival scene seemed to empty Bristol of the people who I associated with. It was a pain for me as the people I'd buy dope from would disappear off to the festivals. This sometimes led me to head down to the Black and White in Grosvenor Road, St Paul's to score. Always nerve wracking and invariably you'd get badly ripped off. My brother was washing up in Greek restaurants in Redland and Clifton at the time, trying to save some money. Increasingly, the people we knew were getting into heroin as it became more and more readily available in Bristol in the early 80s. He wanted to buy a vehicle to get on the road and out of Bristol. He planned that we'd both go. I knew it wasn't what I wanted to do but just didn't have the heart to tell him. Eventually, he bought a converted ambulance and joined the convoy. Later, the travellers squatted some land by a big house in Weston, in Bath, and I went up to visit my brother. The place didn't have a good feel about it. It was January, muddy, cold and the whole place had a bit of a siege mentality about it. The dream seemed to have gone a bit sour. I didn't see my brother for a while but when I did run into him somebody had been messing about on a site somewhere and had driven his ambulance into a river. That was that, he couldn't stay on the road and went home to my parents.

Jake Stratton-Kent: The Convoy did get rougher, because it was more urban in origin, but it was totally demonised by the press, and undeservedly to a large extent. Folks like the TUMT were just gentle hippies. Eventually things got too rough for them and a lot of them moved to France or Portugal to maintain that lifestyle in a more congenial climate. Those that were left behind had to get tougher just to survive. Generally the Convoy would turn up and take a site, and bring the festival with them. It became a much more spontaneous thing, festivals happening in places they never happened before just because the Convoy had to have somewhere to park. Get a stage, get musicians; obviously you got drugs as well because drug-dealing was going on. But the Brew Crew, what earlier on would have been called drongos, they spoilt it for a lot of other people; they spoilt the festivals and they spoilt the Convoy. The Convoy came to be seen as synonymous with the Brew Crew types. The Home Office didn't like the movement and really began to crack down on it at the same time as the Brew Crew arose. So you had these two separate forces. Things are always more complicated than a single issue, but the Brew Crew appeared just when we needed all the good-will that we'd created in the past. It was bad timing, terrible timing. Whilst there were always tough guys on the Convoy and festival scene, they were nice tough guys by and large. When we were parked up on the track leading up to Stonehenge, bunches of yobs used to come and drive their cars at breakneck speed down that track while there were kids wandering about. So we did things like building towers out of stage scaffolding, put a line from one tower to the next… some of these cars coming down would bring down the scaffolding on them. 'Come down here with our kids wandering about, you're going to find yourselves in trouble.' We were being tough guys, but we weren't being bad guys; they were the bad guys coming to pick on the hippies. But the Brew Crew was nothing like that; whenever there was any trouble, the Brew Crew was nowhere to be seen. They made things unpleasant for everyone else but they weren't prepared to take the flak. That was left to the ordinary people who couldn't go on holiday because they didn't have a job, so they went to Stonehenge instead. That's who we were, poor young people, and not so young people, wanting to have some kind of life, some kind of fun.

Martin: It seemed to me in the early 80s that the festival scene fused into and became synonymous with the traveller scene that was coming to a critical mass. The festivals had been self-policing to some extent but the anarchic, chaotic nature just tipped over and it just seemed to become totally centred around the drugs. With that comes inertia, self-interest, greed and paranoia. Things which were probably always there - drugs are about money after all - but which became dominant and caused the whole thing to implode.

Police Roadblock (Steve Bubble)

Glenda Pescado: A lot of people sat up in 1982, after that initial Convoy, and recognised it was changing. Up until then there was a lot of dope and a lot of acid, but that all changed around that time. A lot of harder drugs came in and people were actively using the festivals to deal. People were coming on site to buy a load of drugs and then take them away again. So the Peace Convoy thing, that was a turning point. It wasn't all bad after that by any means, there were some fantastic festivals, like the Nenthead Festivals – the Blue Moon, the Green Moon, the Silver Moon – but it had changed, though that's the nature of the universe, isn't it? Everything changes, nothing is set in stone.

Janet Henbane: In 1982 I helped organise the Blue Moon festival in Cumbria; we had a friend who had the land and we went for it. We went to the Greenham Common gathering in February, 1982 to do 'PR' for it, took some flyers. There were about seven core 'organisers'; we ate, drank, slept and crapped organising the Blue Moon for three months. Because I knew such a lot of folk on the festival scene it was like having our own big party; I was able to spread the word and the TUMT came up here, Thandoy, Nik Turner with his family, and also a band who I'd got to know, who were part of the free music indie scene, called the Instant Automatons, and a band from London called Amazulu. When word spread across the north that a festival was happening we were inundated with bands wanting to play, it was crazy and because this was our first festival we foolishly said we'd pay everyone... when it came to paying bands and performers we ran out of money and the people who really deserved some dosh towards fuel, like the TUMT got nowt, or virtually nowt, so that was a big mistake because a lot of small unknown bands will play for just a bit of fuel dosh or for free just to have an audience. I remember big arguments about what would happen to any money that was made, some of us in favour of it going to CND and others wanting it to go to a Guru but we could have saved ourselves all that hassle because it made a loss! The following two years saw the Green Moon and then the Silver Moon, which has gone down in the annals because the patrolling coppers were pelted with tomatoes and eggs. There was quite a heavy police presence because of the Convoy, but apart from the usual complainers, and sad funless people, most locals and incomers alike loved the festivals.

Keith Bailey: In the beginning, the whole free festival feeling was really liberating and quite wonderful on that level. The police didn't have a government brief on how to deal with the festivals or treat the people involved and the government itself was mostly unprepared for it. So you did have a strong sense of people working for each other. It was very idealistic and probably rather naïve but that allowed a whole cultural movement to be born. By the beginning of the 80s things had changed. I wouldn't blame it on Maggie Thatcher entirely, I think it was that whole neo-con movement and the writing was on the wall that things were not necessarily getting better. That started to radicalise people already within the culture of the festivals who began to wake up and think, 'We can't help ourselves because they have other things to say about that.' Once anything starts to get radicalised you get these extremist elements and I think that whatever shape or form that takes is always dangerous. And that's whether it's religious or political or even in cultural terms. Then the infiltration of the Convoy by all these heavy drug-dealers ... the people who'd started it off in their idealistic, naïve way were powerless to do anything about that. That was because of the ethos of the way the thing was, well, not run... the ethos of the way it was not run, if you see what I mean? So they couldn't do anything about it and of course a lot of those guys [the infiltrators] saw it as to their advantage that the police were made less than welcome.

Greenham Common 1982 (Janet Henbane)

Greenham Common 1981 - 1982

Big Steve: I was involved in the committee that was setting up the Greenham Common Peace Camp. We were living in a squat near Haverstock Hill, by Camden Town. There were a couple of big houses there that had been taken over as a housing co-op and a couple of writers were there, Ken Campbell who wrote *The Warp* and the guy who wrote the *Illuminatus* books, Robert Anton Wilson, they were our neighbours. We were all hanging out together, and got involved with some people at Swiss Cottage who were beginning to get the group together to set up the women's peace camp and I got involved with that. I was good friends with Claudia [Bolton] who was with a [theatre] group called Beryl & The Perils, who had Bill Oddie from *The Goodies* on drums. We'd go to parties with them and with Heathcote Williams because the Legalise Cannabis Campaign shared offices, what used to be the old *Frendz* offices, with Heathcote Williams and Richard Adams, the *glitterati* of Notting Hill Gate at the time. We coordinated and designed publicity and hired a PA, stage and generator, set up two stages at Greenham Common, in the spring of 1981. One stage ended up as a bogus stage because they tried to stop us setting up focal points for entertainments in different parts of Greenham Common. But in the end we managed to set up both stages, one was a pyramid stage and then another, the Tibetans' marquee, which was the women's stage where only women's bands played. Musicians from Northern India, Peggy Seager, Maggie Nichols, The Fall Out Marching Band, ICU with Corrina from the Androids of Mu and Abacush, and also Attila the Stockbroker played there, I don't know how – with a long dress and a wig probably! That was very successful and we were all very inspired by the women's peace camp and what they were doing.

Angel: I was at Greenham Common and that was a very 'festival' experience, we used to hold festivals with a whole political meaning. Dot Clancy was involved in that and her son, Tony Cordy. These were all festival minded people you know, their soul was festival. They were major influences over the whole festival way of life because of who they touched along the way.

Jocelyn (Festival-goer): I started out by going with others to Stonehenge for the combination of music, food, drink, space to smoke without fear of prosecution AND a solstice moment, and then attended various events at Greenham Common between 1979 and 1982, before moving on to Glastonbury and, much later – 1990s, Ashton Court. At all of these the key attractions were the range of happenings – from micro-events such as people singing around a campfire or meditating in public to major happenings like Hawkwind playing 'Silver Machine' for hours as the sun rose, to being part of international news events. It felt like you were doing something important yet having a great time. I must have visited the women's camp at Greenham Common three or four times between 1980 and 1982. I remember going mostly for big events such as the time we made a human chain and tried to encircle the base. It was confusing but exhilarating and I'm not sure if it was achieved. The first time I went, it was with another student from Reading University who'd persuaded me to accompany him. However, he wasn't allowed into the all-female 'protest proper' and I think he spent the afternoon ferrying supplies. The last time I went, it was as a newly qualified technical author working on documenting software for a MoD project – that was kind of a reality check before I resigned the job that I had fallen into following university.

Big Steve: The thing of the Convoy travelling together came out of the exodus from Stonehenge to Greenham Common in 1982, to organise a peace festival at Greenham Common. I think it was Gypsy Dave who made a template with the words 'Peace Convoy' on it and went around spraying 'Peace Convoy' on all the trucks and buses leaving Stonehenge so that it was like people were travelling as a group. Some people were not into being labelled as part of the Peace Convoy, it was a good thing of unity and coming together but some people might have thought that to paint everybody with the same brush could backfire. That was the idea of the Peace Convoy at the beginning; it seemed like a great idea.

Janet Henbane: Gopher Graeme and TUMT refused to have 'Peace Convoy' stencilled on their vehicles, and I knew why. It was a bit of a sensitive issue because of the political situation and the press. I decided I'd go with it and fuck the consequences and 'Peace Convoy' was painted on the boot of the bus, stayed on there for a good few years. The actual journey to Greenham was amazing; Big Steve drove my bus, I hadn't advanced to driving it myself! There were about 140 vehicles of all descriptions, vehicles breaking down left, right and centre, but such an awesome feeling. The coppers never really had to deal with anything like that before, so all they did was watch as the vehicles chugged by.

Big Steve: I'd been involved in Greenham Common the previous year, organising the Women's Festival for Peace. I'd gone to jail for supporting the peace camp as well, so when the idea of people from Stonehenge moving on to support it came, I felt it was an important stand; it was probably the biggest event in the peace movement involving CND and other peace groups at the time. So our involvement supporting the women at Greenham Common was one of the best things the people from Stonehenge did, and yes it was very important. We drove *en masse*, a huge number of vehicles travelling together in a line, leaving Stonehenge and travelling to Greenham Common. They broke through police roadblocks to get onto site, some travelled from the back of the site and nobody knew what was going on because they were all following the person in front. I remember driving a bus onto the Greenham Common base, driving around the back and arriving at a site we'd established, and starting to set up the Pyramid Stage. Organised the bands, Rat Scabies from The Damned came down, Nik Turner, Wystic Mankers, Red Ice, Dream Cycle Seven and we set up the PA and stage in the Tibetans' marquee.

Jocelyn: My most vivid memory is of coloured thread – multi-coloured ribbons woven through the chain-link fence around the base, washing hung out amongst trees decorated with wool, benders with different coloured tarpaulins and the brightly coloured clothes everyone wore. I don't remember the weather but I remember getting muddy and there being muddy children playing around the camp. But I remember most the generosity of people, inviting you to share a hot drink beside their fire and a seemingly never-ending supply of home-made food, including several different varieties of hash cake that visitors dropped off to keep the camp going. I met up with people who ranged from well-wrapped-up grandmothers to nearly naked punks. There was a safe feeling that you didn't get on other festival sites at the time. I shared a tent with strangers without a second thought; we were united in our aim of highlighting the insanity of nuclear weapons. The base itself was vast and I didn't really notice much inside. Occasionally we would chant slogans when a truck went in or out, or shout teasing and lewd remarks at a guard who ventured out of a building. Thinking back there was lots of music, singing when at the fence and people jamming at the camp by the gate but, for me, talking and listening was more important.

Big Steve: There must have been undercover agents on site because of the sensitivity of where we were; they cut the generator lines a few times, someone would be playing and they'd cut the power so we'd have to go back and repair cables, or somebody would try and sabotage the generator. We had quite a lot of problems with keeping the show on the road all the time, everything would go down and we'd maybe have a back-up replacement generator to put on whilst we repaired the other one. But we managed to put on the show. People from the Convoy tore down maybe a quarter of a mile of the perimeter fence…I remember Rainbow Paul singing his twisted freedom improvisations at a nervous security guard across the empty space where the fence had been very early one morning. Russian TV came down with news crews and was interviewing people. They said it was the most important event; some of it was on national Soviet television. So it had ramifications on a worldwide scale. The British authorities were obviously very upset that the perimeter fence had been brought down and they surrounded everybody with riot police and picked out individuals who, they said, were involved

Greenham Common 1982 (Janet Henbane)

with bringing down the fence. In some parts it was quite hairy, or quite bizarre because hundreds of riot police came charging onto the site as we all sat herded up in front of the pyramid and a double-decker blasting out ‘Grocer Jack’ by Keith West. We had a sweat lodge in the middle of the site, after this a load of us had gone in and come out sweating, feeling revitalised and clean, and would go off to swim in a stream on the site, naked, whilst American troops wandered by laughing, mocking, watching the hippies and the punks washing all the filth off; something to tell the folks back home!

Angel: It was a profound place. I actually knew women who lived there; I was heavily involved in Greenham Common. Then all the festival people that came through, the Peace Convoy, they got involved, the consciousness of the people. It was a further development of that, all connected. Those like-minded people, they were drawn there for that purpose, that we wanted a better world for our children. A Better World! I know it sounds kind of fluffy in one sense but actually it was very deep and very real. It hasn't gone today, but what's happened is that oppressive forces have very skilfully made us all think... they're always demoralising it, taking the power away from it. For instance the [Iraq] anti-war demonstration, I stood at the Hyde Park gates and all the thousands of people that passed me by were incredible… it was a movement that brought together all different cultures, which is very much in the festival vein. You have a situation where different cultures are brought together in the sense of Greenham Common and the anti-war demonstration, that political side of things. People from all walks of life and all ages are brought together for that one sole purpose. People were made aware and could realise just what a powerful movement there is, a consciousness all focussed towards one intention. There is so much suppression, lies and deception within the media that people aren't really aware of. They actually stated on the news and in the media that there were far fewer people on the anti-war demonstration than there actually was! They don't want people to realise just how many people came together that day. They had to suppress that information and in the same way many things were kept from the public as regards Greenham Common. I knew that for sure because I knew women that lived there and they had a very hard life. They remained there; they weren't just there on festival days, special days like 'Bringing Down the Walls of Jericho', chanting and singing, creating so much noise. They were there the whole time. So they lived with that stark truth and reality of why they were there, which was the possible destruction of our children. They had their water cut off; they had abuse from the Government. They had threats. These women were put through hell. Some lost their minds, literally, ended up very ill. It was a hard time, a terrible time for them because the same oppressive forces that I'm talking about, in the same way that they prevented Stonehenge from going on, they smashed up, destroyed, the so-called New Age Movement. This is the government's point of view, they can't have kids being born without being registered, people going their own way, living their own alternative life and that's the sad fact of the matter.

Hands off Greenham!

The future of the womens peace camps at Greenham is seriously threatened by a **Land deal** between the Ministry of Defence and Newbury District Council, giving the MOD the land at Green and Yellow Gates to become part of the base

There is increasing **Violence** against women

Evictions are nastier and more frequent

Women are under **Threat** from orders banning them from Greenham

Women are needed to stay at the camps

Contact for more information.....

OR CONTACT

GLENYS 0942 6055

or DI 0703 5544

Getting There

Getting to and from a free festival was often as big an adventure as the festival itself.

Peter Pracownik: I had an old Bedford Van that needed three 'Hail Marys' and one 'Our Father' for it to start!

Wayne Twining: Because you had to! If you had a choice, you'd do it the easy way! Nice new transit… we lost wheels and everything! Sparks on the M25 with our VW, back wheel came off! Note to self, don't go touring in an old VW camper!

Swordfish: It's different from the other side, isn't it? For people who were actually 'the punters.' People who've got nine-to-five jobs, they can afford to use that as a bit of a holiday whereas us as bands on the road travelling from one field to another – we're just trying to survive in those things. Hopefully if the weather's nice to you and it's not muddy… but it's that love of what you're doing, it's just self-motivation. The vibe that you get at a festival is different to any other – and especially the sound outdoors, which is different to anywhere else. There's a different feel to the sound of the drums and the bass booms and there's a freedom with everybody doing what they want to do. Music needs to be free, and the performance needs to be free and as soon as you start putting boundaries and regulations around it you start thinking, 'What the fuck are we doing this for?' You just want to have a good time, have a party.

Claire Grainger: Me and Sarah [Evans, Hippy Slags] bought an old Bedford CA Dormobile which had one of those old gear-shifts on the steering column, which made it very tiring to drive but we'd take it out to London, Folkestone. I was the only one who could drive at that point and there wasn't really room to accommodate a driver as well so it was quite exhausting sometimes. But it was the only way we could afford to travel. We couldn't hire a van and pay a driver as we didn't get paid much from our gigs. Hawkwind [support slots] were the best we ever got paid, we'd get a hundred pounds but a lot would go on transport.

Paul Bagley: Getting to and from a free festival was often as big an adventure as the festival itself. I remember the incident whereby I accidentally imbibed some mushroom tea on 26th September 1987: Worcester, Pitchcroft Racecourse, Summers End Festival. After staring at a campfire by the River Severn for hours babbling away, it eventually got to me through the haze that I had to be at work the next day at 9am. After desperately grabbing what orange juice, coffee and anything else that I could lay my hands on at 3am to straighten up, I finally started to come down and felt together enough to make the one hour drive home by 6am. All was going fine until I hit some road works and it started to rain at the same time. The combination of red cones flashing by, flashing by, flashing by, and windscreen wipers going back and forth, back and forth, back and forth, made me suddenly realise that I was in no fit state to drive. Needless to say I pulled off at some services and never made it to work that day… at some point I somehow made it home. I was in the process of buying a place and was crashing at my parents'. My mother found me late the next evening still in my festival attire staring at the walls with eyes wide open saying, 'Wow…'

Simon Williams: The buzz was that you were in a van, you had a generator and a PA in the back and you were tearing up the countryside looking for this 'happening'… 'Where is it?' Heading down these country lanes with a little map, no GPS or anything, and suddenly you'd find it. And it might just be a couple of buses that gave it away or it might be a big tent in a field and then the gathering would grow and peak on the Saturday night and they were all great.

Janet Henbane: I remember in 1989 me and two female friends, and my two young children, went down to Glastonbury in my bus. We didn't have tickets and were hoping to blag our way in, which you could in those days as the gate setup was different then. I can't remember which gate we went to but we were in a huge jam of traffic down the back lanes. This would have been a Thursday or probably Friday and when we arrived at the gate we started driving in and were asked for our tickets and we said we were with Nik Turner's band… and we got in! Thing is, they had to let us in cos we were in a thirty-foot long old Bedford bus and there was nowhere for us to turn round as the lane chocked up with cars. We ended up parking in what got called the Travellers' Field. We were dead chuffed we'd managed to blag it in!

Daryn Manchip: I went to the Oxford Free Festival in 1986 in the back of a very old van (called Horris) driven by a friend, James. Somewhere close to the site this van broke down just as the police had stopped it. The police informed James that the festival was cancelled. Of course this wasn't the case; they just wanted to stop hippies like us from attending. To the police officer's surprise seven of us jumped out of the back of the van and started pushing Horris towards the site entrance. Bump-started, we all piled back into it and drove onto the site. We had one of those large family tents that were popular in the 1970s, no ground sheet, just tarps. We were all totally knackered from our jaunt up from West Devon and put the tent up fast in total darkness and went to bed. To our surprise when we woke up the next morning there was no tent, it had blown away completely. What remained was a pile of us in sleeping bags in the centre of the site. Apparently a group of other festival attendees were watching with joy as the tent ascended to the high heavens at first light in high winds. We had completely missed it – and the festival had not even started yet!

Bridget Wishart: In summer '84 I went to the Elephant Fayre with my hippy art college buddies, all piled up in the back of a van: lots of colourful clothes, long hair, and beards. We also had some graphics students on board, who had never been to a festival before. It turned out that a few had scored Lebanese (hash) to bring. I said it was likely we'd get searched by the police because we looked so 'obvious', and they'd have to be ready. One of the girls had only recently started smoking dope and had bought an eighth. 'Well, if we get stopped they'll search us and if they find that…' I pointed to her stash neatly wrapped in a pretty, hippy stash bag… 'You'll get busted and won't be going to any festival.' She looked doubtfully at her piece of dope, wondering how she'd manage to eat it all if we were pulled. A mile or so before the festival, at a lay-by, police were stopping 'likely looking' vehicles and searching them, and we got pulled over. Even though everyone was expecting it, it was still chaotic, people trying to find and eat their stash without being seen. I wasn't too worried as they didn't have any women officers present to do body searches on us girls. Five minutes later a woman copper appeared and they were separating lads from girls. I'd forgotten how dry your mouth gets when you're afraid, a bit stoned, and buzzing on adrenalin. Miraculously everyone had managed to eat their stash and no-one was caught in possession. The graphics students were terrified the whole time and couldn't believe that nothing was found. Sadly, the girl who'd eaten the eighth slept through the whole festival and never saw a thing! Though she did say she had some great dreams!

Jocelyn: I have vivid memories of the empty A303 and waiting, waiting then walking for hours. One year I took my bike to Stonehenge – a CB200 – but was dead pissed off that a couple of bigger bikers removed bits of the brake one evening. There was a definite 'anything goes' feeling to Stonehenge. 'My bike has failed so I'll just 'borrow' yours.' 'Oh okay, I'll just nick someone else's to get home.' One year my father – who worked in the Forces – gave me a lift and chuckled all the way home about how he'd been offered drugs and what the MoD police would do when they processed his number plate. Sadly nothing further was said – I feel he was disappointed.

Paul Bagley: There was the time when I pulled into a quarry near Swindon to ask directions of a group of travellers who I thought would know the way to the site. Of course I soon became aware that this was not a bunch of free festival travellers but other travellers. A group surrounded my car and I became acutely aware that they were 'casing it.' As more people started to empty from caravans I decided that a swift exit was in order, put my foot down and sped off past a jeering crowd who luckily were only just in the process of arming themselves with stones, etc, and missed with their attempted throws… A musician friend laughed at this and said that was nothing. He had done a similar thing and, on pulling the band's van onto a site, realised, like me, that he certainly wasn't among friendly travellers. A group of young kids, no more than teenagers, surrounded the van and in true 'mob' fashion coldly said, 'Give us some cash, Mister, or we'll slash your tyres.' He kept a gun under the dashboard in case of emergencies like that and proceeded to pull it out and wave it about to disperse the crowd. It had the desired effect with most of them running off screaming… apart from one very entrepreneurial young kid who never flinched and proceeded to ask the question, 'How much would you want for the gun, Mister?'

Bands in the 1980s

Why do we discuss the festival bands of the 1980s, when we've not given the same specific and standalone commentary to the stalwarts of the 1970s? There was a different reason for existing between the bands that played for free, as part of their overall career, at the festivals of the 70s, and those bands that came together because of the festivals during the 1980s. It's that thing of wanting to form a band to be a part of something, so whether it was that you'd seen the Sex Pistols at the 100 Club or the Free Trade Hall or that you'd watched Hawkwind do their space-rock thing among the Stones, you were part of that mass movement of bands that came together because of what you'd seen and heard, because you wanted to be a part of it yourself.

Some bands crossed over into the mainstream – Ozric Tentacles, then The Levellers – but many continued to exist simply to travel the highways and by-ways of the festival calendar, passing the hat around for some petrol for the van or diesel for the generator, being part of the fabric of the festivals, a soundtrack to, or a backdrop for the gatherings.

Oz Hardwick: From the bands I knew, they weren't that interested in meeting the mainstream unless it came over to meet them, and that vision is why I respected them. You have to start any discussion of festival music with Hawkwind and their various formations and incarnations. Whether they were staging an elaborate ritual with processions and dancers, or at the nucleus of an ad-hoc jam band, they were definitely at the centre, musically.

Swordfish: Hawkwind were revered because of what they'd laid down. The whole way they wrapped the whole thing up, really; the culture and everything.

Oz Hardwick: In contrast to the media version of the 80s, in which everyone had a soundtrack of Duran Duran or Wham, for me it was Solstice up until they split – no-one

Magic Mushroom Band, Treworgey 1989 (Oz Hardwick)

soars with that sort of passion. At that time, to play that sort of music and express an openly idealistic, though far from naïve, vision in your lyrics was, I think, much more daring and challenging than a lot of the shouty punk-based stuff that was going on. The others that need to be mentioned are The Magic Mushroom Band – everyone's favourite psych-space-pop dance band – and Ozric Tentacles… who I'm sure just move from place to place and are still on the same jam they started in '83.

Joie Hinton: The Ozrics weren't called that [originally], it was Bolshem People. I saw them playing, I was living in an ambulance and the people I was living with kept hassling me to go over and ask to have a play. I think it was the day before it all finished that I built up the courage to go and ask for a jam. They said, 'Yeah, sure, make some swishy noises.' It was great fun, really good, and throughout the next year we played at a few parties. You see, the great thing about playing the festivals with a generator was that people would take your number and, the next month, ask you to play at their squat party. That's how it started; we had a couple of bookings after the summer, did a few of them and called ourselves Maya for about six months and then 1984 Stonehenge turned up, the big one, and we called ourselves Ozric Tentacles and did our first gig there as the Ozrics. At that particular point I was a guy who lived on the road; '83 I was in a squat at one point in Brixton. When the punk thing was going on, I was in a squat in Oxford, which was really funny, a sort of parody of posh people and punks! That was about 1978, a really good summer. But you're living in a house with a bunch of types so you just plug in, for sure. The first gig at Stonehenge using the Ozrics name was great, in the Tibetan Tent, a very friendly bunch... just a nice, long jam really. We did it two days in a row, I remember the Car Mechanics playing and being really brilliant. That's how it took off and because you were playing in public you got all these people taking your number and you got bookings and it was great exposure. It's very difficult these days for bands, not having that free festival scene where they could go and force themselves on people. We would just turn up and force ourselves on anybody, so that people got wind of it all.

Swordfish: We [Magic Mushroom Band] made a mistake with our songs having too many lyrics – I think the Ozrics kind of did it better. I always wanted to do more instrumentals but Gary [Masters – guitarist/founder member] wanted to put his vocals across all of the time and there was this sort of juxtaposition of the two. I don't see though that everything you're doing has to have a message. Certainly not a political one – it's not about that, it's taking people on a trip. Sometimes, though, you feel you have to prod a consciousness and the lyrics of a song can suggest that to people. Live, we'd trip-out and the songs would turn into extended jams. But when things are led from the guitar it dictates something in terms of the style of the song writing and as soon as you strip that away it leads to other possibilities and other areas of music that we were exploring. Its eclecticism, the same as the line-up of festivals back then. Now, they tend to be all the same kind of stuff, it's like everyone wants everything put into some sort of genre, like you go to a space-rock festival and it's all the same, whereas I liked the eclecticism of seeing something different, or wacky. I think that's what they're guilty of now, not bringing it all together and having the old and the new.

Simon Williams: The Ozrics were always great whatever they were doing. Web Core, a classic but forgotten festival band was absolutely brilliant. Treatment. A lot of [bigger bands] dallied with the idea of being hip to the scene without wanting to live the lifestyle, and you can't blame them for that. I was playing guitar with Doctor and the Medics and I talked to Clive about this and he was really into the whole scene and the idea of playing the festivals but they had some major commercial success, though they were still part of the underground scene, organising their own clubs and stuff in London.

Wayne Twining: Treatment were those nutters who were like Arthur Brown, they were mental. Weird instrumentation... if you were off your head, they were brilliant!

Swordfish: There was an advert for BMW, shown all over Europe, but not in England, and Ozrics' music [Sploosh!] was used on that. Ed Wynne's father was a sculptor, did a lot of stuff along the embankment. 'Boy on the Dolphin', the boy was Roly who was the Ozrics bass-player. Ed had been set up with a nice town house, big studio, near Wimbledon Common and was already doing library work and work for Channel Four – and there was us in our humble four-track trying to get a decent sound and be commercial. But then, we'd come across that ... people who had the bus that *looked* like it was going to break down but never did, whereas we had the bus that broke down!

Adrian Bell: None of the bands I ever liked seemed to make it in the mainstream. Hawkwind were the closest, but they just ignored the mainstream and did their own thing anyway. The Ozrics being adopted by the music press in the 90s was quite funny actually because it showed the press to be the pathetic toadies they really are. The *NME* was jumping on the bandwagon and attempting to 'Free the Stones', eight years too late! So yeah, those bands maintained the vibe and integrity because they're all still going, long after the mainstream got bored and did something else.

Janet Henbane: I have mixed feelings. You want bands to make some money for all the time they put in, but you don't want them to be slaves, having to fulfil some contract so the music isn't as good any more. But, what happened was that things evolved amongst festival bands to avoid all that commercial music contract shit. Indie bands compiling their own tapes and singles, music for free, a huge, non-commercial, music scene happened – which was amazing. A guy I know cobbled together various 'free music' bands' output into various compilations with such names as *Music for Pressure*, cocking a snoot at 'Music for Pleasure' albums. I still have some of these tapes and the bands playing on them sound wonderful today: Androids of Mu, The Mob. Thandoy never went commercial; I couldn't have imagined that! They were one of those 'best kept secrets' that could have gone further, to a bigger audience, but they stayed a 'festival band' and that was how it was. If they'd gone commercial it wouldn't have been the same. They had a lot of followers who loved the music. I got to know them, recorded some of the festival gigs and decided to put together a compilation tape. I loved the music so much and I knew others did too. The compilation tape was advertised in *Sounds*' 'Cassette Pets', which was where 'do it yourself' bands could advertise their tapes. Sometimes just the price of tape and stamp was needed to obtain the music, a brilliant idea! I did a compilation of the TUMT Wystic Mankers band, also advertised that in *Sounds*.

Daryn Manchip: I'm not going to get cynical about this. Everyone's trying to make a living somehow, many artists supported the free festival scene and, one can assume, for whole hosts of reasons. It's worth remembering that many of these artists were out there anyway, gigging and selling products. That's the nature of earning money. If there are issues, it's with 'pay' festivals where organisers expect free labour to support a few in a festival organisation which makes a profit on the backs of others' free commitments. This is the shadow side, and increasingly in this decade this is what is happening, this even goes with so-called free festivals or community events. There's always a hidden agenda, which is a real shame.

Jeremy Cunningham: The first gigs The Levellers ever played were free festival gigs, because they were the only ones that would have us. You didn't have to 'pay to play' or any of that rubbish. We used to go along and stay at places for months at a time and just play the odd show. We'd play with a generator, or two or three little generators, trying to get them all working at the same time... even played by candle-light once when the generators went down and we had just one working, giving enough power for a PA but not for lights. I used to live in a bus at the time and was a part of that scene, I was a traveller; I was the only member of The Levellers that lived on a bus full-time. Simon [Friend] our guitarist used to as well, but that was before he was in the band. There was us and another band, RDF... Radical Dance Faction... and we used to travel about with them. We were bands who lived that life as well as sang about it. [RDF's] Chris Bowsher is still a good friend of mine. He's one of the best lyric writers I've ever heard. He'd turn up at a festival site and it would be filthy, muddy or if it was hot there'd be dust everywhere, and Chris would always come out with a suit on, looking the height of sartorial elegance. You could spot him a mile off at any festival with his huge blonde dreadlocks and pin-stripe suit, everybody knew him.

Clint Iguana: Not that many of the bands I liked crossed over; I suppose the Ozrics were big enough to fill Brixton Academy at one point. Good luck to them I thought, I've sat down with them many times and they are as down to earth now as they ever were. They never claimed to be anything they were not. But some bands were too lunched out to be let loose on the public; some were too crap to get signed; some were too full on for any record companies to want to deal with them; some were too far ahead of their time and the record companies did not know what was in front of them. The best ones simply weren't interested in a record deal with a 'major.'

Kev Ellis: I suppose The Ozrics crossed over the most. Trouble was, they seemed to have run out of steam by then. RDF could've been big but it never quite happened. A lot of bands only released stuff on cassette, so most of it has now been lost.

Clint Iguana: There were many out there that were good enough to cross over and some, like Back to The Planet and Senser, did achieve some level of success. There were plenty of bands that were better than the nonsense that was in the *NME* week in week out. I suppose it is a shame that the bands that craved that sort of thing did not have the success that they wanted, but I was quite happy that they stayed where they belonged... I knew about them and it did not bother me that the rest of the world did not. Other bands, of course, didn't give a flying fuck about crossing over and were just full on into partying, sticking two fingers up to the man and doing things for themselves. Some of those provided some of the best sets at festivals, and bands that have carried on with that spirit still do.

Tubilah Dog members, including Jerry Richards and Alf Hardy, teamed up with Hawkwind's Dave Brock and Harvey Bainbridge to bridge the festival generation gap by playing as 'Hawkdog' or 'The Agents of Chaos', filling a void in Hawkwind's free festival commitments and re-energising Brock's own love of the festivals.

Jerry Richards (Tubilah Dog, Hawkwind): Dave Brock said to me, 'The times we spent doing Hawkdog/Agents of Chaos/Tubilah Dog gigs were really good for Hawkwind, because at that time the band was a more straight-rock band and some people were a bit disenfranchised by all of that.' So by Dave and Harvey effectively joining our group, it re-established the link between Hawkwind and the free festival ethos.

Oz Hardwick: Rather more low profile, but special to me, was Omnia Opera. I remember one of the 'woods parties' that used to happen up in Woburn in the mid-to-late 80s, with campfire smoke drifting into the early dawn and their 'Oracle of Knowledge' following it into the trees. Heady days!

Simon Williams: The first festival I ever went to was Knebworth in 1979 to see Led Zeppelin when I was fourteen. Then I started going to festivals in the early 80s – 1982, 1983. The first Stonehenge Festival that Mandragora actually played was 1984. That was it; have van, have PA, will play, you know? It was the ideal circuit, we were all into the other bands, like Hawkwind and Gong and Here & Now and that scene, but also the post-punk bands. There was a lot of respect for the likes of Hawkwind because they were doing, and had been doing for years, that great thing of being at the festivals. And everyone knew that Nik Turner was supplying the stage, or Hawkwind would be supplying the PA. I mean, some bands were seen as 'old duffers', bands like The Enid, but Hawkwind had a lot of respect, they were seen as the chiefs of the scene. A lot of bands would do versions of their songs - punk them up a bit or whatever - and I thought that was a great thing. Mandagora once got booked to do a gig in Israel but were also committed to playing at Glastonbury Festival at the same time, so we got Steffi, the guitarist from Here & Now and Steve Cassidy, their drummer, to play drums and guitar as, I guess, Here & Man, at Glastonbury whilst we were in Israel. I like that stuff! Bands don't have that thing these days. They might have a guest performer but the vibe of, 'Come on. Let's just get up and play' has gone. The influences were a great melting pot; there was obviously that space-rock thing but then it could also incorporate jazz, electronic, and ambient; reggae was a big influence, punk... that made a thriving scene. Mandragora started off by seeing Hawkwind and Here & Now at festivals and being really into their music. We got together, started jamming, and realised that the festival scene was the real deal. We got a bus and an old PA together and from there it was like a family of bands: Magic Mushroom Band, Dr Brown, Hippy Slags... the list is endless. That made a thriving festival scene; because they were all from different areas of the country, word would get around. But of course, no e-mails, no mobile phones; I was thinking the other day how different it was from now. It was just "Look, can you make it?" or, "Oh! So and so has turned up" and that all added to the camaraderie.

Keith Bailey: Hawkwind were much heavier both in feel and musically whereas Here & Now leaned more towards the Gong side of psychedelia, jazzier and a little bit more commercial. I think Hawkwind were tolerated because they had Angel connections, they had a number of Angels as roadies at that time. So I think the radical elements thought, 'Yeah, these guys are heavy enough to do it.' With Here & Now, they kind of felt we were a bit lightweight, which we were, and so they treated us with a degree of disdain.

Gary Bamford: You had Radio Mongolia from Liverpool who were a six, seven piece over-the-top psychedelic Butthole Surfer type thing, all over the place and out of their heads on acid but they came over brilliantly. Live they were the thing, really – an hour of that and you just had to have a rest you know? Poisoned Electrick Head, from Warrington, they were very rocky, very psychedelic; then Screech Rock from Burnley who looked *really* psychedelic but played very full-on punk stuff with heavy guitars and three screaming girls on vocals, all painted up. Like a real good Sigue Sigue Sputnik, but in a field all muddy and painted up. And the Hippy Slags, from Bath, Smartpils, Zygote ... just loads of great bands.

Jah Free (DJ): Poisoned Electrick Head were a bit of everything – music and theatrics. Dub Warriors, in their early form, made a severe impression on me. Boris and his Bolshie Balalaika, he was quite cool, he was wicked to see, what a shock! He'd just turn up with his balalaika and all these effects pedals... 'Hello everybody! I'm Boris and this is me bolshie balalaika... and I'd like to play Voodoo Child!' I'll tell you, he made Voodoo Child sound *wicked*, that balalaika sounded like Hendrix's guitar through all those pedals... he was *gone*, mate! It was like, 'What the bloody hell is he *doing* there?' He looked so strange, but he was really good, a good in-between act, because while he was at the front doing his one-man thing, we'd be rearranging the stage at the back for the next band.

Travellers Aid Trust LP Cover (Sourced by Jon Wright)

Gary Bamford: The Hippy Slags were one of a kind because they were a full-on all-girl band who were good at taking the piss and getting out there. They were all quite clever, educated girls who were part of the Bath scene.

The story of the Bath-based all-girl punk band The Hippy Slags is typical of the interconnectedness of the festival scene at this point in time.

Claire Grainger: I'd joined the Smartpils in 1983; I was living in the same house in Bath as Richard Chadwick and Steve Bemand and we played lots of festival gigs, lots of squats and it was the typical hippie/punk ideology. The Hippy Slags started in 1986. I wanted to set up a new band to have *fun*. I got together a drummer and singer and then we got Sarah [Evans], who was playing in a band called The Roach Club to come along. We played our first gig on 12th April, 1986 and our second gig was on April 26th at a Stonehenge benefit gig. Then we started to do Festivals, Twmbarlwm in Wales, Bannerdown on the outskirts of Bath.

Sarah Evans: The first Hippy Slags gig collided with an important gig my other band was doing and I had to make a choice. I chose the Slags and that was the end for my other band. We were quite different really, weren't we? You were more punk and I was into the Doors, the Velvet Underground.

Claire Grainger: And Rachel, our first drummer, loved heavy metal… and reggae! At the time she lived in a bender down by the railway and was really into the Convoy and living the lifestyle. Because of Rachel's travelling lifestyle she couldn't always get to the gigs so Richard Chadwick would help us out. He knew all the songs!

Sarah Evans: The rest of us liked our baths and our home luxuries. I was a weekend traveller, definitely! But for Rachel, she lived on the sites and we'd find her at festivals living in benders, whereas we'd turn up with tents. We used to get told off for having nylon tents.

Claire Grainger: We were asked by Culture Shock to do a Stonehenge Benefit EP with the Rhythmites and Military Surplus; we wrote a track for it called 'Sunlight in the Truncheons' which was about all the trouble at Stonehenge. 1987 we did the Orpington Festival, then Rachel left and we got Angie [Bell], who was going out with Richard at the time. She was quite familiar with our material and was a basic but solid drummer who gave us the sound that we wanted. Then our first singer, Kate Batty, moved to London so Bridget joined (October '87). Bridget was my best mate. We all got on with her and thought she'd be the ideal replacement.

Bridget Wishart: I met Claire in the college common room. She was an old school punk, dressed quite smart with blazer and tie, like the guys in Buzzcocks. It was a really exciting time of boyfriends, parties, music, and my first Free Festivals: Walcot Festival and Stonehenge. We both joined the Demented Stoats, but Claire didn't like singing so left before the first gig. The band gave out twenty-one free joints at the start of the gig, and everybody had a good time! I moved into Stoat Hall, the squat where the band lived. Claire moved to Bristol and lived in a fabulous squat called Turdy Way, so-called because the bog never flushed. I went to Art College in Newport and Claire came back to Bath and moved into Stoat Hall. The Demented Stoats had broken up and Smartpils formed around Steve and Rich. Claire and another girl, Jenny, joined as singers. I rented a house just up the road from Stoat Hall. Pete, a friend from Art College, moved in and we got a band together called Next Year's Big Thing. The house came with a dog, Sirius. The first winter in the house we only had a stove in the kitchen so Sirius and I shared a mattress in the front room for warmth. I spent a year at the house playing and recording with the band, doing local gigs and festivals including Ashton Court and the Elephant Fayre. Then I was accepted onto a Masters Degree course at Reading University. I continued to come back at weekends and kept the band, the house, the boyfriend and the dog together. Claire needed somewhere to live, I was finishing my degree and it seemed a good idea for her to move in. Not long after she moved in, Pete and I split up and I was accepted to do a Fellowship in Cheltenham. Somehow I ended up with £50 'for the furniture' and Pete had the house and the dog. Claire was now playing bass and had formed the Hippy Slags. I lived in Tewkesbury for a year teaching and working at Gloucester College of Arts and Technology, then one fine day, on a visit back to Bath, Claire asked me to join the band which was the start of just the best few years. I loved being in the Slags, our practices at Stoat Hall were hilarious vodka-fuelled jams and we all contributed to writing the songs - and playing live was really good fun. When I finished the Fellowship I came back to Bath and moved into a garden flat that became my base for thirteen years. I got a part-time job teaching ceramic sculpture at a private school and played local gigs and festivals with the Slags.

Claire Grainger: The rest of us would have part-time jobs, working on the land, picking or whatever. We'd practice quite a lot and spent a lot of time writing songs. We didn't record much, though we did do eight tracks for a demo tape which we were quite proud of. We did two tracks for the *Travellers Aid Trust* album that Dave Brock was doing. But that was a disaster. We'd recorded a slow song and a fast song to show the differences in our styles, and the fast song got recorded over and somehow in the process of recording and getting the song onto the record, they slowed the slow song down even more. I can't listen to that track to this day as it's really disappointing and the representation of us isn't like us at all.

Gary Bamford: 2000DS were on that *Travellers Aid Trust* album and it wasn't really us at the end of it all. They even gave the song the wrong name. OK, you didn't have texts and mobile phones back then but you'd think they'd want to get it right. It's the wrong name or the wrong song, wrong everything. So for me it seemed like a [Hawkwind] management ploy to make it seem as though they've got all these other underground bands *under them* or *into them* or *around them*, when it wasn't really their scene. It's like a relay and you hand over the baton but they just don't and it becomes a marathon instead. Individually, great, but they had their management so they couldn't really turn around and help you. You could sit in a field and get stoned with them, and they loved our band. Every time we played I'd look into the audience and they'd be watching us but it was just a little bit too raw and mad for them to go 'Yeah, come on tour with us.' You could have had the energy from that time and this time and then looked for something new coming along as well and that would have kept it up.

The Festivals' Pinnacle: Stonehenge & Others

1981 -1984

Whilst the festivals were myriad in number, peppering the countryside throughout the summer months, what had started in a low-key manner at Stonehenge had been built upon until it had reached the point of becoming the focal point of the scene, running for several weeks leading up to the solstice and coming to represent the alternative society in all its forms. This wasn't a perfect meshing of the disparate elements of the counterculture by any stretch of the imagination. The old agendas of the Hells Angels, the hippies (or what remained of the hippie, transmogrified into the crustie in many instances) and the more recently arrived punk, represented chiefly by its anarcho-punk wing, were originally set on a cultural collision course. Leading anarcho-punk commune band Crass, with its links back to the 70s festivals and Wally Hope represented by Phil Russell's friend and admirer Penny Rimbaud, were instrumental in organising the main stage in 1980, only to come under fire from the bikers, exposing a deep gash in any anti-mainstream solidarity that might have been perceived to exist.

In his essay The Last of the Hippies, Rimbaud noted, with transparent despair, how one hippie newssheet turned the actions of the bikers, pulling punks from their tents and attacking them wherever they could find them, into a defensible act of misunderstanding. 'If... the first Stonehenge festivals were our first flirtations with hippie culture,' noted Rimbaud, 'this was probably our last.' Yet in the broader sense, Crass biographer George Berger added to this observation how 'in a couple of years' time, punks would infiltrate Stonehenge as surely as the ravers would at Glastonbury...'

In this section, our contributors recollect the way in which this disastrous initial combining of cultures at Stonehenge would eventually lead to the assimilation of different groupings into the main body of the festivals, creating a golden-era of free festivals in the first half of the 1980s. They also reflect on the dangers, challenges, thrills and joie de vivre of the free festivals.

Ello 'Ello - Policing Stonehenge 1983 (Boris Atha)

Dick Lucas: Hitching to Stonehenge, ten or so punks from Warminster and Trowbridge, we were picked up by hippie types in a Day-Glo stripy VW camper. We were approaching the unknown in a van full of quiet hippies. Anything could happen. I forgot to take a blanket and slept under my coat; some of us didn't have a tent so squashed in someone else's. Fact is, most sleeping started at comatose central, smashed on cider and spliffs; you awoke forgetting where you were and what you were doing before you fell over, so a basic tent with next to no camping gear did the job. It was just formative, learning-curve stuff all round at Stonehenge in the early 80s. I spent most of the daylight wandering around amazed and full of trepidation. Punks were new to this scene and Crass were supposed to be playing, so for the first time a lot of punks were there.

Steve Lake: Zounds were playing Stonehenge, we'd always been taking amps and guitars down there, drums and what not, setting up, hassling somebody for a generator or getting on the main stage or something. So Crass decided, and I don't know what year this was, maybe 1980, to come down. Crass and Flux of Pink Indians played, I think The Mob played. Crass

Stonehenge Stage 1981 (Daryn Manchip)

had provided the stage and I think there was this feeling amongst some people that these punk rockers had come along and taken over the festival, which was a bit weird considering Penny Rimbaud's involvement in the early days. I mean… Zounds had been going there before we were even called Zounds. As far as I was concerned I was as integral to Stonehenge as anyone else. But it was the bikers who were really fucking pissed off about the whole thing. 'You punks coming over… you lot coming in and taking over our festival, we want biker music.' Then a few bottles got thrown, I think we'd started to play a song or something and a fight broke out and I could just see this whole fucking Altamont sequence building before me. We just put our instruments down and went off the back of the stage and I went and found some mates in a far corner of a field and had a quiet night. There was actually a lot of fighting and stuff going on. But I never went to free festivals to fight. I went because it was a refuge from that sort of mentality, although you would get problems, particularly people on motorbikes late at night, who've had a few drinks in a big open field with no lights… it can be difficult. But it's not like I'm slagging off bikers, I love bikers.

Penny Rimbaud: That sort of Altamont situation. It was appalling for us when Crass went to

Nik Turner at Stonehenge, 1984 (Adrian Bell)

play at Stonehenge, which for me was a very significant and possibly sentimental journey, but I thought how beautiful it would be, something I'd been a part of creating, to perform at it and that it was really violent… the most extreme violence I'd ever experienced.

Dick Lucas: The bikers didn't like the punks, it was said, they felt we were invading their territory, and back then the Hells Angels were a force to be avoided. Their anger resulted in the total chaos the year that Flux of Pink Indians played and Crass didn't. The bikers attacked the main punks-in-tents area with brutal violence; Crass and friends were vanning punks to hospital all night, I was told. Our group of locals were luckily camped somewhere else and missed the madness. It wasn't all love and peace.

Big Steve: I remember one time, this huge twenty-stone Hells Angel coming across stage with a gallon container of cider, and he'd taken a lot of acid. I was trying to get a band on, and I said, 'Look, you can't do this', and he had an *axe* in his hand and I thought, 'Fucking hell, I'm going to get my neck cut off.' I don't know what happened... I think I must have hypnotised him for a moment and managed to steer him off stage but I don't know how. I remember the bass player of Conflict getting attacked by somebody backstage and I managed to pull the attacker off him. 1981, 1982, they were really difficult years because there were huge gang wars on site. We were always calling for peace from the main stage, trying to get people to calm down and enjoy the festival, help pick up the rubbish, help their neighbour or hand out lost kids notices. Stonehenge was not an easy gig!

Nik Turner: One time at Stonehenge, there were a lot of bikers there who'd been throwing bits of scaffolding at the stage, I think it was Crass or Poison Girls playing, and I went up to these bikers and said 'What's the problem?' And it was, 'Those punks, we hate them', that sort of thing. I said, 'Look, they're not much different from you, mate.' They pointed me out to this really drunken Hells Angel who was being abusive and who I grabbed and said, 'What's up, mate? Come here and have a joint,' and sorted the whole thing out. But that's an example of a lack of communication between groupings, where the bikers couldn't see that the punks were just like them. I think the bikers sort of aligned themselves with the hippies and saw the punks as an anti-hippie movement, which they weren't at all really, even if they talked about them as boring old farts.

Big Steve: There were generational movements [in the attendance], you could see on site some of the older hippies who'd been around since the 1960s, who were now getting into their thirties and forties and had families, had a different perspective from the young punk crowd who were the next generation coming through, in terms of interests and organisations. There was a generation gap appearing on site. At the heart of it, this is really going to the hard-core of hippie ethics and the punk perspective, at the hard-core of both of those youth movements' politics there was a lot of symbiosis between the cultures. This was in their beliefs, in their concerns about the peace movement, against war, for animal rights or green politics and legalisation and control of drugs. Both groups had very similar ideas and a lot of things in common. Where there was conflict it was mainly between people with different agendas on site, people who were into it from a more commercial point of view, trying to make money, and people who were into it from an ideological point of view. Then you had groups of motorcycle gangs, like the Hells Angels, the Windsor Chapter, Satan's Slaves, who were in rivalry, so there was a problem with some degree of violence and riots breaking out on site. This could create instability on site, on a large scale, and it was difficult to try to maintain peace. The Peace Convoy, the hard-core of the festival, tried to maintain some of type of order but it was very difficult. It only took a drunk, twenty-stone, biker to go off on a wobbler and all hell could break loose, which happened occasionally. Then it would involve the whole group, maybe facing off against another group and so cars and trucks got trashed, motorbikes got trashed, motorbikes were ridden over tents. Sometimes it was like Dante's *Inferno*, you'd see a Harley-Davidson motorbike going up in flames and a lot of very angry bikers stomping around. From the stage we just tried to get people to stop acting violently, tried to promote peace and to get people to calm down because from running the stage and putting on the groups, it wasn't something we wanted to see. We wanted to get people to chill out, enjoy the music and have a good time as opposed to getting involved with unnecessary conflict. I think generally, though, the consensus on site was that people wanted to calm things down; people went up and talked to the bikers, talked to the people who were fighting, an amazing collective attitude trying to bring things back to some degree of normality. It would blow up, and some people got black eyes or got some injuries but there was nothing, thank God, too serious. In 1981 there was a guy who was arrested for smoking a chillum on the edge of the festival, down close to the entrance. Somehow this got around the site like wildfire 'Hey, somebody has been pulled out of a tent and arrested', and everyone ran down to the car park in front of the Stones where there was a police control communications vehicle with the boy who'd been arrested inside. Everybody started rocking this caravan back and forth until eventually the police had to let this guy go free and then everyone walked back to the site very pleased that they'd liberated the boy. The police, at that time, were very wary. There was no policing on site; you'd have the Police Constable of Wiltshire walking across the site in the mid-morning just seeing that everything was okay but when things happened at night, the police didn't want anything to do with it. Probably they thought if they'd come on site things would blow up even worse and it would cause more problems.

Penny Rimbaud: I mean, the huge majority of people at Stonehenge, when it was at its best, were there for purely hedonistic reasons and then the Hare Krishna people on one level to the Socialist Workers' Party on another trying to see what scraps they could pick up from that huge mass. Brew Crew… you'll always have pissheads wherever you go. There are doers and there are *not* doers.

Big Steve: In 1981 Nik was there helping us put up the base of his Pyramid Stage; unfortunately, while we were putting up the pyramid itself, two hippies who must have been a bit out of it, dropped an eighteen-foot scaffold pole, which fell on my head. I ended up in Salisbury Hospital unconscious, needing five or six stitches on my eye, but somehow managed to convince them that I had to go back to Stonehenge Free Festival because I had bands coming on stage. I had two very black eyes, but I managed to get back to the site quickly. I'd brought loads of records with me from years of DJ'íng and from working in Bonaparte Records in Kings Cross. There was an open-air market at Stonehenge and I managed to pick up some cool Hendrix records like *Rainbow Bridge* and *Band of Gypsies*, and records by The Doors, and others, to add to my collection. I'd brought a record player and we had a twelve-kilowatt PA. A guy who'd inherited some money had bought it, then had freaked out and became a born-again Christian and somehow we'd managed to get his PA which had been left aside, a bit of luck! Before we could get the stage running, we went off to a builders' yard in Devizes to pick up a generator, scaffold poles and planks to complete the stage design. Everything was set up; we thought we were going to do it better than the previous people and had no real idea that Crass had been running the stage the previous year. We just didn't think it had been done very well. Ours was a combined effort by the Islington Squatters Group. We brought along some mates who had a couple of buses and had been helping with the Smokey Bear's Picnic. Everybody brought along something, the people on the Convoy… if we needed a tool, a spanner or something, or needed some help with the construction of the pyramid, someone would help. Again, it's that thing, what's so impressive about free festivals is that people all mucked in together and helped, so if someone asked for volunteers to do something, people would come together. It was pretty hairy getting on site with the stage. We'd been stopped by the police and had some problems, but we got onto site despite having some hard times. You can imagine how we must have felt, but it's difficult to explain in retrospect. Ten years after Stonehenge, I was still being followed by the police if I was down in that area. Margaret Thatcher said she'd give the police every resource possible to crush the whole free festival movement. A lot of us had pretty well put our necks on the line. Not that I thought I was doing anything wrong, but I was getting stopped and pulled over a lot, getting hassled. It's difficult to say what it was due to. You could get paranoid delusions about being hunted. I mean, poor Wally Hope, who'd started the Stonehenge festival, was a victim of it, being sectioned and ending up disappearing off the map. You get those sorts of preoccupations that are always there, because if the State didn't like what you were doing they had ways and means to make your life very difficult. But Nik Turner and I, the Tibetans, all these people, like the Polytantric, the bands and the Convoy, who put their neck on the line, we were taking it all on with a great deal of humour. I was good friends with the likes of Gilbert Shelton, who used to draw the *Furry Freak Brothers*, who lived in Notting Hill Gate at the time, and Anthony Henman who wrote a book called *Mama Coca*. There were a lot of cool people who managed to keep my head to gether at the time, helped inspire me to keep it all together. When I ran the stage in 1981, I camped on it with my girlfriend because I was paranoid about people stealing the mixing desk and all the expensive equipment we'd got together for the festival. The main stage ran for six days and six nights and I organised it on my thirty-quid dole cheque and a lot of blag. I started work on the stage and line up three months before the solstice, often, once I got my dole cheque, from a telephone box! I was in Amesbury in the middle of June with a mass of 10ps, phoning up bands going, 'You're on tomorrow night', and giving them a running order – that's just how it was. We put it all together, and then bucketed everyone in the audience. People say it was totally improvised, totally anarchic and spontaneous, but there was a lot going into it beforehand. In between bands I'd be playing music, making announcements, changing drum kits, setting up guitar and bass amps, mic'ing stuff up, getting everything set up – for six days and nights! Quite a ride!

Painting Wango Riley's Stage (Dave Fawcett)

Dick Lucas: I ate hash cake or hash fudge; spent time running about in the shadows amongst the vans and stalls and back to the tent then off again. Talked for a million words and couldn't sleep because someone was near the tent playing some very repetitious keyboard space music all night. I saw the inside of vehicles made to live in that weren't mere holiday homes or caravans! Where did these people go after festivals? It was like a whole new version of society that existed under the radar. There were non-shops that sold cigarettes and home-made cafés selling tea. Anyone with an ounce of planning and a cardboard sign could set up a DIY 'business.' One chap had set up his badge-making machine; I got a thin pen and fitted all the words to one of my songs (song no.35) into a one-inch circle, instant badge! I had a shit in a field. This sounds vitally unimportant, but it was another first! It was part of the back-to-basics de-civilising process that a week at a festival was becoming. A lot of modern-day taken-for-granted things were just not there, people had to improvise and think round basic situations that had never come up before. No port-a-loos here, no nappy-changing facilities, no security people to run to, no refunds (no fees!), no laundry….get used to it. The process involved asking people for help, helping others, but mainly rethinking your whole existence! After a week of this my perspectives were shattered wide open and I felt like I'd grown up a lot.

Wango Riley's Travelling Stage (Jah Free)

Jerry Richards: It was all this fabulous creativity. Lots of people from all over the country with their ideas in this sort of collective unity where you could sit down in anybody's tent or at anyone's fire, smoke a joint, have a lovely time and talk about anything you wanted to. Talk about the weather, if you want! It was a wonderful situation and for us, Tubilah Dog, we spent seven years on the road from the start of summer-time right through until November playing as many festivals as we could possibly get to – I saw us as the entertainment, really! We'd turn up and we had a blackboard … people would roll up, 'We're a band, we want to play.' Well, okay, put your name on the blackboard, when your name comes up you're on, there's the PA tent over there, go and have a word with whoever's manning it. Or someone might ask, 'Who are playing next?' … 'Go and have a look at the blackboard.' We'd all mix tasks, we'd all put the lights up and get different things together and take whatever drugs we needed to keep ourselves going for the duration! Of course there were loads of us in Tubilah Dog and we had quite good organisation so we quickly got a reputation that if we'd turned up at least there'd be a light-show on site, a PA, a generator. Something was going to happen. There was going to be entertainment, then the Ozrics might turn up and they'd want to use the gear and that's how it worked. If you ran out of petrol for the generator you'd go around and ask people if they'd spare some petrol, refill the generator and the gig would start again. It was lovely to be a part of that kind of sensibility.

Big Steve: I think there's lots of [name] bands that, in retrospect, we wish we'd been able to get to play at Stonehenge, but the ethos was that there was always a place for free festival bands. We'd have bands, for example, like Red Ice, whose singer, an Irish guy, was a very famous figure on site called Belfast Brian, a hard-core punk who was musically speaking, let's say, sometimes rather dodgy, but whose spirit summed it all up. There was a tendency to try to make [the quality of bands] better, but there was always a space, maybe not a prime spot in the evening, but always a space for bands to turn up who wanted to play.

Simon Williams: Then, of course, you can't mention the Free Festivals without mentioning Wango Riley's Travelling Stage, which is just legendary now. I believe it got sold to some raver dudes in the early 90s. That stage should have been filmed... much better than watching people now doing *X-Factor* or whatever, that stage was the real deal. Now, all it was, was a travelling stage on the back of a truck but it was painted up beautifully and was always at these events. There was something really cool about the whole thing, it might just have been a bit of wood on the back of a truck but it brings back that circus thing, the travelling freak show. It just had more character than something that's built for one event and gets sponsored by Coca-Cola or McDonalds.

Jah Free's Story: Wango Riley's Travelling Stage

Jah Free: I was in a reggae band for quite some time, which developed into Bushfire, a pretty capable band; looking at what we achieved it was quite amazing. At the time we had our own PA, mixing desk and sound engineer, our own stage set-up. We were quite efficient, when we moved around we took our environment with us, never had to rely on other people. During the final years, Dave Ashley, from Southend at the time, acquired the Wango Riley's Travelling Stage… I'm not sure *how*, or from whom, but he actually bought the stage itself, the lorry and everything, great big Pantechnicon. The side used to come down and form an outward platform which would become the forward stage area. The back of the lorry itself would be used as the drum booth where the drums, the speakers and the bands' amps went, then with the sides pulled out you couldn't see the lorry. It looked like something from the fairground, as the whole lorry was enveloped in structure all round it. But there it was, hey presto, quite a sight to see. It took about two hours to set up from scratch, getting all the poles out and the big awning over the top. Dave acquired the stage and I think he felt he took on the commitment. If you bought the Wango Riley Travelling Stage, you bought the commitment that goes with it, to take it out and do with it what's supposed to be done with it. And that is, to make free festivals; that's the heritage of the whole thing, you can't buy a thing like that and shelve it, stick it in your garden and use it as a toy. He felt it was his duty to carry on the cycle. Realistically, when it first started, we were all, 'What? You bought what?' But it became his whole life until he couldn't do it anymore. From the circles he'd bought the stage from, Dave learned about the festivals and places that it normally went to. Other people assisted, and away he went doing festivals here, there and everywhere. This was around 1982, 83, 84. So that was the first involvement, because Bushfire was a self-made thing and I was one of the founder members; being in a band for eight years you learn things and don't know that you're learning along the way. 'Blimey, I'm a sound engineer now.' You've got to learn to do a mix of some sort, we had our own lighting system… we'd learned certain things. Because of that, I was handy to be on the Wango stage, to look after the bands' needs. We were hiring our PA out to other bands and going and putting them on, we knew what to do in terms of mic'ing up the drums and the bass, knew what was needed. Now I'm an artist in my own right, I tour in Europe quite a lot, but the whole thing started at Wango's stage because at some point I had to start talking to the people. 'I've lost Johnny, he's got a red jumper and blue trousers.' 'Can you get George to meet me at the front of the stage?' People were coming up asking so I had to talk and make announcements and over the couple of years that I did that I developed a feel for the mic.' There was a certain shyness to start with; if you've got to speak to a load of people through a microphone and you've not done it before, it's 'Gawd, blimey…' but I got comfortable and it helps me now as a reggae DJ when I play my music at them. I'm talking to people like I did back then learning it on Wango's.

Because Dave was part of the band, Bushfire started going out and playing on the stage and we actually did a tour in France with it; by that time it could be done anywhere because we had our own generator, our own PA. In the middle of that field? OK! We didn't need power, didn't need lighting, it was a complete entity, the way the stage was dressed, everything. We went to our first festie, bands were coming up and the only tax was getting them to bring some petrol for the generator if they wanted to play. Put your name on the list, you've got a spot, come back at three o'clock, bring some petrol. Many a time we'd run out of petrol in the middle of the night and had to scamper around; for the festival to carry on we'd have to find someone willing to give a gallon of petrol. People used to follow the stage around, particularly bands, Poisoned Electrick Head, they'd find where the stage was next and come and we'd do it again. We'd do things like Torpedo Town, White Lady, but we'd find our own places as well. There was a guy who used to go ahead and find a place where we could do it, by the time the police had turned up and got the eviction order done we were on our way anyway. There were snack wagons, an organic food guy who did falafels, an egg-and-bacon type van that came around with us all the time; they'd follow wherever the stage went and do business at the next festival, like a small entourage. Reach the venue and start putting up the stage and it wouldn't be long before we had egg and bacon brought up to us, we supplied their living so they fed us. You could go up to any of the food sellers, as a worker, and you'd get your food. Nice bit of chocolate cake went down lovely at two in the morning, even better when it was free. Or there'd be coin gatherings with the bucket, pass that around to help with the petrol and stuff but there was never any profit. But the crunch came and you were hounded everywhere you went, 'You can't come into our county.' It was very hard; Dave took the stage to France, stashed it there for three or four months to let things cool down a bit. Then he picked it up, drove a bit down this mountain, stopped at a bar for a coffee before making the journey back, and saw all this smoke going past the café window. When they looked out, the whole thing was in flames… the whole thing was just gone, all the photographs, the PA system, everything… there were hoards of photographs, that was the saddest thing.

The Festivals Pinnacle – Stonehenge & Others 1981 - 1984 (continued...)

Michael Dog: My first Stonehenge was 1981. Like everybody who visited Stonehenge, apart from people who had a specifically unpleasant experience, I was just blown away by this gathering that must, even at that time, have been twenty or thirty thousand. People turned up at this place for a month and brought stages and equipment... the entire infrastructure... just for the love of the event. I kept going to them right up until 1985 and then carried on going to the gatherings that marked the summer solstice for several years after that. Then I got involved with the Stonehenge Campaign, the campaign to allow access to the Stones and make a festival happen again. I was involved with that for a number of years.

Swordfish: Stonehenge 1982 was the inception of the Magic Mushroom Band. I wasn't in the band then. I was in the same field but with another band; but that was where it all started for me. I'd been to free things before, like at the local Arts Centre, but Stonehenge was the eye-opener. Everything about '82 was quite magical. The Angels buggering around on motorcycles late at night was a bit heavy, but apart from that … there was strict policing to try and keep the smack and stuff away even though everything else was blatant. It was, well, *disorganised* chaos.

Peter Pracownik: People just wanted the freeness – just like at Glastonbury in 1971. I was there for six days and six nights and it was well managed, there was no dysentery, there were free soup kitchens and everybody just put in what they had and made something happen.

Swordfish: Peter was a witness to all those early things … The Isle of Wight and the first Glastonbury. I was a bit younger and coming from that heavy metal thing and being in London and having no experience of music in a field, apart from Reading and that sort of stuff which I don't class as being in any way similar to that kind of festival. It was really that thing of going to somewhere that was free and experiencing it for the first time. Like, turning your back and there's Tony McPhee playing in a tent or the Invisible Opera Company and all these other people doing magical things.

A theatrical camp site, Stonehenge (Bridget Wishart)

Big Steve: In 1982, I'd been working for the Legalise Cannabis Campaign during the winter and was organising gigs and benefits. In 1982 we organised The International Cultural Herb festival in Brockwell Park, in Brixton. We got in contact with Lambeth Council and Mr Ken Livingstone, and the local MP Tony Banks, and got permission to put up a stage. I don't know how much we paid. We took Nik Turner's Pyramid Stage there, got in contact with various Sound Systems, organised a festival for the legalisation of cannabis and had about seven thousand people turn up. Tony Banks came backstage and congratulated us on organising a very well-run event. This was back in the days of the GLC [Greater London Council]. As a left-wing local government in the Thatcher-era they were supportive to a certain extent, as long as we went through the official channels, exchanged correspondence and negotiated the conditions of organising the event. In terms of modern health and safety requirements, they were probably not as strict as they are now. They were supportive to an extent… in the background. The stage at Stonehenge in '82 was a little bit better organised in terms of the preparations beforehand. Though financially we were all living off the dole and constantly being evicted from squats, it didn't dampen our spirit. We had the experience of how to build the stage and the ramps, the lighting and PA requirements. We increased the size of the PA, from 6k up to about 8k. All these additional bits and pieces that you needed, all the tools to put the equipment up, organising generators, were better organised that year but still fresh and improvisational. We just hoped when we started to bottle the audience for contributions, we would have enough money to cover the costs. We started to make contacts with many bands months before the festival which was essential work. It was amazing the crew that came together on a free festival site. People volunteered to help for free, for the love of the festival.

David Stooke: Before I started at Art College, I spent two years doing crappy jobs around town. Going to Art College was a bit of a spur of the moment thing, but the minute I got there I started meeting people. The college was full of hippie types. I'd had no idea about the festivals, travellers. Salisbury in that period [circa 1982] was just Hippie City – people were saying, 'Wow, have you been up to Stonehenge?' It was very Bohemian, there were a lot of thinkers, hippie types and it was inevitable really … it drew me up to Green Lane which was the ultimate place to go if that was your interest. By the time I'm up at Green Lane, meeting people living in caravans and in buses and telling me about the festivals – I'm changing from an eighteen-year-old art student who knows nothing, into someone who is totally drawn in. I loved it. If you weren't into these things, the festival didn't happen because there were no posters for it in Salisbury, nothing in the local papers. It was like the festival wasn't there. I'd kind of heard of it but didn't really know *if* it happened because I'd never seen any posters or seen it on the news. The first time I went was the summer of 1982. From an artistic viewpoint, the buses with chimneys, the tepees, stone circles – this was the imagery I was dreaming of, something I could almost claim as my own. It was so visually rich, and I was drawn in. I wanted to draw it, wanted to paint it, to say to people, 'This is what's happening.' And before long, I was living that way. The people that I met at Green Lane were a million times more interesting, more fun to be with, more invigorating than those who lived in town. It felt like that Johnny Depp film, *Fear & Loathing in Las Vegas*. The colour is cranked up and watching the film is like a trip. In a way, going into this scene … the colour was mega, the characters, the lifestyle.

Peter Loveday: The influence is just there, it's such a wonderful fund of great stories. I have got the notion of doing the great festival retrospective comic. Treworgey [1989] would be a huge volume in itself. I'd messed around with comic strips and cartoons, and Russell the Hippie originally appeared in a community newsletter in a decaying pit village in Derbyshire under a different name. I had this fund of stories that I'd built up over the years and I just wanted to get it out on paper, a sort of *Freak Brothers* for Britain. Russell got his name from various sources, but partly because Wally Hope's [real] name was Russell, and I wanted to balance that with a sort of sceptical mind so went for Bertrand Russell. It was only once I'd started attending festivals, and doing stalls at festivals, that it became possible. A festival is a city that creates itself overnight and even the most regulated festival can never be sure what city it's building. Things do get wildly out of hand. It's like re-enacting a whole civilisation over the course of a few weeks or, for most people, over the course of a few days. The stories become very intense and people's experiences can be very intense; it's just the easiest place to find stories, really. That gave me the impetus to get started and provided me with an annual harvest in the mid-80s when I was self-publishing comics. I could do a comic, put it out at Glastonbury festival, and go back and pay the printer out of what I made. That gave me a starting point in two ways that balanced out in getting me started and making sure I never made any money! You've got to be cheap to run if you're going to think of a festival as a way of making any money, and don't have too many expectations. Russell was based on people that I already knew, and a bit of him was me as well. I'm never quite sure; it's varied at different times. I got very into 'clowning' and the traditional history of the clown in Europe, so the early Russell is very much the clown figure who was always operating at ninety degrees to what was going on around him. Solving things as much by luck as by judgement, which is really what a lot of people do. But without festivals I don't think I'd ever have taken off on the comics. I'd always had the do-it-yourself ethic. I'd been brought up with it. I'd been working as a Community Arts worker and if ever there's a DIY ethic, that's where you'll find it, particularly back then before it became a profession, but it was a thing to do if you weren't fit to do anything else! It was more about discovering festivals, because I'd been bumbling around in the 70s as this uneducated Trotskyite, politically uneducated, and it all seemed to make sense and fitted with what I'd seen in my childhood. My father worked on fairgrounds and was very at home in the London street markets like Petticoat Lane, and when I was very small he'd take me around this bizarre world of Dickensian characters. I think [laughs] that had my father discovered psychedelic drugs he'd have been very at home at festivals. It's that thing where you discover your parentage in yourself. It became very natural for me, doing stalls at festivals already having that DIY background. I found ways of doing Glastonbury Festival on the cheap, I doubt if I could now, but it was the one place, let's face it, apart from the free festivals, it was the only festival that survived; had it not survived I'm not sure we'd have any other festivals now. I do think it's beginning to reassert itself, and a nice little change in the economic situation will make people appreciate festivals all the more – bread and circuses.

Daryn Manchip: I recall music lessons at primary school, around 1971-1973, where our teacher used a music narrative textbook written using cartoons as an educational guide around 'demos.' These songs were about how groups came together and protested and celebrated through protest. This reflected a time of popular discontent within the existing social world. I think this implanted the seed for the future as I recall at a very early age how social division and inequality affected participation [in society] or not. Having an older sister, herself radicalised in the 70s, also affected my social outlook. Katrina worked for a school in Devon, for children excluded from the mainstream, whose ethos was 'humanistic.' Many of Katrina's associates at Kilworthy were involved in the free festival scene from the mid-70s Stonehenge

Festivals to the creation of Tepee Valley. Looking up to big sister and respecting what she was involved in, I wanted a piece of the action. At seventeen, I attended the 1983 Elephant Fayre at St Germans, Cornwall. Two weeks after this event, I organised the 'Tavistock Free Festival' with a group of other disaffected young people, an event supported by the then Devon Youth Service. This one-day festival was held at a place called The Meadows. We had the use of a 38-ton curtain-sided trailer as a stage, a generator and eight local bands. Unfortunately for us it rained; in fact it poured! We were concerned that the bands playing would be electrocuted so this event was abandoned and a hastily arranged indoor venue was found in the town for the evening. We were closed down by the police; they'd received loads of complaints about the volume of the music. The first proper free festival I attended was the 1984 Stonehenge People's Free Festival. There was another world out there, which was going on alongside mainstream society. I recall how anarchic Stonehenge was, being both disturbing and exciting all at the same time for an impressionable young adult.

Jerry Richards: It was a coming together of people, with lots of different talents. And people with no discernible talents, who would simply be there, who would always be at festivals that you'd turn up at. You'd start bumping into people all the time and in the end it'd be embarrassing not to say, 'Hello – didn't I see you at Blowinghouse Fayre?' or Torpedo Town or somewhere ... anywhere! That's how I met Dave Brock because Dave and Harvey [Bainbridge] or Nik [Turner] who I knew before, would always be at the festivals we'd go to. I was in a band back then called Tubilah Dog, a musical collective, a *legitimate* collective, signed up with Somerset House, which got us off the dole. We got money from the government and loans and things off banks - which we never had to pay back because they forgot to get us to sign anything! Someone was looking after us!

Joie Hinton: I really liked Jerry's guitar playing, really mad about it. Tubilah Dog was a good Hawkwind covers band... well, not covers, but similar – I liked them a lot. A lot of bands were influenced by Hawkwind, but more just the *word*, what it is, really; I think Ozrics were inspired by what Hawkwind really stood for rather than it itself if you know what I mean? Dave Brock is an icon for thousands of people.

Jerry Richards: We got together, all like-minded people and thought, let's get some equipment together. 'You play drums, you can be the singer, I've got a guitar, he can be the bass-player, let's get this thing together.' My friend Alf [Hardy] and I, we got these things together. Get yourself a vehicle, get yourself a light show, get yourself a tarp and you had an instant stage.

Simon Williams: That was another great thing about the festival scene. It was a really good apprenticeship because you had to do it yourself. If you wanted an album out, save the money up, go and do a few gigs and put your album out. Or if you wanted to get a light show together, go around the boot fairs and pick up some old slide-projectors and do it on a *budget* but just do it! A real hands-on way, do it and put it out there.

Mushroom Tom at Winter Solstice (Bridget Wishart)

Jerry Richards: You could go anywhere. Put it up in the middle of a field! If you had a generator, pass the hat around for a bit of petrol, which was no problem as everyone would chip in for that, and just have a really nice time anywhere you wanted to put a festival on. That's what happened to us at the Rollright Stones in '87. I saw Douglas Hurd there... he was the Home Secretary! He came around with his wellies and his green flak-jacket on and he had the Chief of Police with him. But he had no armed guards – he just came to the festival to see what everyone was doing! Now, *we* put that festival on, we just took our gear and put it up and we did that a lot and consequently we bumped into people all the time. That was how we met Scouse, who did Wango Riley's Travelling Stage, and who was always at the festivals; and we did the Hawkdog/Agents of Chaos gigs with Dave and Harvey, and whoever would turn up really. We played at Aldermaston, bands were swapping over and people would stay on stage for a while, then their band would go off but some members would stay and play with the next band.

There'd be a constant merging of things going on and a kind of unity. And it'd be under close scrutiny, you could have five hundred police all ringing the site.

Richard Chadwick: You couldn't get any information on the radio about where the next festival was going to be, it was all via flyers and black and white photocopied bits of paper that had lists of where the next festivals were. There were very few periodicals or magazines devoted to it, apart from *Festival Eye*.

Oz Hardwick: *Festival Eye* still plods along, but there was a huge and varied 'zine culture. There were the band-zines, of course, but there were some really talented people producing and contributing to some fascinating publications. The decidedly un-punk *Sniffin' Flowers* was an inspiration, the bridge from the 60s and early 70s underground mags. *Yellow Gnome* was easily the funniest, and beautifully drawn, too; *Calculated Risk* had a darker edge in places and I was a big fan of, and a regular contributor to, *7th Dream* – used to sell it down the Hammersmith Clarendon, Marquee, etc. Oh, and *Encyclopedia Psychedelica* which was completely up its own backside and all a bit proto-rave-culture, but they printed the first glowing review of my poetry, so they're ok in my book!

Richard Chadwick: The thing that made those festivals work was the same thing that made punk work, that underground culture. What you'd get is a crew turning up with the basic wherewithal to put a band on. They might have the backline, amplifiers, a drum kit and a few instruments and another crew might have a generator and you could combine these things and then other musicians would turn up with more gear. Rollright Stones is a good example. The only equipment there was owned by Tubilah Dog, we went down there on the [laughs] first date of our Smartpils headlining tour and I remember saying, 'Where are we playing at this Rollright Stones Festival?' And Pete the roadie said, 'Just *at* the Festival, you know what it's like.' We turned up and it was slamming with rain and there was a stage with musicians and stuff going on. We went down there, said, 'Can we play?' They said, 'Sure' and we just did. That was what it was like, people sharing stuff.

Paul Bagley: At Rollright Stones the rain was so heavy that the Tubilah Dog crew who provided the stage had to build it from the ground up so that they had shelter whilst erecting it. This meant that there was a nice covered area under the stage. As the rain continued through the day and night it became a hangout and shelter point for many passers-by. It was a weird sight – a band jamming away above and a crowd of folk underneath the stage skinning up and generally having a good time. It was also a safe point from the roving police cameras surveying the site from the nearby hill, trying to hide but looking obvious.

Mark Wright: Organisers? There weren't really any in the conventional sense. Despite all the years of confrontation the police could never get their heads around it, and would always ask to speak to who was in charge. Occasionally someone would have to put themselves forward for legal reasons. I remember once when three of us, despite being concerned that it would all come back on us, put ourselves forward to oppose a local council's attempt to get an injunction to stop a festival late on a Friday. If it was unopposed we would be immediately moved on, but just by turning up in court the hearing was postponed till after the weekend. The council had tried to do it all on the quiet but fortunately someone from the press had let us know and passed on the necessary legal advice. It worked out to our advantage because we were interviewed for the local news afterwards and managed to get in an excellent plug for the festival. Perhaps there were those people who tried to identify sites before each festival, and I'm sure that the likes of Wango Riley's must have had some organising to do, contacting bands etc., but for most festivals it was just a matter of chance who turned up with what kit.

At the Campfire

David Stooke: The people were a major attraction, and the thought of living in an old bus totally appealed to me. When I was up at Stonehenge, I hardly heard any of the music, didn't go and see the bands. For me, the festival was about the people, about wandering around and the things you saw. You could have as much pleasure sitting by a campfire watching the people coming and going. That would be as amazing as being sat in a crowd watching a band. The music didn't play much of a part.

Bridget Wishart: Big things, small things, *anything* can happen round the fireplace. I remember the longest spliff at the free food kitchen fire, about 20 inches and it smoked very well! It's about meeting people, connecting with people on a deep level and never seeing them again. Making things on the fire: tea, toast, soup or stew, always getting lots of advice from visitors, some of it even helpful, then sharing what had been made with whoever was there. Fireside Joe was a festival character who suffered from epilepsy and had severe burns from collapsing into fires but he still loved them. Everyone knew him as Fireside Joe, because that's where he'd be, by a fire, tending it, keeping it burning and playing with the flames. You'd think he might decide to do something else but fire was his thing and that's where you'd find him, even during the brightest, hottest, and sunniest of summer days.

Angel: It really is a very powerful and profound thing when you find yourself in that campfire situation and the fire is going and the music is playing and people really connect. Things are born out of that situation. It seems that life doesn't allow that in our everyday existence. We're bombarded with things all the time, but get into a festival situation and all your values change. What you value in a city or in your everyday life is completely different when you're actually living it at a festival. You have all these influences from these *earth* people, all these experiences, and it does shake your values up.

Chris Salewicz, in Redemption Song (Harper Collins, 2006), his definitive biography of Joe Strummer, talked about Strummer's reconnection with the festival campfire vibe, Joe having experienced first-hand the free festivals of the 1970s. "I've been to a few free ones," Strummer told Salewicz, "They were the ones where you felt, 'This is getting there, everyone pitching in together.'" And interviewing Film director Julien Temple on his documentary, The Future is Unwritten – Joe Strummer, Craig Erpelding later wrote how he felt Strummer saw the campfire as "any loose assembly of people bonded by the rising flames and the advancing dawn." Joe had created his campfire at Glastonbury, the original 'Strummerville', and then metaphorically took it back to his Somerset home so that Temple would say how he had, "People from all walks of life sitting by the fire... in the firelight everyone is equal."

Angel: That beautiful thing, like Joe Strummer, I'm sure he offered beautiful things around his fires. It must have been lovely, what lucky people they were. That interaction! Those experiences, they're deep you know, they're things that you take with you for the rest of your life.

Jake Stratton-Kent: The camaraderie was massive; you never knew who was going to turn up at your campfire, people you'd never met before in your life… it connects with witchcraft, strangely enough. A circle with a fire in the middle, the gathering… the old idea of Celtic or Pagan hospitality, you can't turn away someone who comes seeking hospitality, it's almost instinctive. I met some incredible people who turned up at my campfire, or I turned up at theirs, Wally Hope being one of them. I woke up one morning in my incredible exploding sleeping bag, feathers everywhere… and he turned up with a mess-tin and made coffee for me and this biker type that I'd never met before in my life but who was in the next sleeping bag. Before you knew it, there was a little gathering, completely spontaneous, or so it seemed, and that was the beginning of me really liking Wally Hope because I've always been a coffee addict! First thing in the morning on Salisbury Plain with the beautiful smell of coffee… and despite his background he certainly had the common touch.

Joie Hinton: I moved over to Ireland for a bit, four years or so, got the Oroonies together properly; came back in about 1983 looking to find someone who I'd met, who was a great guitarist, who'd actually disappeared and I've never seen him since. But that's when I bumped into Ed and Gavin from Ozric Tentacles, though they weren't called the Ozrics then. Stonehenge was getting so big, that was the crazy thing. '83 was really an amazing year; really pivotal for meeting people, '84 was just the biggest one ever. It went on for a month, completely free, and it was like a small city had developed in the field opposite the Stones. I was there for about two and a half weeks, but with that going on you could go home for a few days [laughs], sort things out and get a lift back. People were hitching back to London or wherever, and then you could go back to the festival if you felt like it! You came down with your own generator and you played by the tents, plugged in by the campfire and suddenly you had a gig going on. And anyone could do this, anywhere they liked, at any time. That was a really wonderful thing, go for a wander around the site and you'd come across these gigs happening completely unadvertised. No stages, nothing!

Angie Bell: The days when festivals lasted long enough to go home, sign-on, get the giro… and go back again! That was the highpoint!

Angel: I gave up on Glastonbury because it became such a massive commercial thing. I was at Stonehenge. We'd go to Glastonbury and gather all the food that had been left there and we'd take it back to Stonehenge. We really knew about recycling because all the sleeping bags and the things they'd leave, the people at Stonehenge really needed that stuff. It was a great way to redistribute.

Stonehenge 1983 (Kev Ellis)

CRAZY!!!
STONEHENGE
SOLSTICE
RIT
FREE FESTIVAL
JUNE
THE WORLD
M3
A30
THE STONES
BRING A FRIEND
OR TEN!!"

Eleanor's Story

Eleanor: I grew up in a village called Newton Toney, a few miles from the Wiltshire town of Amesbury. For as long as I can remember, once a year all the youngsters from the surrounding area would join the party that was the Stonehenge Festival; local people had always had a good relationship with the festival organisers. I remember visiting Stonehenge many times and being able to actually sit on the stones to eat a picnic. As midsummer drew nearer, local businesses would welcome the festival and I recall my parents telling me that when I was older I would be able to go and join in; but sometime during the early 80s the atmosphere changed. Travellers have always been part of the countryside way of life; many supporting farmers by providing a seasonal workforce. Around the time of one festival, however, a particular group of travellers wreaked havoc and, I believe, were one of the main causes of the festival's demise. Several shops in Amesbury were vandalised and looted and a small group of travellers who camped for a couple of nights in woodland near the Boscombe Down Airstrip cut down and burned over two hundred healthy trees, leaving untold damage and litter in their wake. Other travelling families suffered severely from the behaviour of this small group of idiots who left their BMWs and public schools for a weekend, pretending to commune with nature and get in touch with their spiritual sides. Many families who had visited the village for years and happily integrated with local people found a less than warm welcome when they returned and no longer felt comfortable coming to the area. The police were very heavy-handed at this time and my mother told me that she remembers a time when hundreds of people were targeted and attacked in a brutal and unfair fight. One must wonder whether it was perhaps the policy of the police to stir up trouble in order to speed up the process of banning anyone from the site altogether. I never truly understood why, as the police were stopping and searching cars at random as they headed in the direction of the Stones, that amongst the slow-moving trail of beat-up VW campervans and modified Transits sporting flower designs and 'peace and love' slogans, they chose to stop me, aged seventeen, dressed in Laura Ashley as I returned from a music exam driving my parents' Volvo. I was obviously an anarchist in disguise! In addition to this, the distribution of illegal drugs radiated further from the festival site and the largely peaceful and friendly festival-goers were branded in general as drug-dealers and trouble-makers. Local youngsters were encouraged to stay away from the festival and many people felt that 'their' celebration had been taken away. I lived in Newton Toney until I left home at eighteen and have never once seen the sun rise over the Heel Stone on midsummer's morning.

Photographer: Boris Atha

Dealing with the Locals

Daryn Manchip: I've spoken with local people, many have supported events, and many have also used these events to vent their hatred of other human beings too! Some have been opportunistic to place demands on organisers which have very little to do with the festival itself other than power demonstrated towards a group of individuals who were perceived as 'lesser people' by their fear. How silly we are? I recall around Stonehenge in 1985 the hospitality and warmth shown towards us, the Convoy. People were clapping, waving and smiling as it went past – these were local people. Then of course there were others who demanded that occupied sites be sprayed with disinfectant… Penzance Sun Festival 1988, as reported in a local newspaper.

Richard Chadwick: Watchfield Festival went on so long I ran out of money and I went into the village, which notoriously, because the festival had been advertised in all the music papers, had closed its doors and all the shops were closed. Signs everywhere saying 'No Hippies', but I went into the village and got a job digging someone's garden, during a really hot summer, and went there for several days. They knew I was camped up at the festival, we'd got ourselves established with a camp there, so they came up the night that Gong played and it was like having your parents coming to visit! It was so sunny and nice and they were really captivated by it all and thought the music show was stunning.

Adrian Bell: Hanging Langford 1986 was the best example, when a camp of 400 'Stonehenge Exiles' descended on their sleepy settlement. They loved it. I even got invited into one house for a chat, and the local school kids were enthralled. The landlord of the local pub cleaned up, and I assume he retired to the Seychelles not long after as a result of his "Hippies Welcome" policy. I watched England beat Paraguay in there…

Angie Bell: Often we'd run out of petrol going to or from festivals. Knock on random doors and people would be quite obliging… 'On your way', probably!

Steve Bemand: They were scared, often, of damage and depravity. But there would always be a few local traders who knew the benefits of an influx of hundreds or thousands of temporary punters would outweigh the debauchery going on under their noses.

Tipis at Stonehenge 1984 (Boris Atha)

2000DS's caravan… punk it up! (Dave Fawcett)

Stonehenge 1984 – The Beginning of the End

Somebody put up a sign on site saying,
'1984, mind your head.'

Keith Bailey: The rot had already set in, but in terms of just sheer numbers Stonehenge in '84 was enormous, it must have had at least one hundred thousand people there [police estimate was seventy thousand]. Fifteen, twenty thousand people are manageable whereas once it had got to that size you've basically got a city - with only rudimentary sanitation. Small was beautiful. There was a bunch of people who took it upon themselves to dig latrines but there was no real hygiene ... then you'd get five hundred Hells Angels all roll up at once and that's heavy. Stuff like that began to get intimidating - which was totally wrong. They were a law unto themselves and by '83 were already imposing their law on all sorts of people. If they thought a burger van was charging too much they'd trash it. That's not the solution as far as I'm concerned.

Joie Hinton: I remember in '82 or '83 when this bunch turned up and no-one could believe what they were like. They called themselves The Warped Ones and they arrived on this *chassis*, the bottom half of a bus, just the wheels and the steel girder with an engine. They turned up on this machine and were rampaging around the site, all these weird Mohican *nutters*, a bit like the guys out of *Mad Max II.* Apparently they'd been into Amesbury car park and completely trashed every car in the car park; no one could deal with them. Nobody knew who they were, where they'd come from, nothing. They were absolutely just out of this world, they could have been aliens, you know?

Jake Stratton-Kent: After Wally Hope's death I was at every single Stonehenge Festival, though by 1984 I was becoming disenchanted. The Brew Crew had appeared and they were climbing all over the Stones and giving other people a hard time. There was this Celtic harpist that used to turn up and the Brew Crew were hassling him, 'We've got as much right to be here as you have.' Well, nobody was saying they hadn't, but he had a right to be there too, why were they giving him a hard time? That was the kind of thing that pissed me off with the Festival towards the end; but then they banned Stonehenge and, right, I was ready to walk away but you tell me I *can't* go and that's another matter.

Big Steve: Stonehenge 1984: I was involved in a traffic accident with my bicycle; I was going to a Tai-Chi Chuan yoga class and came off my bike. I went flying over the handlebars and ended up under the wheels of a juggernaut. Woke up in hospital about five hours later, regained consciousness with a broken right arm – and this was about three weeks before the festival was due to start. So from my hospital bed I was trying to get in contact with bands and make sure everything was okay. I was in hospital for about a week before they let me out, so from a personal point of view it made things much more difficult for me, not being totally able to use my strength and energy to organise and put up the stage – I'd taken quite a heavy blow. My arm was in plaster and a sling. I hitched down to Stonehenge with a little tent, and arrived there on the 15th of June. I had to organise the bands, and be the MC and DJ. The stage base had already been put up by the Polytantric by the time I arrived. Fortunately I had some good people helping me, but it wasn't the same. For me, 1983 was the peak in terms of the quality of everything; in '84 it *was* okay but different, it had got so big. The miners' strike had occurred, I remember talking to Arthur Scargill in the queue to the Screen on the Green in Islington after Orgreave and I started arguing with Scargill, saying that he'd provoked Margaret Thatcher into reacting with the police and all the rest of it. I think I called him a wanker, which obviously didn't go down so well. Though I supported the miners I was pissed off. He must have thought I was crazy. Dealing with the miners gave Thatcher and the police the possibility of taking on the festivals and '84 was the precursor to that. Somebody put up a sign on site saying, '1984, mind your head.' The writing was on the wall, there was something almost Orwellian about that year, there was a transition. People were taking it to the limit and there was going to be a karmic backlash, a reaction. There were problems with burnt out cars, rubbish… I was attacked on site by some people from the so-called Peace Convoy; the Convoy had been infiltrated by the SAS and all types of thugs.

People, *agents provocateurs*, the authorities were trying to destroy the free festival from within. I got beaten up by a group of heavies with baseball bats. Nik rescued me on a Harley and took me to the St John's hospital on site. There were supposedly people doing freebase in a caravan or so the rumour went, I couldn't believe it, *in 1984* people were freebasing, and walking around site wielding baseball bats. There was some heavy shit going on. Rumours and lies and madness reacting. We had always tried to keep things cool from the stage and told people where to go to get help from festival welfare with drug abuse problems. The abuse of drugs or otherwise, like in any big festival, was caused by a minority of people but as always this reflected badly on the majority. Despite all of this I refused to be intimidated and managed to keep the stage together, got all of the groups on stage on time; things went well despite the initial problems. At the end I did my best. We took everything down, cleared up the site around the Pyramid Stage… picked up another can... as another police helicopter rat-

(ABOVE) Smack dealer's car burned out (Boris Atha)
(BELOW) Getting around at Stonehenge, 1984 (Adrian Bell)

Hawkwind with Jenny Chapman Tibetan Tent 1984 (Oz Hardwick)

tled overhead. There was a barbed-wire fence next to where the stage had been which was covered with broken strands of cassette tape. The juxtaposition of images wasn't lost on me. I came away from Stonehenge with mixed feelings. In retrospect, if there had been some kind of coordination with the authorities, or there had been willingness by the authorities to communicate and work with people on site, then it could have continued in a form that was more stable. But there was no willingness from the Conservative government, or from English Heritage or National Trust, for it to carry on. That July there was a protest against Porton Down, against the animal experiments laboratories, there was some protest from the Animal Liberation movement, there were various peace camps at Boscombe Down in July as well. There was supposedly a secret underground nuclear base under Salisbury Plain or near Boscombe Down, so the rumour went. It was like a pressure cooker in some ways. It was beginning to fracture. Politically they'd decided we were causing too many problems and there was no willingness [for the festival] to continue.

Policing

The police are being curious - be the same to them

Klive Krainger: You could talk to an individual policeman, someone who was standing at the gate or somewhere like that and they would engage with you and they weren't just behind

Smiley Coppers, White Horse Hill, 1985 (Adrian Bell)

these transit vans with big screens, you could talk to them. They didn't quite understand, but some of them liked the music and some could see that people were having fun and weren't hostile but [generally] they were made to stand there all day watching this thing that they didn't understand at all… which was part of the fun, doing something that these ordinary people didn't understand.

Adrian Bell: I wouldn't say I had dealings with the police, but it was pretty hard to avoid them between 1985 and 1999. A lot of them were friendly and happy with the overtime we brought them, but others were out and out hippie haters, and made that quite clear. You could normally tell the two distinctions just by looking at the photos I took of them. The ones who smile for the camera are the overtime-happy ones, and the ones standing next to them, scowling, are the *Daily Mail* reading Thatcherite coppers who think we should all get a job…

Keith Bailey: There was a whole alternative scene starting to evolve, and Here & Now were spearheading it, bands like us and Crass were fiercely independent; the more we preached that gospel the more hassle we got from the police and Special Branch. One example, we'd just started one of our 'free tours' in London and were due in Brighton the next night. We were stopped eleven times between London and Brighton, basically every five miles. Twice by the same bunch … I recognised one of the guys from an earlier stop and he said, 'Ah, you *have* got your eyes open,' and pulled out a warrant card. Special Branch. 'We've got a file two inches thick on you lot.' They were out to harass us to destruction. Every time we'd get stopped the whole bus would be turned over and stripped down, everyone would get searched and they'd bully and harass us. I got pushed around in numerous police stations – bollock-naked and shoved around by some sergeant with black leather gloves on; it's a test of your resolve. But we had so much support from the people, from the ground and that gave us the inspiration and the energy to continue.

Mick Farren: It got a whole lot harder to organise festivals, farmers wised up about renting the fields and you had this whole 'Not in my Back Yard' thing that got better organised and it got more difficult. [On Harold Wilson and Edward Heath being more benign than the Thatcher years] I totally agree with that, but that's the five-percent of difference. You didn't quite have the same mad Police Chiefs that you did under Thatcher, plus you didn't have external things like the Miners' Strike. In 1972 the cops hadn't acquired riot shields. It was very much down to the local town clerks and chief constables of the county and how they reacted.

Angel: All those years that people spent going [to Stonehenge] and honouring that sacred place, feeding and giving to that energy! The government in no way could allow this; already people had become a thorn in their side because festival life actually gave way to the movement that was the Peace Convoy. That was born out of that whole festival life. They were trying to devise ways to smash that to bits, to destroy it, because they can't have people being born and not registered, people burying their own dead. You have to be numbered.

Jerry Richards: The police physically attacked me just across the road from the Heel Stone, when a thousand people came through the fence and started beating people up. You know, there were women and children, dogs playing, people playing flutes … it didn't stop the police, they were totally out of control.

Simon Williams: The one time I really remember getting hassled by the police was during the Stonehenge festivals. We got pulled over on the way home. I mean, it was quite obvious that we'd been to a festival, we had a generator, a PA and a big stage on the back of the van… and we got pulled over on the way *back*. There was a young copper who started searching a friend of ours, Suzie, who was with us, and he found her contraceptive pills and pulled them out and was going 'I've got you now.' We just started laughing at him because we knew what they were, so he showed it to the WPC and got this look that said, 'you idiot.' And that was it, 'Okay, you can go now.' We were chanting 'Monday's Acid. Tuesday's Acid,' and really taking the piss!

Jerry Richards: The authorities were frightened, no doubt about it. There was that pervading sense, going to a festival, of keeping a close eye and listening to the police waveband to find out what their response to all of this was. It brought the police presence into a sharper focus for the public, and brought the police into a really sharp focus for the police themselves, because their public image was under scrutiny. I personally stood on the Hampshire-Wiltshire border watching the two Chief Constables of Hampshire and Wiltshire arguing over which force was going to pay the bill to move us off Devil's Dyke. When you get to that level, it's ridiculous. There are eight hundred people there and they are arguing about who is picking up the bill for moving these hippies out of the area. And of course, by stopping free festivals in that way, they split everybody up, everybody went off doing different things and the police got spread more thinly on the ground.

Swordfish: When it gets too much, that's when it gets too messy, which there have been testaments over time for. The classic is Woodstock; when it gets too big, how do you control that? Because by nature some people aren't too good, are they? They lose it. If we'd all had the correct teachings, about drugs and stuff and how to use various things and had the discipline maybe things might have been different, but there were too many out of control characters. Take Stonehenge, when we were there, '82, '83, it was only in three or four fields centred round the hill, with Nik's Pyramid Stage, and the following year it was in nine or ten fields and really expanding out. So you could see that next year it just wasn't going to be allowed and the police were patrolling the perimeter and it just killed it.

Ribblehead Free Festival 1988 (Janet Henbane)

Nigel Mazlyn Jones: It ruined Rougham Tree Fayre. In that one year it blew up the whole scene, which Margaret Thatcher then loved, 'Beware the Peace Convoy', and it gave them an excuse right across the nation. That became the training schedule, to this day, of how to handle group civil disturbances. That really gave the Thatcher Empire the reason to bring in the Criminal Justice Bill and all the subsequent things we've now got that have eroded civil liberties. I remember the Devon and Cornwall police at a folk festival in Skinners Bottom [near the Cornish town of Redruth], it wasn't a free festival... it was a *folk* festival with no more than fifteen hundred people for the whole two days. One travellers' coach turned up, and a *kerfuffle* starts... everyone is rushing up to the gates... what's going on? 'The *travellers*' coach has arrived... [Mock horror] with *travellers* in it... it's the Peace Convoy.' The Cornwall police had never seen any trouble, the Devon police had at Stonehenge, being involved with the Somerset and Wiltshire police, but the Cornish hadn't. So the Cornish police decided to use it as a training excuse and turned out *en masse* with *jam sandwich* cars and personnel and one or two truncheons out... and there's *one* travellers' vehicle. An old Leyland truck crammed with about twenty people, with five or six people on top shouting abuse down at the blue uniforms, who were shouting abuse back up. I went up there, and unfortunately I was shaven by that time and it was raining and I'd borrowed someone's blue anorak, hood was up to stop the rain, beard was gone in those days, they didn't recognise the old 'NMJ' from Stonehenge and all the rest of it, and there they were hurling abuse at me! But it was one vehicle, and the way the police treated it... and all it had started from was one vehicle they didn't want on site, *one vehicle*... and it was 'the Peace Convoy'.

Jah Free: One time, we were going to a festival, I think it was the one in Cornwall near King Arthur's Castle in Tintagel, we were all sleeping in the bus and we decided to have a stop and a fondle of the Stones because at that time there was no fencing [around Stonehenge]. We just decided it was respectful to stop at the Stones and have a half-hour break... clear our heads or cloud our heads, whichever! We'd only just pulled up and got out when all these police came roaring up, 'You're not setting up a festival here,' all this sort of thing! They actually thought we were going to put a festival on there and then. We'd only stopped to look at the Stones, and there were four police vans, three cars! Several times we'd get turned away at borders, 'You're not coming into our county.'

There was a situation once, it was supposed to be the Ribblehead Festival but somehow it had all been cancelled. We found this lovely big expanse not too far away and had a lovely festival there. The police were a bit pissed off about that but again, by the time they got their eviction order we were starting to go. We all lined up at the gates to leave, but the police didn't want us to go that way, they wanted us to go out through the other gate. Three hundred vehicles all facing one way in a semi-circle, waiting to file out and the police are saying, 'turn round and go out the other gate.' They'd all turned up with no numbers on and it got quite hairy, lots of pushing and shoving. The first vehicle was getting, 'Move your vehicle back.' Well, where did they suggest it moved? There were another five vehicles behind it! The guy actually dragged the driver out of the cab, 'Well, I'll move it back then.' As soon as you put hands on, certain things happen. The people who are most easily ignited, they start grabbing someone and it all starts going off. In the end a Chief of Police turned up, 'All right, you can go that way but you have to go only five or six vehicles at a time.' So it fizzled out and we all left in small bunches and amalgamated at the next festival. Sometimes you'd just drive, drive, drive, head towards Kent, then be waiting in Kent for the advance party to say, 'I've found a field.' One particular one that comes to mind was next to a pub, and the landlord was well pleased! The other local people weren't all that pleased but it went off wonderfully. At one festival we had the local mayor turn up, bigging up what we were doing, 'I think it's great the young people are doing such a thing.' My experience of local people was generally good, they'd come to it. A rumour would go around the first night, second night they'd want to come and have a look. That mayor invited us back the next year. Over the course of three days there was some construction going on in a distant field, they actually built a mock Houses of Parliament, you could see what it was by the Saturday, then on the Sunday night they set fire to the bloody lot! It was huge, all made out of pallets and cardboard; Sunday night, when the mayor was there, all the music stopped and everybody came out and watched it burning!

Keith Bailey: Towards the end of the [1984 Stonehenge] festival, a whole bunch of guys from the Convoy trashed the police mobile command centre – and I mean reduced it to rubble. I think that was the point where Maggie and her crew said, 'We've got to do something about this,' and it caused the [1986] Police Order Act. 'Two people proceeding in a given direction can constitute a procession and can be arrested as a threat to civil order.' They made it very clear from spring 1985 that the Stonehenge Festival wasn't going to happen.

The Festival Scene (Mel Owen)

The Beanfield and Beyond – Stonehenge 1985

The Beanfield was the end of the Convoy proper because after that it did kind of fragment.

Keith Bailey: Post '84 there were still good people involved but a lot of the festivals were Convoy organised and I had issues with those guys. Even though we'd, in a way, planted the seeds for it, we were viewed as outsiders, not radical enough and as an outsider you tended to see the heavy drug-dealing side of it first. I think we knew, driving away from Stonehenge in '84, seeing the police command centre being trashed… I remember saying to the keyboard player at the time, 'I reckon that's the last one.'

Chris Hewitt: I think it's very sad that it did polarise into this whole thing of, you either run a commercial festival with a big fence round it or you have totally chaotic events with no-one being responsible and there were elements within the Convoy and the Brew Crew that just messed the whole thing up long-term, didn't they? It always amazes me, I've got several friends who claim that they're anarchists but they all sign on the dole every week! If you're an anarchist then why do you take money from this government that you want to want to depose? It's a very comfortable position to be in, isn't it? My business that I run now [Ozit – Morpheus Records] is still fairly unconventional and chaotic but one has to run it within a certain amount of rules to survive. There were people who, even though a lot of them had everyday jobs and considered themselves to be quite political, argued that festivals should go ahead even if the authorities objected and we shouldn't bend to any rules. It was a big fight for freedom but the problem with that is sooner or later someone has to be responsible for things like damage to the farmer's land… or sanitation… and once you get up to twenty thousand you have got to start planning these things. If you do a graph of the growth from three hundred to three thousand to twenty thousand, if [Deeply Vale had] carried on in that growth situation it would have become totally unmanageable, it would become a disaster like many festivals did.

Jerry Richards: You had lots of different people who'd come through the free festivals of the 70s and early 80s leading up to Stonehenge in '84, by which time that had become massive, world famous, and was about to become a heritage festival. If you had a festival for twelve years at the same site it becomes a legitimate fayre under common law, so '85 was the last year that the authorities could stop the festival happening. The next year would have been the full quota and we'd have had common law on our side. That was one of the reasons they stopped it. You had all these disparate groups that would come together at these free festivals: artists, musicians, and jugglers... people who just lived on the roads and would be moving around all over the summer and doing the festivals. Then they'd move to Europe for the winter, take their buses over there, there wasn't so much pressure on the people who were moving around. You'd have people like Screech Rock – a wild punk-rock art-house who'd paint themselves in Day-Glo colours or Mutoid Waste Company who seemed to turn up at nearly every free festival I ever went to. They'd build structures of scaffolding, bits of wreckage and cars and bits of trucks and weld all this stuff together on site and created these fantastic sculptures. They did one at Tewkesbury Festival which was the same day as [Hawkwind's] Bob Calvert died [14th August, 1988]. They built this absolutely massive dragonfly with about a twenty-five, thirty foot wingspan hanging up on this derrick all painted psychedelic Day-Glo colours and lit up by UV at night. Or they built a huge spider using scaffold legs, again all painted-up; they'd make different things at different festivals and it'd always be ... well, when I was at art college we'd call it an 'installation'. You'd go to do this week's 'installation' on some

Mutoid Waste - CarHenge (Janet Henbane)

new theme and that's what they tried to do, keep different things happening all the time. That was what was so thrilling to me at the time about that period of British free festivals, that common theme.

David Stooke: The Beanfield was the end of the Convoy proper because after that it did kind of fragment and even though a lot of the people hadn't changed, they probably weren't *together* in the same way.

Big Steve: It was well-known, we were in the eleventh year [of the Stonehenge Free Festival] and there was an old piece of common law related to fairs held on common land that if a fair was held for twelve years running you could obtain a Royal Charter to hold fairs on the land in perpetuity. Legally, I don't know if that really would have been the case, but certainly that was the understanding and belief on site. [The authorities'] take on it was that there was this huge, anarchic free festival on Salisbury Plain which unfortunately had excesses, in terms of clearing up a few burnt out cars... people would drive cars down to the site and leave them there... and a lot of rubbish, though we cleared up a huge amount of it. There was this breakdown in communication between the authorities and the people on site, and it had got so big, it didn't have the infrastructure to deal with all the problems and things that needed to be organised. So there was a feeling that 1984 would be the last one. There were problems with some of the Convoy. In '84 or '85, in April, they squatted the Wells Fargo plantations and had supposedly used up the English Heritage or National Trust budget for the festival. There were indications that things were out of control, and that, even with the willingness to try and solve them, some people had already made it very difficult for those who were trying to allow it to continue. There were plenty of scapegoats to justify the clampdown. Also the politics of the newly established English Heritage and their plans to obtain World Heritage status for Stonehenge could possibly have had an influence. But if everything had continued, it could have been great, we could have organised it really well, had there been the willingness from the authorities. People loved the festival so much, you get people twenty years later saying it was the best experience of their lives. There was a real willingness from a majority of good people who would have liked to have seen it continue; it would have been well organised, a national event.

Paul Sample (Salisbury Council): During the 1980s the local [Salisbury] Council was controlled by a particularly obnoxious bunch of right-wing Tories and we spent quite a lot of time debating various exclusion zones with them. My view is that there was quite a bit of tacit support – not a majority by any means - for the free festival in the local community, though not amongst MPs, the farmers and landowners, and English Heritage. Obviously there were some bad incidents, but by-and-large, the main problems to local people were caused by the road blocks and restrictions to movement, rather than anything that may have been done by the festival-goers themselves. Most took the festival and its consequences in their stride and knew it was a seasonal problem. Quite a few local Councillors, from 1990 onwards, wanted to see a more co-operative and less antagonistic approach and I think, over a period of time, we got our views across quite well. The relatively peaceful events in recent years at Stonehenge are, in large measure, a testament to those who took a more enlightened approach to the festival. The aggressive approach of the 1980s simply resulted in a massive policing operation which was financially unsustainable and hugely disruptive to local people. It couldn't go on.

Big Steve: The main channel of communication with the authorities was through Festival Welfare Services [FWS], through the teams that were working on site, and through St John Ambulance who had a hospital on site. That was the main contact with the police. English Heritage and National Trust didn't want people on the land and were not willing to enter into any discussion. English Heritage, at the time, was taking over the custody of the site. There was no attempt [from them] to channel communication through FWS or through established organisations on site who could have been used as conduits for discussion with the Tibetans or the Pyramid Stage or people from the festival like Sid Rawle, or members of the Convoy, to try and look at ways of improving the infra-structure and safety. In 1985, when they banned the festival, there were attempts to have meetings with English Heritage in Fortress House, in Savile Row, London, which we went along to, to try and discuss the lifting of the ban. But it was impossible; you were dealing with this huge quango that had no desire to talk to us. Even Michael Eavis came up for talks with the press. I apologised to him for the chaos and huge numbers of punters that were being exported to Glastonbury and wished him well. The first I was aware that Stonehenge 1985 definitely wasn't going to be allowed to take place was that they'd put up posters in the London Underground. I caught the tube down from Camden Town and there was this huge English Heritage poster, 'No Stonehenge Free Festival 1985.' It's difficult to describe, but I was under a lot of pressure, getting stopped and searched a lot. I was seriously concerned. For me it was like, 'I'll do what I can.' I was on to the next project, the next gig, looking for another tract, doing other creative things.

Peter Pracownik: At the Beanfield, Thatcher needed to make a point - people couldn't gather in great masses without rules and regulations.

Big Steve: After Orgreave, and taking on the print unions at Wapping, the police were well up to taking on the free festivals. Margaret Thatcher had pronounced that she would do anything she could to make life difficult for free festivals and the Peace Convoy, so she was allocating huge amounts of resources. They decided they were going to take it on, and they did at the Beanfield. When the Beanfield occurred, I was in Nigel Planer's flat in Clapham with my girlfriend and it came up on the BBC News about the Beanfield, I looked at Nigel, who was Neil in *The Young Ones*, and he goes, like Neil, 'Oh, what a bummer, man.' I couldn't believe it... surreal! I was dis-gusted, angry and saddened by all this brutality that my brothers and sisters were facing just for trying to celebrate the summer solstice at Stonehenge. My friends told me not to go as I would be targeted. It seemed there was nothing I could do.

Matty's Story

I was seventeen years old – I'd already made up my mind to be a musician, right from a very early age. I'd always had a feeling of being different, of looking for something in life that I couldn't ever describe. I was always with musicians, smoking some pot, taking trips on LSD – that sort of thing. It's like smelling the most beautiful scents but not ever knowing what they are or where they come from. I couldn't get into the nine-to-five thing; I didn't want to get trapped in that kind of situation. When I was ten I had a copy of Bob Marley's *Rastaman Vibration* and connected with that, and I used to spend a lot of time at my grandmother's place in Southall. You could hear the reggae and blues parties going on and I had an attraction to that.

I was with a guy, let's just call him 'G', we were in a little Wiltshire village in the English summer, on June 20th 1985. My travelling companion was an old festival head, nine or ten years older than I was. I'd known him for years. He'd run away from home when he was something like twelve years old and ended up getting into the festival scene and travelling around. He lived near me when I was a kid, with his tattoos and his hash, and there was a whole lot more to him than just the everyday things. When he wasn't at school, or wasn't out in the city, he'd be in someone's tepee or in a bender or down in Wales with people that he knew. But he had a £50-a-day smack habit ... and that was in 1985.

There we were in this Wiltshire village; I've no idea how far away from Stonehenge we were. G had spent the night in one of the old red telephone boxes and was shivering from withdrawal; a big bust had prevented him from scoring and that's why we didn't get to Stonehenge until late on the 21st. I'd taken some Black Bombers the previous night and I was buzzing because I'd never been to Stonehenge before; I was only seventeen, whizzing my tits off and rolling him some joints and saying, 'Don't worry, you'll get sorted when we get to Stonehenge.' I was a naïve seventeen-year-old but I did love G, even though he'd ripped off half of my so-called mates. I understood that he was addicted and could see past his addiction because he had a lot of pain inside. But life's a journey and people who don't suffer don't get to appreciate and see that life is such a temporary thing and that suffering can be turned around. Life

Trashed coach at White Horse Hill, 1985 (Adrian Bell)

throws up different obstacles but I see that as a blessing. You can't appreciate the sun until you've been in the darkness.

Evening of the 21st, the sun was shining and the birds were singing. G said, 'Matty, if you hear a motor, stick your thumb out.' A bus picked us up; I remember the air-brakes coming on and the doors electronically opening and the driver shouting, 'Get in quick; we've got to get to Savernake Forest.' This was my first experience of Stonehenge ... why were we going to Savernake Forest? The driver of the bus was called Pete and he'd either heard through CB radio or simply had got away lightly ... but he was driving his bus around and getting stopped at roadblocks and being told to 'Get the fuck out of Wiltshire.' We arrived late at Savernake Forest, and I remember his lovely missus, who'd fed and watered us, watching *EastEnders*, which is quite bizarre! The police were at the entrance to Savernake Forest trying to prevent any more of the Convoy and festival-goers entering. Pete wound down his window a crack and the police demanded 'Name? Registration number? You can't come here.' Someone yelled, 'Drive!' and before we knew it, we were in Savernake Forest.

Joie Hinton: All the buses with their trashed windows and people recovering from all of that... I had a few friends who'd been involved in that and they were telling us horrible stories. It was like the 'walking wounded' you know? But they had to go somewhere, immersed in their bruises and wounds and weren't so much into flying the flag of festivals at that point. It was like a refugee camp in a way, but then it turned over in a few days to be quite a groovy time at the end.

Matty: There were mixed emotions. Hundreds had suffered at the hands of the SPG and Maggie Thatcher and it was the beginning of the end – and it was only my first time, I must have cursed it, man! I hadn't slept and, heavily stoned, I was dead on my feet and needing to sleep. G jumped off the bus, I gave him a tenner to keep him going, and said goodbye to Pete and his missus. I stumbled around, fires were blazing and towed-in vehicles from the Beanfield were all around, some just shattered and twisted metal that represented what was once a family home. It was just a whole vision of destruction, people standing around the campfires discussing what had happened, with a few spliffs and a bit of booze. G found me, and actually had a cup of tea for me. I'd seen this guy consume vast quantities of stuff and still walk in a straight line better than anybody returning home from the pub after a few pints.

I mean, this guy was hard-core. I had a couple of Hot Knives for fifty-pence or a pound and scored a bit of hash and the next thing I knew, the muscles in my face were twitching involuntarily – G had put something in my cup of tea. I was in the forest, tripping. The sun was shining, there were fire breathers, jugglers, fires going and a reggae sound system and I was just blissed-out. People were there making the best of a bad deal and keeping their heads up, you know? That was down to Lord Cardigan. I walked up to the festival drag and this Convoy geezer was asking his little kids to thank Lord Cardigan for letting them stay on his land. He was all done-up in his tweeds, with his beagle dogs and he was just checking out the scene. The Thatcher government, through the power of the police, was trying to stop it and Lord Cardigan let everyone stay there, so it's a duality. I got a blanket and plotted-up about five foot from the nearest fire. People were conversing and telling stories and just sharing what they had with one another. It was something I'd never experienced before – that openness. It was: I'm going to pick you up, man. Pick up your spirit, come on.

Ozric Tentacles at White Horse Hill 1985 (Adrian Bell)

Paul Bagley: A group of us ended up in Savernake Forest, including, coincidentally, others of the Omnia Opera crew. We didn't know each other at the time but realised years later that the familiarity when we did meet up was due to the fact that we had shared the same campfire as we recalled the conversations that had been flying around. Word came out that there was an alternative free festival at Westbury White Horse where Hawkwind ended up and so I made my way there via home where I picked up a blind lady friend of mine and some provisions. The weather turned as if the elements were in protest at the events of the Beanfield and by picking up some hitchhikers we found out where the festival was. The police had already blockaded the roads and were towing vehicles away, so I parked up a mile away and walked through the torrential rain, guiding the blind girl. Eventually we reached the inevitable blockade across the road and a police sergeant took great delight in telling me that the road and the festival were closed. I protested, pointing out my now bedraggled blind friend, and also raised the fact that there couldn't have been an injunction passed to close the road so quickly. At that moment one of the police started piping up that I was a troublemaker and should he arrest me? I thought this a funny turn of phrase to use and then suddenly noticed, with abject horror that, apart from the sergeant, all the other police at the blockade had the parts of their uniform that displayed their numbers patched over with black tape. I quickly made my apologies and left… I could have made my way across country over a forested hill along with the other festival-goers, but it was dark, I was soaked and I had my distressed blind friend to look after. I went home…

Jake Stratton-Kent: I wasn't at the Beanfield because I was coming up from the South West whereas [The Convoy] was coming across from Bristol so the police had two bunches of people to deal with. We'd arrived in Amesbury when the Beanfield kicked off, thought this was our chance and marched to Stonehenge on foot, several hundred of us. When we got to Stonehenge there were only about a dozen cops in sight, then suddenly there were bloody trucks full of blue uniforms, no numbers or anything, and the people they were beating up were mostly very gentle people. We'd avoided the roadblock, and I'd have been happy to march on the 'Thin Blue Line' myself, but most of the people in that crowd who'd marched from Amesbury started going over the fence into a field to try and take the site, with no confrontation in mind. Then trucks full of thugs, some of whom may not even have *been* police, pulled up. Alsatian dogs being let loose on women. I got a truncheon in the kidneys. They eventually pushed us out of the field, down the road. I was getting pretty annoyed by this time, then this riot cop guy came charging into the crowd with a baton and one of those small shields that the snatch squads have rather than the big plastic shields that they make walls with, and he was looking to hit somebody. He came running into the crowd; I looked back, saw him coming and just stuck my foot out and he went down like a sack of potatoes. Naturally lots of folks moved in on him then, but I kept walking; I didn't want to be spotted as a troublemaker. I went there because I thought I owed it to the old hippie ethos and Wally Hope who was no longer around. 1984 I didn't like, Stonehenge had the Brew Crew and biker riots. I was ready to walk away from it until they banned it, then I thought I'd better go and show my face for something I used to believe in. And take the flak. I was there to drag people out of trouble, if necessary, and get them away; I took a couple of youngsters under my wing and got them away from the trouble – that was why I was there. It was something I believed in and I wasn't going to let it down when it needed me.

Jeremy Cunningham: The Beanfield thing was almost what got The Levellers together in the first place. I mean, none of us were at the Beanfield, though I was at Stoneycross the year afterwards, but we all saw it on the news, independently. I remember all my friends at the time saying to me, 'Did you see that on the telly? There were all those people who looked just like you, getting the shit kicked out of them.' And I was, 'Yeah, I know some of those people.' That was one of the things that made us all, individually, want to get up and say something, and the only thing we could do was to play music, which was the only way we knew how to do it, apart from me as I was doing paintings about it as well.

Jerry Richards: Lord Cardigan took everyone in after the Beanfield. He said, 'I saw what was going on in the press and heard it on the radio and I couldn't believe it and had to see what was happening.' So he went to see where the action was going on and said, 'I've just witnessed the British police force running amok, out of control… not under the control of supervising officers.' And he was horrified, this upstanding citizen of the State, and it really blew him away, and so he said, 'Come to my land, come and stay on my land.' So we owed him a great debt of gratitude because he took loads of people in who otherwise… you know, pregnant women were being hauled through the windscreens of their buses, shocking behaviour. So this whole wonderful, beautiful vibe that we thought was in motion began to become dissipated by all of that and split off into different factions.

Oz Hardwick: Really, it was the criminalising of people simply for gathering together. You could be woken up by the sound of helicopters and a tooled-up policeman sticking his head in your tent for gathering, as people had always done, on common ground. I stopped going in the late 80s. Obviously festivals were being stamped out, but there was an element by then which, in spite of any rhetoric, was as Thatcherite as you'd find anywhere, with a thuggish disregard for anything or anybody beyond themselves. I still feel that the real, unspoken objection was to so many people gathering and having a good time without spending and consuming to any significant extent.

Daryn Manchip: Hippies became the next scapegoats after the miners. We were used for political ends by both the government and the media in some form. This disintegration caused more problems than any solution. The powers that be exploited the fragile nature of the Free Festival movement and promoted fear of it to the wider population.

Jake Stratton-Kent: It wasn't anything to do with cracking down on drugs; it was cracking down on a social movement. Thatcher used the same police and the same tactics that she used on the miners. An interesting thing was that the travellers were up in the north of England, part of the Convoy, around 1985; the police arrived, trashed all the vehicles, dragged the men off to prison and said to the ones who were left, 'If you're not off by Monday, your vehicles will be impounded.' A bunch of miners turned up with welding gear and tools, got them all back on the road. A couple of years earlier, the miners wouldn't have given a thought to the hippies being in trouble but suddenly there was common cause.

Angel: It was a highly political time and for me it all centred on the Molesworth Festival. Before the Beanfield, the Peace Convoy had been hit quite severely in Yorkshire. There were lawyers going to the courts, trying to help people... and the miners actually helped the Convoy because where the government had slammed into them, bust up their homes, taken their kids, their dogs... these people were given an ultimatum that they had to mend their vehicles by a certain time, literally only hours, and their vehicles were actually their homes and their livelihood. If they couldn't, their vehicles were going to be trashed. So the miners actually all got together and they helped fix things. At Molesworth, I ran the free food kitchen with my friend Myra. We were feeding hundreds of people a day. They had teachers, so children were being taught. A lot of these people had degrees, they were very well-educated people who had decided to go and live in tepees. They knew how to grow their food; they were ploughing the land in order to sow the seed. They were people who had the crafts and the skill to make things that people needed. We were seeing [TV] footage and that was when I had that harsh realisation that what you see in the media isn't actually true. That it's all staged. We knew what was really happening, we had the inside information. Of course, it all ended desperately sadly, with the authorities invading to secure site for MOD [February 6th, 1985], smashing the whole place up, terrorising people and frightening their children. They annihilated the whole place, which had been the ultimate realisation of all the festivals that I'd ever been to. That was one of the most incredible festivals.

Dick Lucas: Travellers suddenly became a very selective collective noun that forced a focus on anyone in individualised vehicles, as if travelling was suddenly something that we don't ALL do. While I'm here, people wouldn't be travellers so much if they were allowed to stop and stay somewhere without getting moved on all the time! Once there was an exclusion zone, the freewill and spiritual desire to get to the Stones at the solstice became politicised, as did a broader issue of freedom of movement. It wasn't just the Stones now; it was about the right to go anywhere we liked! The right to gather in numbers and be left alone seems to have been a big threat to the State's way of thinking. They weren't really thinking we were going to smash up city centres or trash their cars, houses, or possessions, which was the violent angle propagated to the press, they just knew the power of numbers, and the power of an *idea* once sufficiently put into action. If these travellers were seen getting away with self-sufficiency and not paying taxes, it might catch on! The State loses control when it can no longer scare the population into submission via laws. So the full force of State power was brought in to stop all this wanton behaviour. From '85 to '88 the mission was to get as near to the Stones as possible come June 21st, which meant gathering around the edge of the exclusion zone on the eastern border of Wiltshire. Get a van, get people in it, go looking; no mobile phones, but a few CB radios, and local radio news would often guide us to the very point of the 'traveller problem' they were reporting on! It was also possible to have a CB radio tune in on the local police transmissions, which helped. Gradually people would build up in side lanes off the main road until someone decided we were a large enough convoy to head off onto the main roads to find any field we could plonk in and set up a festival site and get the music going. Often meeting more trucks, coaches, and vans on the way, always aware of overhead helicopters assisting the overstretched Hampshire police, who themselves had little experience in, or enthusiasm for, dealing with what was actually just a bunch of people travelling about causing little damage bar the occasional traffic jam. Later on, the cops had the Criminal Justice Act, and all its numerous updates throughout the 90s. Although that was brought in when the ravers had upped the ante from a few hundred hippies/punks/anarchists in a smattering of vehicles or on foot to thousands of well-connected car-owners, it was created based on the experience of trying to quell the post-Stonehenge movement. And it's a fact that the lack of these sweeping powers of detention had allowed us to carry on in fields at all: we used the inexperience and comparative powerlessness of the police to get what we wanted.... up to a point. That point was the metal barriers along the road-edge of the Stones and a line of riot police with batons charging us down.... to stop us sitting or standing in or near an ancient stone circle! It was fucking insane! But at least back then we still managed to gather and stay at Cholderton Woods for a few days, set up, play music, socialise and make the most of feeling outside the systematic life for a while.

Simon Williams: I've thought about it a lot and I just think that Margaret Thatcher absolutely hated the idea of people having sex and drugs and rock 'n' roll in a field, for free. There was nowhere for her to make a buck or to tax it and so she hated it. People having a good time in Thatcher's Britain? She wasn't into it.

Oz Hardwick: It's a dangerous phenomenon to advanced capitalist ideology. It did infiltrate the scene, though, whether in the form of the criminal elements within the camp, or those who thought there was cash to be made from packaging it up and selling it. Think of *Acid Daze* at Finsbury Park. Fenced into a concrete pen with a string of bands going through the motions (and going through an awful PA), with foul, overpriced food. Was that feedback, or the tolling of a death-knell? I was affected on a very deep, personal level. I felt a profound despair – for a long time; I lost the belief that one could make a difference. It took a very long time to regain a sense of purpose.

Simon Williams: Now, the best bits of the festival culture have lived on and they've noticed they can make money out of it. A compromise: everyone can go to Stonehenge for the Solstice but with no bands playing, no month-long party. Back then, we'd park up at the beginning of June for the festival, it'd hit its peak over the Solstice, hang around until the end of July and then we'd go down to Glastonbury.

Michael Dog: [Press coverage] was split down the middle. The right-wing press, who used that classic strap-line of Medieval Brigands, summed up their feelings that there was this travelling mob wreaking havoc in the countryside that had to be stopped at all costs.

Then the other side was the complete opposite, especially after the Beanfield, and their coverage was extremely sympathetic – why shouldn't people do this thing, they weren't doing any harm. But it ceased to become an interesting story to the media. There wasn't any more mileage to be gained by journalists turning up at festivals and reporting what was going on, the world had moved on. Unfortunately at the same time there was the flight from the festivals because thousands of people who would have gone instead kept away, so it became this minority interest. But there was positive coverage because inevitably a number of journalists had gone to festivals themselves so they were keen to write about a subject that was close to their hearts.

Big Steve: We organised a nude peace rally on Hampstead Heath after Stonehenge one year. One of the guys there, Kristoff, was holding up a sign saying 'Ban the Bomb', completely naked, and his picture appeared on the front page of *The Sun* the following day. 'Nudes Against Nukes'. We were certainly aware of the power of the media and that we could use it for things related to the peace movement, which was the main focus of our attention at that time. As far as the right-wing press, *The Daily Mail*, they were probably very wary. On the fringes of that Notting Hill, Islington scene there probably was contact with left-wing journalists from *The Guardian*. With things like the Legalise Cannabis movement, if we thought we could get favourable coverage we would send out press releases, but we didn't think we were understood by mainstream media. There was quite a lot of alternative media on-site, people like Don and Golly, who printed a daily newspaper on a Gestetner [stencil] press, this festival news sheet with information about what was going on. The most important annual publication was Willie X′s festival lists. Other alternative magazines would write about the scene, like *Time Out* or *City Limits*, but in terms of mainstream media… we got in contact with *The Guardian* and they did an article about the Mushroom Festival, and the Ad Lib column in the *Evening Standard* did a piece about the free festival at Stonehenge in 1981, but other mainstream media? No. [We didn't work the media] in the same way that Wally Hope, or the people who organised Windsor did. They were interested in using the mainstream media to publicise the festivals. We were too busy organising the music.

Stonehenge
pilgrimage
JUNE 1st 2pm : PEACE PAGODA . BATTERSEA PARK
also walks from Bristol . Exeter . Oxford . Doncaster & more ?
JUNE 10-12 : WEEKEND PARTY
CALLEVA ROMAN TOWN . BERKSHIRE
JUNE 17-26 : FREE FESTIVAL
JUNE 21st : SOLSTICE RITUAL & CELEBRATION

Food

More often than not someone would spare a crust or even a curry.

Dolores Dina: I was so desperate to get away from home. I'd be going out with very little money, with no food or transportation. When I went to Windsor I packed a tin-opener, for some bizarre reason! I didn't eat very much at festivals. I lived on bananas and crackers and there was muesli, which I think was free, that I got from the back of someone's van. They had muesli with apple juice in a cup, which wasn't very pleasant but then there wasn't a lot of food around. That's how I got through the festivals, asking for handouts here and there and people were kind enough, no-one ever asked me for money. That was how I got by.

Steve Bemand: The Hare Krishnas saved me a number of times. I had a bad trip at Stonehenge 1977 - consumed 'too many' whilst we were taking the site. When I could eat again, there they were with the free food. I did get worried I owed them allegiance for the food, but didn't join! Then I got involved with the Big Yellow Tepee free food; going round with a bucket collecting up change, getting food from the town or on site, cooking it up and giving it away to whoever needed it. Also of note was Mr. and Mrs. Normal's Fudge Café, which was brilliant, they were such great hosts, Rico's Coffee House with its top-notch liqueur coffee and The White Vegetarian Food Van which was always immaculately turned out and provided very good food. But if you had no food or money you could just go up to a camp of people or a food stall and ask to be fed. More often than not someone would spare a crust or even a curry.

Janet Henbane: I've eaten many times at the Hare Krishnas, it was part of the festival experience. HK food can be a bit hit-or-miss but it's usually good. At Glastonbury's 'mud bath year' [1997] the HK did spaghetti one day and when my son came to be served he was given a small amount, which he obviously thought was inadequate, so he pushed his plate forward towards the server, who wasn't happy about this and gave him a black look, but he kept his plate there waiting for more, and pushed it forward again! He was given a further piddly helping. It was a bit embarrassing at the time but we have a good chuckle about it now and I like to think it was some kind of test for the woman concerned!

Decker Lyn's Café at Cyro Court 1988
(Dave Fawcett)

Angel: Vegetarian food in the early festivals was really quite a remarkable thing. People hadn't been exposed to vegetarianism. That really was a place where it all took off and made people aware of exactly what it was, and people could get to taste it. I had no money when I went to those festivals with my kids. I used to hitch with two children to get there, and we would have to somehow survive and make it work. Quite often I'd get involved in free food kitchens or whatever I could do in order to survive - you were able to do that. There was a wonderful bartering system, a way of working and receiving; it was this massive support network.

Bridget Wishart: Most people who were there for the duration were eating at their camp, using pans or plates and small amounts of cutlery. There weren't many of the take-away containers that make rubbish so prevalent at festivals these days. Food was sold from vans and camps. You ate nearby and gave the plate and cutlery back afterwards, or, like chapattis, the food didn't need wrapping anyway. I had baked bean chapattis, peanut butter chapattis... or just chapattis! Just for the record, peanut butter chapattis are very hard to eat and stick to the roof of your mouth like glue!

Oz Hardwick: I recall a member of a fairly high-profile band of the day, who'd been pretty much living on a cocktail of diverse chemicals for a week, haranguing a burger-eating friend 'for putting *that shit* into your body.' Another time, I remember wandering around Stonehenge early one morning and finding a veritable smorgasbord of recreational drugs on offer but nary a bite to eat.

Sarah Evans: Double-decker buses would get turned into cafes, which would be really cool places to hang out but you'd also get creative stuff going on, hair cutting and hair dyeing and it's really people *living* and doing things. I was amazed how *organised* Stonehenge was considering it wasn't an organised festival, because you had the main drag that just kind of organised itself. Hard drugs weren't tolerated. I remember a black car, right in the festival entrance, upside down and burned out with SMACK DEALER'S CAR written on it as warning to people going in there.

Mark Wright: Post-Beanfield there was virtually no-one selling food on site. My partner, Claire and I started selling food for the first time at the Wick Tip festival in '88; egg butties, veggie burgers, veggie curries and cups of tea and coffee. I'm not a vegetarian, but it was generally accepted that food for sale, or for free with what was called a 'pot-mess' where everyone put in what they could, was veggie. For quite some time we were virtually the only food-sellers at the festivals. Later on we also started selling dog food, Rizlas, mineral water, and a few beers. At the Birkenhead festival, with DIY and The Free Party People, we had dozens of Easter Eggs, each with a mug. For years afterwards you could tell people who'd been there, because they had the mug! When we had more money, we started selling a lot more beer and cider, our speciality was super-strength cider, pound a can. There was quite a move against the selling of Special Brew, though by this time there were slightly fewer problems with Brew Crew types. We were probably one of the main sellers of cider and beer at many of the 90s festivals, most of which were quite small, so we're not talking lorry-loads but for the first day or two the trailer would be pretty full of the stuff. We were in quite an odd position because of course we were well-known by the likes of Black Max and his Brew Crew cronies; they weren't friends, but they knew we were usually the best chance of a drink. We were up and about reasonably early, which was one of the Brew Crew's main drinking sessions. Often they would be completely wasted by lunchtime and you wouldn't see them again until the evening. We never had any trouble with them, but there were lots who did. I was one of the only people with a cash-and-carry card, so somebody would usually sort out transport to the local warehouse. At the beginning there wasn't much money about so beer, drugs and food were usually sold as cheaply as possible, nobody had any time for 'bread heads.' This all changed a bit with the arrival of Es, raves and easy money.

Klive Farhead: I'd have three or four different vegetables and some water, a very few spices and no stock or anything like that. I'd have this little dip in the ground with some dried wood and it would just get enough heat in the pan to boil up these few vegetables. And the rain would come and put the fire out and it took three or four hours to cook these few vegetables… some carrots and a bit of cabbage! My utensil to eat it was an empty baked bean tin that had some juice in it, which became the stock. But you were really out of it anyway, really fucked and if you hadn't eaten anything for days it just became the most amazing food because of the effort you put into it.

Mick Moss: One food kitchen was run by a guy called Skip. Never knew his real name. The work mostly involved chopping up vegetables and boiling them to mush with rice, brown of course, while trying to stay as stoned as possible! It was usually quite wholesome food, prepared by disgustingly filthy kids with dirt and shit and fag ash under their nails, but good intentions in their hearts. As far as most of the other food stalls, they served a purpose and made a bit of cash. Good luck to them. Then there was the kitchen run by Nigel Leech. This wasn't 'free food', but good and cheap. The staff were volunteers; a hard core of about six plus whoever we recruited on site. Anyone who was hungry… wash some spuds, have some food, that kind of thing. It developed into a little scene of its own. You'd see the same faces turning up again and again.

Kev Ellis: Our guitarist had a food stall, 'Crucial Cuisine', at all the festivals we went to so there was always plenty of food around our camp!

Janet Henbane: What makes me laugh is all the Health & Safety, environmental health, and food hygiene you have to comply with nowadays. Back in the 70s you just got organised and did food; I remember a stall called 'Magic Munchies' that did wholefood stuff... there's no way they'd pass all the requirements needed to trade now! When I travelled with the TUMT we sold food in the blue and white marquee. Once, for a gig in Hackney, we made 'Tibetan Food Parcels' the night before - beans and veg pasties, delicious! When I acquired my bus, we knocked out a bit of food as we had enough space to make it and had an oven on the bus. It helped make a bit of derv dosh to keep the bus on the road. We made apple crumbles and custard, chilli beans and rice, banana cakes. I'd bought a box of organic ripe bananas for £2 and there was the inspiration. At the Aktivator festival, late 80s, we decided to do some pakoras but we didn't quite get the mix right, too much water in the batter mix, so when fried they didn't stick together and we ended up serving a pile of battered bits of veg! I did feel a bit embarrassed but the young student types didn't seem bothered at all and went away quite happy.

Mark Wright: The authorities liked to paint a picture of loads of dirty hippies leaving rubbish everywhere and virtually never cooperated with the provision of skips and the like. However most people did their bit, we understood the potential for negative propaganda. During and after the festivals, people would clean up and there would be bin-bags available to be used by the more educated punters. It wasn't like all the dirty scumbags that frequent Glastonbury. Anyway there was only one person who could claim to be a real litter picker and that was 'Martin the Litter Picker.' Martin was a really nice guy; he didn't do any drugs, and hardly drank, if at all. Of course in the days before mobile phones communication was a real problem and it was Martin, continually updating messages on his answer-phone, who was central to many people actually making it to the festivals. You

A shop like no other; Longstock (Mark Wright collection)

have to remember that usually we didn't know exactly where the festivals would be, and as often as not, due to the police or local authority injunctions, the site would change at the last minute, sometimes more than once. Martin would spend most of the time ensuring that the site stayed clean and trying to educate others into doing the same. He often ate with us, and there were a few others on site who would also ensure he was looked after.

Bridget Wishart: At Stonehenge the only time I remember any litter was around the Pyramid Stage on the weekends and after a night of bands. Mainly it came from outsiders coming in for the night, eating and drinking and chucking their litter down. The site was so clean that when I bought a tab of sunshine acid, picture of the sun on the front and green on the back, and I dropped it on the grass on the way back to our camp, I took the same route back and found it again, green side up in the grass! Toilets on festival sites could be dodgy and over-used. At one Stonehenge, '80 or '81, the only shit-pits I found were holes dug in the ground with a white circle painted round them and in full view of everyone. I wasn't ready to use them! So, like others, I took a spade and used the woods. It wasn't the best solution, but it wasn't the worst! Many people didn't use a spade and the woods ended up a real mess… that was the worst littering of the festival. I worked at WOMAD in the mid-90s, designing, painting, and hanging décor for the festival. During the festival itself I didn't have any work to do other than check and maintain the décor, so I would visit the halls and marquees and look at the drapes we had made and how we had created a peaceful, beautiful and ambient atmosphere for people to listen to music in - and be really upset by the amount of mess that people would leave, spoiling our beautiful arenas. I did try wandering around with black bin-liners, picking up rubbish and asking people to put what they could reach with an outstretched arm into the bag. It was so obviously their rubbish but it was like talking to a brick wall.

Steve Bubble: I saw 'Rubbish' Martin, who was the guy you were guaranteed to see at the end of just about any free festival clearing up rubbish the minority had left behind, getting beaten senseless by a gang led by a girl with a cricket bat at Bramdean Common in '88. He'd exposed a bender full of gear stolen from other festival-goers and paid the price…

The Travellers' Field

Getting in for free was a real mission!

Emily Eavis (from an on-line discussion in 2004, organised by The Guardian): "A lot of the old school travellers now run certain areas of the festival and are still as involved as they were in the beginning – go to Greenfields or Lost Vagueness."

The relationship between Glastonbury Festival and the free festivals has always been something of an odd and detached one. Though it originally rose as part of the first wave of free festivals, and then remained fallow through most of the 1970s, and whilst on its return to the calendar clearly embraced the social aspirations of the free festivals, being inclusive in the type of entertainment and acts that it offered (Hawkwind headlined alongside New Order and other mainstream bands in 1980), there's a sense of unease and mistrust that permeates through the commentary of seasoned free festival-goers. At the time of the Beanfield, Glastonbury's organisers were faced with a harsh dilemma, to support those who'd felt the wrath of the authorities and to risk 'guilt by association' in the eyes of an, at that time, often unsympathetic local council, or to reject the travellers and be viewed as betraying the original cause. So it was in the face of an almost unsolvable dichotomy that Glastonbury established the concept of the Travellers' Field, separate from the main festival and on the edges of its boundaries but still as something that had a place within the framework of Glastonbury as an entity.

Bill the Boat (Festival-goer): What was the original Travellers' Field?

Steve Bemand: It was after the Battle of the Beanfield, where the Convoy got turfed-off and Michael Eavis gave them a field at Glastonbury.

Angie Bell: So it was the Convoy that *took* the field originally. [Then it was] run by that saloon, Lost Vagueness, but it was originally the Convoy that *took that field.*

Dick Lucas: Citizen Fish [formed by me and Jasper, of Culture Shock] played at the Travellers' Field at Glastonbury, and very good it was too! Especially as it got us into the main festival for free! The difference between there and, say, Stonehenge a few days before in the calendar, was all about money. It always cost 'too much', and, after a week or so at a free festival, merely *having* to pay to get in was a massive barrier in the head. Getting in for free was a real mission! Luckily bands did get in for free, but once when we weren't playing I crossed a field, as crouched as possible, to find the newly erected wall being beaten by an occasional ladder that one of several shadowed types were charging twenty pounds to climb up! Having forked out, the ladder was taken away for fear of impending security doing the rounds, and then I had to pay again to get it five minutes later… over the wall, big drop! Money was the filter that kept the travellers out to a large extent, and a security blanket for those who preferred their festivals to contain as many home comforts as possible, which didn't include the 'medieval brigands' they'd read about. Hence the mental invisible block between inside the Travellers' Field, when there was one, and just outside it. Gawkers ahoy! Come on in! It's the people who make a festival; when anyone could get in, one way or another, it was fantastic. Spontaneously bumping into free-fest faces amid lager loons and suburbanites was heart-warming. It was a meeting of minds that had come from and would always go back to the free festivals, as though Glastonbury was a crazed holiday extension of the real thing!

Steve Bubble: I went a couple of times and particularly remember them as extraordinary. Even the journey from a site a few miles down the road was memorable; thousands of people were living on the road by this point, and most seemed to head for Pilton. It took eleven hours to go the four miles from a site down the road, as buses got jammed on corners in the tiny country lanes. The fields, when we arrived, were just filled to the brim with vehicles of all shapes and sizes. I'd never seen so many travellers' vehicles in one place.

Mick Moss: It was okay. It's not my scene. But they're welcome to it. What's the phrase? I'm not sure if I like their 'Chosen people with a God-given right to everything' attitude. Not all travellers obviously. But some of the more annoying people have this thing that they're *it* and everybody else isn't.

Paul Bagley: The Green Field, full of alternative workers and therapists, was the closest thing to the free festivals; especially in later years when a stone circle was built there, attracting the pagan and more peaceful people. However, you were constantly reminded that the 'city' of people, as the Green Field people called them, were only down in the valley. The peaceful Travellers' Field that stood next to the Green Field in the early 1980s was very different from that of 1990, which was my last visit there. That year the travellers had been segregated away from the Green Field and the rest of the main festival. Consequently as I walked around the site, I felt there was a feeling of fear and suspicion. People didn't want to talk to you if they didn't know you; the complete opposite of the free festival scene. To make matters worse, one of my friends foolishly dropped an acid tab and was trying to deal with it. We were doing okay until a pack of travellers' dogs came over and he freaked out. The dogs set on him and I got him away and to the first aid tent, with the sneers and laughter of the travellers ringing in my ears. The first aid tent exclaimed how brave we had been when they patched him up and that most of their customers during the festival were people beaten up there. Helicopters circled in abundance and I did see an amusing sight of the travellers throwing everything they could up in the air at one, as if they stood a chance of hitting it! Later I heard there had been a big fight between them and the security. That was my last ever visit to the field and to Glastonbury in general.

Michael Dog: It was the last year that Michael Eavis made a Travellers' Field available that was a separate but conjoined entity to the main Glastonbury festival. If you knew about it, you could enter the festival from that field for nothing. He'd made this available after a gap of a couple years when one had not been allowed and I guess that someone had prevailed on him. We ran a sound system there and we had very happy memories but it was marred on the Monday morning. I remember wandering around the Travellers' Field and there was a huge gang with sticks and stones descending, claiming that someone had been attacked by security when they were tacking, going around the site when it was finished picking up the pieces of junk. Suddenly this mob of a number of hundred people gathered and marched into the main festival site and wreaked havoc. They set upon porta-cabins and Land Rovers that were used by the festival and set fire to them, and it was awful to watch. I was there with [key Stonehenge Campaign figure] Alex Rosenberg, and we were so incensed by what was going on and were shouting to people, trying to appeal to them, 'Don't do this, this is biting the hand that feeds you. This isn't going to end well.' And people turned around and attacked *us*. I got punched in the face and Alex got assaulted and this was the last time I remember seeing him. I think he bowed out completely after that. This was a turning point. Michael Eavis was never going to make a Travellers' Field available again, at that minute, and sure enough that *was* the end. It was just heart breaking to see what things had descended to; these idiots, off their heads, who, at the drop of a hat, would turn into a mob. And it was sad that someone who I had a lot of respect for, who'd stand there saying, 'Look guys, stop, don't do this,' they'd just go and beat up.

Bridget Wishart: I hadn't planned to stay for the Hawkwind gig in the Travellers' Field on the Monday night as I was supposed to be back at work. I had a lift sorted to get back to Bath on the Sunday afternoon but after sitting in a traffic jam on site for three hours I gave up and decided to stay for the gig. My then boyfriend, Mark, was involved in production for the Acoustic Tent, and had a Land Rover and radio so he could move equipment about, stay in contact, and respond to emergencies. On the Monday afternoon I wanted to go over to the Travellers' Field and find out what time the band were due to play. Mark was heading that way, so said he'd give me a lift. His site radio was talking about a disturbance that had hap-

pened between some travellers and security. As we drove down the Acoustic Field, we saw a line of figures running across the field below, many carrying tools as weapons. Voices on the radio were cutting in, in a panic. Festival workers and Land Rovers were being targeted. Mark didn't have a festival Land Rover, he had his own, but as we drove closer to the running men he ripped the official pass off the windscreen, and we decided to return to the camp. Haggis, from the Circus Field, was caught in trouble and radioed for help and then his partner Bella came on crying out for him. It was all very chaotic and frightening. A bit later we heard an ominous beating and hammering sound, which, we found out later, was some travellers attacking the onsite security building at the farm. I heard someone break into the radio frequency, making violent threats. Apparently, radio frequencies had been tapped into throughout the festival, with emergency vehicles being misdirected and people being verbally abusive and disrupting communications. A short while later I watched scores of police in riot gear run down Muddy Lane and disappear in the direction of the Travellers' Field. Having been at the Smokey Bear's Picnic when the Police raided it, I was really worried about what was going to happen next. I still needed to get over to find out if we were playing and to tell the band what I'd seen. When it got dark we wandered over and found the guys. There was a very charged, tense atmosphere in the field. We decided that the best thing would be to play the gig so everyone would have something to watch and lessen the chances of trouble and confrontation.

Hawkwind played. People watched. They were an audience and not an angry mob. At some point during the night, the police returned to their coaches. The night remained peaceful and the next day I made my way back to Bath and my job.

Paul Bagley: The anarchistic protest group had turned, in my opinion, into the very thing that they sought to protest against. They'd become a part of the problem, rather than the solution. Reasons for that varied, including, in their eyes, Michael Eavis turning against them. This is a general thing, this isn't a statement about travellers, but rather travellers placed in the hotbed of a commercial festival where cultures clash. The two didn't fit, creating a 'them and us' mentality rather than one of, 'We are all one community', and violence was the inevitable result.

Gavin and his Albion HD23 arrive at the Traveller's field Glastonbury 90
(Dave Fawcett)

Outside Inside – Late 1980s

There were all kinds of indoor events that were more than just gigs

Let's not think of the festivals solely as an outdoors countryside-based phenomenon. Thanks to the development of squatters' parties, and the work of the Club Dog organisers, the ethos of the festivals didn't stop when summer drifted into autumn. Instead there was a strong attempt to take the free festival agenda 'indoors' at clubs and squats, as reflected upon here.

Oz Hardwick: I think terming it as 'the scene' is interesting, since the peripheral gatherings were really important. From 1986, there were a lot of Stonehenge benefits, for example – mainly at the Hammersmith Clarendon. Indeed, there were all kinds of indoor events that were more than just gigs. We don't have the weather for festivals through most of the year, so all the characters would be at these different places where, and this is a crucial thing, the gathering would be as important as the bands.

Nik Turner: Inner City Unit played a lot of gigs in London, at underground clubs, which were like festivals. ICU came out of the Sphynx thing, the band was a bit more flexible and could go anywhere without being preoccupied with money. ICU was doing what I used to do with Hawkwind, benefits and festivals and events of different types. I still saw it as being part of a celebration. I liked that and wanted to put my energy towards that.

Keith Bailey: [Here & Now] put the hat around in the middle of gigs to try and shame people into coughing up [laughs]. We did that for two and a half years and toured that way all over Europe. It was that ethos of bringing the free festivals to the people! It was amazing when we started, getting a few thousand people in, because it was a free gig, but we'd be coming out of it with more money than if we'd done a deal with a promoter. People were really into it for the first year or so, but what really killed it was playing Central London Poly with twelve hundred people there and we got something like thirty quid and I thought, 'No, this has finally played itself out.'

Ozric Tentacles with John Pendragon (Oz Hardwick)

Swordfish: It's that *Electric Tepee* thing. When we were at Brixton Academy, the *Return to Source* events, and they put the flat floors in with the Tepees… this was *Electric Tepee* and Dave Brock should have been there to witness the legacy he'd started. Okay, this is psychedelic trance music but it's the same thing. We're having a party and everybody's being free, and to take away the stage took away that whole ego thing from the performance. I'm hoping we have another revolution because it's about time and something needs to happen. The homogenised scene that we have, it's stifling something that's still got to burn.

Simon Williams: For every Glastonbury, there were twenty or thirty little festivals that happened on the fringe, on the outside of Oxford or up in Yorkshire, and that was a great thing … from Cornwall to Shetland. As for festivals in the culture of Britain, it was a really important underground scene, but it was away from the music scene which was run by a few record labels, a few publishing houses that have control over all the media. Let's face it; they weren't letting the smelly hippies in [laughs]. 'No, we're not having this.' People like Michael [Dog] and Richard Merry and the *Whirl-Y-Gig* saw that energy and took it to a club during the time of the dance music scene. *Club Dog* was a magical event, it was the indoor music festival, and they'd have different rooms for different things and would put a lot of effort into making the ambience of the place special, a very psychedelic environment with lots of décor. Taking that kind of energy from the festivals and putting it into the clubs and the urban environment really helped as a contribution to British culture; rather than some coke-head running a club going 'Oh, I know what the kids will like.'

Peter Loveday: The sort of people who predicted, and were instrumental in making it happen, that move from Acid House music to trance music and world music… the Dog brothers and Fraser Clark who was the man behind the *Encyclopaedia Psychedelica*, a wonderfully flawed fake-guru, these guys were magicians, shamanistic people who were part-fake, part-misunderstood and who made a lot of enemies along the way. The Dog brothers less so, but Fraser Clark was an extraordinary character. Those people saw themselves as shamanic figures… I don't think *Club Dog* saw themselves in those terms but effectively they were that way. There was a lot of spirituality driving that, sometimes slightly spurious, but that's necessary to become a good magician otherwise you'd become a hermit, and that mix of spirituality and shaman-ship is an interesting one, and they always generate good stories, which is my game, anyway.

Michael Dog: I squatted for a while in the late 80s, but by then myself and some others had started running *Club Dog*, and that was a way of life for us because we ran these festival-like events on a weekly basis. Though it never generated serious money it did pay us a basic living and I was able to rent – but for two years I squatted. *Club Dog* was a rolling group of about twelve people… we never sat down and discussed a manifesto, we just really enjoyed putting on events that were like festivals without actually having to run a festival. We all had an interest in music and arts and put on events that had the colourfulness and light-heartedness of the festivals. That gave a platform to the bands that played at festivals and other performance artists… otherwise, what were they going to do with themselves all through the winter? We provided them with somewhere to play and it was a self-perpetuating thing, if no-one had come we'd have stopped, as we never set out for it to take up such a huge chunk of our lives. It's just something that we started doing and people kept coming so we kept doing it.

Joie Hinton: The Dog brothers were good friends and they had the nerve to do this, *Club Dog*, and it became a bit of a cult thing. They had a remarkable DJ called Richard Monkey Pilot, he actually ran *Whirl-Y-Gig*, he was the resident DJ at *Club Dog* and was a very inspiring source of interesting new music; he crossed a lot of things over and brought in a lot of World Music. They'd have a couple of rooms, a really weird band in one and a name band in the other, great atmosphere, really good fun. It was almost like a gig version of a rave and a chill-out room – a mad band and a weird band but it was good stuff.

Michael Dog: *Club Dog* ended up running for about seven years and only stopped because the venues we ran it in became too dangerous. The core of the performers we put on was the family of Ozric Tentacles. The Ozrics themselves we put on twenty or thirty times but then also the Ullulators, the Oroonies, the Rhythmites and wider members of the scene like Underground Zero who were a Hawkwind-style band, various reggae bands, and African performers. Then as time went on the people who would be the nucleus of what became the live dance music thing eventually started to come through. Wooden Baby, who became Eat Static [Merv Pepler and Joie Hinton, of Ozric Tentacles] who started experimenting with just using sequencers and synthesisers, and Banco de Gaia who was also one of the early people in that scene.

Wayne Twining: Joie [Hinton] and Merv [Pepler] are the sweetest guys you're ever going to meet. I think between them, with the early Eat Static singles, they're responsible for the entire early psychedelic trance scene. You can follow it from there.

Swordfish: Whereas, I think, to this day, Hawkwind kind of stuck where they were and didn't move on into that next phase. They embraced it a bit, maybe for commercial reasons or perhaps spiritual reasons but perhaps it was a bit alien because it involved dance beats and they had a different kind of mantra.

Joie Hinton: There was loads of trance-y dance-y stuff being played years before we started doing it, but not so much of a live thing. I think we got into it about two years after it kicked off; we had a band that could do it on a stage, but there were loads of other people doing it as well. Maybe we were in the early bunch, but I can't boast that we were pioneers! I know some people will say that, 'Oh, you guys were the originals,' but I don't think that was true. Bless 'em, though! Maybe we brought some of the dance stuff into the scene that we were in; in that respect it would be true. The *Club Dog*, underground music scene in London, we were kind of the token dance band because we were originally the crustie hippie band Ozrics, then suddenly two or three of us were doing this dance music.

Michael Dog: As time went on the space-rock side of that scene died away and it turned into the psychedelic dance scene. We went on to form Mega Dog and that was what Mega Dog became. The thing that linked all of these bands was that they weren't doing three-minute pop songs; it was music to bliss out to. The style changed, it wasn't that we stopped putting on space-rock bands - there just weren't any, apart from Ozric Tentacles. The Ozrics took it to a wider audience, but probably they were just at the wrong time – just at the point where they'd broken through to a wider audience, that audience stopped being interested in that kind of music and got into dance. Ozric Tentacles didn't really move with the times, and that was all it was. A year later and the huge mass of people that were into that music were now going to dance events.

Gary Bamford: Ozrics were doing big venues, weren't they? But could they handle it? Lots of these bands are capable of getting there but are they capable of keeping their heads on while they do it? I prefer to just stay as we've stayed, not have massive sales but we've got our kids, our motors and our music and never really took part in trying to sell anything to anybody because that whole scene is shit. All those bands, they're capable of getting there, they're good bands, even some of what they're saying is good but they can't handle it when they get there. Then they want to come down to Earth and hang around on the edge of the scene. Which is okay, but I don't see any of those bands helping others to punch through. All those bands, Levellers, Ozrics… bands that got on the verge of being big – I wouldn't say that any of them have kicked doors open to get live music back in. The Levellers came in at the end of the travelling scene and were a cool bunch but they walk in with their management team and their roadies and forget it. But individually, we have a good laugh.

Michael Dog: What was going on in tandem with all of this was what was developing in the festival scene, or rather what was not developing in the festival scene. Sadly my memories of the late 80s and early 90s festival scene is gradual decline into the ground. We would do our last gig at the end of May and stop doing *Club Dog* or *Mega Dog*, whichever it was at the time, and we'd stop through to the first Friday in September which would usually be our first gig of the season. We'd stop for the summer and go to festivals as punters and we'd also go as stage and sound system. There was still some good events in that period, one of the ones that most comes to mind, which is lovingly remembered but which also is a sad tale, was an event called Torpedo Town.

Torpedo Town 1990 Poster Collection of Steve Bubble

Torpedo Town – Mid 1980s – 1992

I saw an amazing mixture of music, from punk bands to folk bands, weird bands, *unlistenable* bands, it was all there!

One of the paradoxes of the festivals, Hampshire's Torpedo Town festival was politically motivated, happened on an annual basis, was visible and public in its promotion and yet, for most of its history, ran with if not tacit support from local authority then enjoyed a 'hands-off' approach in its policing that other festivals would have envied. And yet here is another example of a positive approach to festival organising that eventually suffered from internal and external pressures of quite unbelievable proportions.

Simon Williams: Torpedo Town was great, it got bigger and better every year and it was nice that there was a political message behind it; that we didn't want torpedoes being made locally. It was a good excuse for a party and everyone was up for it! I remember it also for not having too many hassles.

Steve Bubble: I met some people, in Cholderton Woods funnily enough, who ran the Solent Free Information Network, or F.I.N., part of a network of 'F.I.N.' publications, who published festival lists and news for the local area. A couple of the people involved organised the Torpedo Town Free Festival, which was traditionally held on or near the site of the Marconi arms factory in Waterlooville a few miles outside Portsmouth, and grew out of a protest against this company. I had been to Torpedo Town in 1986, my first free festival in fact, and was blown away by the nature of the event. People living in the most amazingly decorated old vehicles and buses, a feeling of togetherness, an appreciation of music and art and an 'anything goes' attitude. I saw an amazing mixture of music, from punk bands to folk bands, weird bands, *unlistenable* bands, it was all there! It was an impromptu 'town' of around four thousand people who were mostly off their heads on acid.

Michael Dog: Torpedo Town was one of the best organised and most lovingly produced of the southern Free Festivals. With the southern festivals, it was kind of hit and miss really. The date would be on the festival list and you'd go along and it might be a really amazing event with great things happening or it might be a glorified park-up in a field with a few people hanging around getting stoned. You never knew until you turned up, but Torpedo Town was different. My understanding was that one specific guy, Kevin, was the organiser and he took it upon himself to put on this event in his local area as a protest against the naval base at Portsmouth. He approached it with the same ethos that we approached Club Dog, which was why we liked it so much and actually formed a lot of personal links to the guy. We recognised the same dedication to quality. He publicised the events and found a site each year and saw to it that the festival happened annually and did exactly what it said on the box. There were always a number of stages, lots of facilities and water, and there was a consistency that made it stand out head and shoulders above the other events that were happening at that time. It would be in a different location in Hampshire each year but would go off without any trouble, with the local police completely supportive of it at a time when in other parts of the country the police were being extremely Draconian in the way they policed the festivals. The organiser seemed to have a different relationship with the police in Hampshire – they would actually direct people to the festival site! You'd turn up in the locale and be stopped by police and instead of turning the vehicle over and strip searching everyone they'd go 'Oh, you're here for Torpedo Town?' You'd go, rather sheepishly, 'Yeah' and they'd say, 'Right, well it's up there. Follow the lane, go left and right and you'll find the site.' It was almost as though they really wanted people to go there and get off the road and out of the way.

Kev Ellis: We turned up for one Torpedo Town. 'You're Dr Brown!' says the copper on the gate. 'Follow us!' And we were being given a police escort onto site, to avoid the mud! Later the police pulled their paddy wagon round to the front of the stage to watch our set.

Michael Dog: It was a great event, but the sad twist to it was that as the festival scene descended into this madness that is now referred to as the Brew Crew, that was the end of Torpedo Town. The last one I remembered going to, I don't think I ran into Kevin because by the time I arrived, at the latest on Friday morning, he'd already been attacked by a bunch of Brew Crew on site who'd set a dog on him. He was in the local hospital and that event was finished. It was horrible. It was like how I'd imagine it was if you were camped next to the Hells Angels at Stonehenge, except it was all over the site. You couldn't get away from these people; they were on a mission to intimidate and bully everyone around them. From that time on, festivals became dangerous places to go. People stopped bringing their children to them, whereas it had always been a huge aspect of previous festivals that families came along. You stopped seeing children, you stopped seeing any 'fluffy' people at all really, because the only people who still went to them were people who could 'do alright in a fight', who felt comfortable that if someone started on them, they could defend themselves. Anyone who was a more gentle kind of person stopped going, because what was the point of going to a festival if you might get your head kicked in? It was just tragic to watch and it just spiralled downhill from there.

Kev Ellis: Many people did take kids with them, though I thought them very brave most of the time. It really was not ideal for young kids.

Steve Bubble: I loved Torpedo Town and wanted more. I was hooked! The following summer saw Torpedo Town on the road; police were out to prevent another festival happening. There were rumours claiming Butser Hill was blocked off, whilst a phone number announced Bramdean Common was the actual site. We raced off for a forty-minute drive to find vehicles struggling to find the site, which was tucked behind a village on the A272. It's an ancient common where gypsies used to gather, indeed there is a little tin church at the edge of the woods, built in 1883 for the gypsies who used the common. This could have been a fantastic festival, if not for the violence that marred the event. It was going to be the last Torpedo Town because the organisers were so disillusioned by the theft and violence and the air of intimidation that prevailed at some of the festivals at this time. I'd met Kevin, one of the organisers, by this time and the following summer tried to persuade him to carry on and not be defeated by a minority, but he was having none of it. Again in 1989 he was not convinced, but I told him that I was going to advertise it for 1990, so he'd have to sort something out then. I designed a poster and sent it off to *Festival Eye*, where it duly appeared listed as a 'mystery festival' despite having happened for years. I don't think Kevin was *that* impressed, he didn't say as much, but he did nothing to make me think he was going to be organising anything so I started phoning people up, starting with Bob Dog at Club Dog. Bob helpfully gave me a list of bands most likely to want to appear at a free festival and helped by spreading the word too, but it was all a bit last-minute. People and travellers were gathering near Petersfield and I'd sent out maps to many people via the 'Friends of Torpedo Town' address that had been traditionally used for correspondence. Unfortunately it was for an area which, rather stupidly, I hadn't realised was designated as a 'Site of Special Scientific Interest' due to the rare flowers and fauna found there. I was working right up until the start of the festival, listening to local radio keeping listeners up-to-date on the numerous encampments of festival-goers springing up as the weekend drew nearer. On the Friday morning, a number of vehicles attempted to gain access to the initial, badly chosen site and it was getting pretty intense. I was getting calls saying we desperately needed somewhere else to go! We eventually found a large common that hadn't previously been looked at, right on the Hampshire, Sussex and Surrey border. This was ideal; the police couldn't quite decide whose area it was in, and each force just wanted us out of their own particular county. A friend with a massive breakdown truck, who just happened to have one of the early mobile phones, was up near the A3 with a convoy of traveller vehicles. I gave him the name of the new site – and people headed up there. By this point I'd hopped in the truck and bombed up the A3 myself. There were vehicles everywhere, all somehow heading to the same point. By 2pm people were at the site entrance and having to dig to make it wide enough to get the coaches in – the main site entrance was on the actual dual carriageway. Police, meanwhile, had coned off one of the lanes to allow vehicles to queue and enter. The site was massive, about 650 acres, a huge dustbowl on one of the hottest weekends of the year, and a great festival was had. There were a couple of sound systems there, the first I'd ever seen at a festival, booming House with some nice lights flickering around the valley that mesmerised onlookers as the darkness closed in – it was a new sound to many! There was a bit of aggravation between travellers and the younger 'free party' goers, especially when it emerged that some young entrepreneurs were charging an entrance fee to unsuspecting arrivals. There was a rumour that a couple of coaches arrived for a rave that they'd paid twenty-five quid for. There was a massive amount of fine wine and port on site, liberated from one of the local houses' wine store. People kept coming – probably eight hundred to one thousand at any one time, as the TV and radio stations stated clearly where the site was. Sarah Greene apparently owned one of the nearby houses and stories of people using her swimming pool circulated. The festi-

Rave at Torpedo Town (Mark Wright)

val actually lasted a fortnight as the police insisted we had another week because they didn't want the whole site crossing the county for the Cissbury Ring Festival the following weekend. The second weekend's party was entitled Tornado Town, and the site filled up once more for a second celebration!

It was a good year for festivals. The numbers were picking up and cross-pollination was occurring between the travellers and the rave posses. The buzz was amazing, and I started work on the next year's event, already thinking that this was a great site but unlikely to be accessible again. I was right; the site was blocked almost as soon as the last vehicles had moved off, but there were plenty more open spaces that we'd already looked at. Spring saw many visits out to various commons, and as we visited the previous year's site we crossed the road to look at some M.o.D. land, a reasonable space, we thought! Bands were contacted, another list from Bob Dog; they themselves were hoping to bring a small stage and P.A. with them. Wango Riley's Travelling Stage was keen to come, having recently been acquired by Elm and Ash. Bands were phoning up, stalls, a circus, sound systems; it was feeling like it was going to be a good one! This time I'd persuaded Oxfin to run a phone line, a single number, to tell people where it was going to be. A few people knew in advance, but I'd stressed on the posters that the site would only be announced at mid-day on the Friday. It was at 1pm when we actually arrived at the site to find large festival vehicles heading up and down the A3 once more. The police duly arrived, a couple of high ranking officers who seemed slightly impressed that by the time they'd found out where it was, dozens of coaches and trucks were already on site. 'So you're the advance party then?' the more senior one asked. 'Yep, the rest will be here shortly,' I replied with a grin that stretched from ear to ear! I stayed on the gate by the main road for hours, watching people and friends arriving. A never-ending procession, it seemed. When I walked round the corner back into the site a festival had begun. Wango's were there, and Spiral Tribe had turned up and picked a wonderful circular clearing behind and to the side of the main stage and the Club Dog stage. There were smaller party rigs all around the site and still the vehicles kept coming. A fantastic festival was had with no trouble, bar a coach catching fire from a candle, and all round good press in the media. There was footage of parents dropping kids off for the day on the local TV news! Sadly, Dinah McNicol went missing on her way home from the festival, and her body has only recently been found. She'd been murdered by her lift. That was the only downer on the weekend; I thought at the time that it didn't look good for her, and it was very sad.

Planning started for the next one. Sites were checked out and bands and stages contacted. Then, at lunchtime a week before the festival, a dozen Special Branch officers arrived at the little reprographics-cum-stationery shop I worked at. The shop was turned over, artwork was found – the original poster for that year - and I was in trouble! They wanted to search my house, but my girlfriend was due to go to work and I almost persuaded them to wait until she had; I explained that she wouldn't be happy and that I didn't want to stress her out. They took me to a police station near Fratton in Portsmouth, before changing their minds and dragging me home to turn it over and upset Annette! My heart was in my mouth as they searched. I had hundreds of flyers for the festival hidden on a shelf, and they missed them by *millimetres*. I was denying any responsibility for any involvement in "organising" anything. Then we were on the move, this time to another police cell in Alton, about 30 miles up the road where I was charged with 'Conspiracy to Cause a Public Nuisance', the charge that Spiral Tribe were infamously faced with a year later. The journey to Alton was full of questions, revolving around anarchism, due to the literature and the pile of Green Anarchism magazines they had discovered at my house. I evaded the philosophical debate as much as possible. I realised they were trying to get into my head, and managed mainly to stay silent. I maintained my right to silence throughout the repeated bouts of questioning, sticking to my story that I wasn't an organiser! I was merely 'helping' to find a site away from peoples' houses and making sure that welfare teams and emergency services were on site – the festival list was nothing to do with me, I claimed, and the date was set by someone unknown, as were the other festivals. I hadn't realised there were friends in cells nearby. Kev had brought the mail for the festival down to the stationery shop where I worked and been followed from the alternative wholefood store 'Time for Change' where the mail was delivered, and was seen handing over the pile of envelopes by one of my questioners. This was Kev's only involvement, but they were trying to get evidence for the conspiracy charge to stick. Another person in the cells was the poor owner of the shop – who had nothing whatsoever to do with the festival at all, other than letting us use the shop as a 'care of' address. I wish I'd known they were in adjoining cells though! Home Office permission was granted to allow questioning to continue for a second day, as suspects could at that time only be held for twenty-four hours. At this point I realised that I was in potentially serious trouble. There was no solicitor around to help but I was allowed to speak to one on the phone, who agreed that I should maintain my silence and get proper representation as soon as possible.

My girlfriend was in complete panic by the time she had left work. No-one could find me and the police refused to say where I was for hours. I think they called 'Release', who managed to track me down and she arrived at the police station and, after persistently being told 'no', was eventually allowed to see me. Having seized my address book and electronic organiser, the police proceeded to call every band and contact and tell them that the plug had been pulled, that I had cancelled the festival. The questioning was going nowhere, the police told me that I would appear in court the next day and would be sent to Winchester prison for the next week or so. I panicked and told them that I was unable to do anything regarding the festival and that it was now out of my hands; I couldn't stop it and they were now responsible for what happened. They changed their minds, unless they had never intended to try and get me put inside (probably more likely, in retrospect), and instead asked the judge that I be put under curfew.

I was made to report to a police station three times a day and was not allowed to have anything to do with the festival and had to stay in my house from 8pm until 8am. I had no choice but to agree.

By the time I was released there were two massive sites in Hampshire, one near Romsey and the other at Otterbourne, both near Winchester. Police were fighting pitched battles in the lane approaching the Otterbourne site as they tried to prevent more travellers, who were still arriving, getting to the festivals. Despite the High Court injunctions and my rather stringent bail conditions, I duly signed in at the local police station, went home, shaved off my dreadlocks and blagged a lift after dark from a visiting friend and headed off to Otterbourne. It was chaotic in the vicinity, police had managed to seal the site by this time, preventing more vehicles entering, but we parked with hundreds of other vehicles that were abandoned on the roadsides and headed for the sounds of music. The weather that night was drizzly and miserable, but the size of the gathering was huge, probably about twenty thousand, and this was just one of two sites! I stayed a few hours before slipping away, but not before I'd explored the council recycling centre that the festival was right next to, climbing over the vast piles of bottles and other salvageable materials, interesting! The next morning, before I visited the police station round the corner, I switched on the TV to discover the headlines were that travellers had burned down a council incinerator... in the very same place I'd climbed all over. I was sure I was being set up and paranoia kicked in as I headed out to see the police! It was to emerge later in the morning that a fifteen-year-old had set fire to the port-a-cabin next to the incinerator. So the sabotage that, the tabloids screamed from their front pages, cost one million pounds, was actually about twenty thousand pounds worth. But the damage had been done and it felt like the end.

88
AKTIVATOR
AUGUST 12·13·14
COME AND CAMP
AT BUSHLEY· NEAR TEWKESBURY· GLOS.
PLEASE LEAVE PETS AT HOME
·LIVE MUSIC·
NIK TURNERS' ALL STARS
RYTHMITES · JONAH AND THE WAIL · WORMS
GOD ONLY KNOWS · DYNAMIC PETS ·
HOT STRINGS · RAILTOWN BOTTLERS
OZRIC TENTACLES · GOING CASE ·
CHILDE ROLAND · SONS OF
SPOCK · HIPPY SLAGS ·
DJIBOUTI ROO ·
SOUL SARANS
· HET ·
STALLS
TAI CHI
CIRCUS
DRUMMING
CAFÉ
DANCING
BENEFIT
FOR
TRAVELLERS SCHOOL
£5
· ON THE GATE

Aktivator – 1988

The doctor's wife went around and told all the old people to get their relatives to come and stay with them and lock up their garden sheds.

Aktivator '88, named after a Steve Hillage track, took place over the weekend of 12th – 14th August, 1988 and featured a collection of West Country bands, many hailing from the Bath scene. Nik Turner's All-Stars, Rhythmites, Jonah and the Wail, Ozric Tentacles, Childe Roland, and the Hippy Slags were all listed on the flyers for this festival, whilst it also passed into Hawkwind folklore as the first appearance with the band of drummer Richard Chadwick, who would go on to become their second-longest serving member.

Not a free festival per se, it had a gate charge of £5 to raise funds for the travellers' 'Skool Bus', a mobile educational establishment intended to follow the travelling community across the country, the registered keeper of which was Richie Cotterill. "Conflicts are arising amongst the travellers over where the Skool Bus should be," noted its newsletter the following year. "The Skool Bus is a large, symbolic accumulation of the energy which has been put into this project but is only the beginning of this manifestation. It may not be long before the poisoned attitudes of our critics will destroy what little faith the travellers had in the whole project and after that, nothing will work."

Sheila Wynter (Landowner): The farm was about ninety-eight acres, and then we bought another twenty, so it was quite a small farm. We had four fields down by the Severn and when it flooded, which it did every year between November and February, most of it went underwater, which was most inconvenient! We had a Rainbow Camp just before Aktivator started. They'd get in touch with a farm and say, 'Can we do it?' and they wouldn't tell people where it was until the last minute. They'd get people signed up and then they'd say, 'You go to this place on the OS map.' They came with beautiful tents and organised a lot of talking and practical workshops. They knew me from the Farmers' Third World Network. It was well organised, people came with tepees; they put up a wonderful shower that had a big boiler and they lit a fire and people would run out of their tents, all completely naked. There was a stuffy old Colonel who lived near the bottom of our garden and he was out with his binoculars every morning… someone caught him doing that! I sat in on some of their workshops and they'd have a talking stick which was passed around, and if you had something to say you'd say it while you held the stick, and if you didn't you just passed it on. They talked about all sorts of topics, philosophy and religion; they had speakers and wonderful food in their kitchens and it was lovely.

"The Rainbow Circle is primarily dedicated to planetary healing, personal awareness and inner growth. Our aim is to provide a beautiful and protected village atmosphere for people who seek genuine human communication. The camp provides a focused space for experimental learning, knowledge sharing and ceremony."
Quote from Rainbow Camp information flyer

Nigel Mazlyn Jones: At the last Stonehenge I remember a meeting of the people that had 'organised' it saying that its mayhem gave the authorities the excuse to dump on it big time. That 'spiritually' it was indicating these events had become too huge. That was the core issue. It was suffocating the beauty, the mystique and the atmosphere that Stonehenge could give to a smaller gathering. It had become out of hand, thus creating the reaction it got from the establishment. What came out of the meeting was that those who cared about having a gathering that was sacred and mystical should go and celebrate the other sacred sites in Britain in small gatherings. I was astonished that it worked, because out of it came the Rainbow Circle camps which were always paid for by a hat gathering and deliberately *not* advertised and avoided getting the druggies from London coming to deal and people abusing it. It very much spawned lots of little festivals that took on various cloaks of what they were trying to achieve. So whilst it appeared to all blow up, it actually created a whole other thing. Rainbow Camps were acoustically based and there were no generators allowed, no electric music, no star names, and no huge expenditure. No massive drug use – some of them were very specific: no drug use at all. I know lots of people who helped run these things and had children, and I've seen *them* grow up and become fine people, education professionals out there in the world doing all sorts of things. Children of those, if you like, wandering, searching adults.

Sheila Wynter: My husband was an alcoholic and had got himself into a really bad state and had taken himself off to a treatment centre, where he was for a very long time. [My son] Adrian talked about hosting a little music festival; I suppose I said 'Okay,' but I didn't think much about it. Adrian had been saying, 'We're doing this for the Skool Bus' and he kept talking about this young couple who were organising this collection to keep it running. Aktivator took over nearly the whole farm, we estimated about seven thousand attendees. We heard there were great queues of travellers coming down from Wales, which is when the police got interested – they were very worried. As the travellers came into the village, we got them in at a gate before the farm and we'd put a fence so that we could get lots of vehicles in all the way down. Then we got the caravans with horses into the paddock at the end. They were lovely because they brought with them their chickens and goats, and all their horses were having foals.

Bridget Wishart: [On travelling with horses]. You were, at that point, still able to do it. You needed the support of the people around you but you could just take to the road. Because of the animals' needs they tended to park in one place, they weren't part of the Brew Crew types because they had responsibilities to their animals. Yet they partied like other people but they had responsibilities that other people didn't have. Some [normal travellers] would steal a vehicle to get to festivals and then abandon them and move on.

Sheila Wynter: The travellers didn't pay on the way in, but they paid on the way out because they'd had such a good time. The weather was good, there were no accidents - but there was one case of sheep-worrying and the villagers were terrified. The village didn't really like us anyway and they were furious. They'd had the Rainbow Camp, which didn't do any harm at all, but then all this lot came and the doctor's wife went around and told all the old people to get their relatives to come and stay with them and lock up their garden sheds. All sorts of things, winding them up and saying it was dangerous – these people with earrings and coloured hair! They didn't phone up or come around much, but there were a few threats.

Bridget Wishart: There was that whole thing… it would be portrayed on the news as 'travellers are coming to your area' and they'd have kind of, 'Farmers, lock up your daughters and protect your land.' Farmers and other landowners were blocking access to their land with huge stones so that travellers couldn't pull onto it.

Keith Bailey: At Megan's Fayre, up in the mountains of Wales, a small festival with maybe five or ten thousand people, the local farmers got together and drove around spraying everybody with pig shit, which got rid of us for sure and we ended up on some barren hillside with no water or anything. The people who'd put it together had spent weeks and weeks on the site putting up these amazing facilities. Everything was made from wood and the people who set it up were just such nice people and the whole vibe was excellent. And that got turned over by the local authorities because the farmers around it hated us doing it. You'd get the progressive thinking people in any area who'd welcome it with open arms and say 'look, it's good for local businesses,' because the shops would sell out of everything nearly overnight, but then you'd get the Colonel Blimps who were dyed-in-the-wool nimbies.

Sheila Wynter: There was a strong police presence; they took over a barn just up the hill, and there were helicopters as well. It was really feared that 'things' were going to happen. We sat around the kitchen table and a lot of the police chiefs came and Adrian explained what we'd done, and what we were doing. They said that they were going to keep an eye on it and it all seemed very solemn but there wasn't any trouble, apart from the one sheep-worrying incident. The dogs were the worst thing, a lot of the travellers had dogs and they fought a bit and then they'd run off and there was one sheep killed, which was a bad thing and caused terrible anger. But nobody was defecating on the village green, which was what the villagers had all been warned they were going to do!

Bender being set-up, Aktivator '88 (Sheila Wynter)

We thought that if we fed and watered and rested the people who were in charge of those coming in, and made sure they all had wood for their fires and the loos worked and laid on water... if we serviced them really well, the thing was much more likely to work. Adrian hired a digger and made two really big pits and had eighteen-hole loos. And he'd managed to find a timber yard that was selling up and said 'I'll buy all the wood' and found some lorries to bring it all up to the farm, because otherwise they'd have taken down all our precious trees to make fires to cook with. So this wood was brought in, and Adrian arranged to have skips brought in each day to take all the rubbish away. He was only twenty at the time, but he was a brilliant organiser. There was a chap that did a morning and an afternoon newsletter letting people know what was happening. We had the Aga and we made bread constantly, and as soon as it was made we cut it into vegetarian and vegan sandwiches and took them up to the people who were dealing with things and taking the money. And we took all the money and put the cash in margarine containers in the fridge and then someone else took the cartons up to Tewkesbury and hid them under a bed! So when Adrian needed to pay the bands, someone else went and got the cash – and in the end there was about three thousand pounds left over for the Skool Bus. At the end he went up to the barn and said to the police, 'Well, you've had a great time while we've had the festival. You've sat here the whole time playing cards, you haven't had to do anything. Could you give us a donation for the Travellers' Skool Bus?' I don't know whether they did, but they were fine and were really surprised

Richard Chadwick and Childe Roland Aktivator 88 (Bridget Wishart)

I liked the travellers and met a lot of them; there were bad ones of course and a lot of druggies. But you know, when people were really down and out and they got below the social services [radar] and they didn't have an address, they were advised to go to the Salvation Army. The Salvation Army couldn't really help them, because it had rules, quite reasonable rules but some of them couldn't take that either, so the Salvation Army suggested they join the travellers. There was one woman who had a London bus with forests painted all over it and she had her own children but she'd also taken in some very sad cases and helped them. I thought she was a wonderful person. Some of the kids she'd taken in were from middle-class families, who'd got chucked out because of their behaviour. The travellers had their own First Aid unit, who were a lovely lot because you couldn't get the Red Cross or St. Johns to come in. I had some old sheets and they wanted those to make bandages and stuff, not that there was much trouble… and there wasn't too much trouble with drugs though we did have one chap who came into the farmhouse and said he'd been spiked and was very ill. He was all right, he got through, but that was a bit frightening.

Bridget Wishart: Jock, who was a healer and a homeopath, he and his wife Sally used to help people out; there were people who you knew, like you could say 'Go and see her on the red bus, she's got some herbal teas.' But there were a slow but steady stream of people who would go and visit Sally and Jock to have various injuries and traumas tended. Sally always had her homeopathies with her. And she cooked the most amazing pea fritters!

Steve Bemand: Many times people off their heads or drunk would cause a rumpus of one kind or other. But it usually got chilled by people around them before a mass brawl could erupt, and the trouble-makers were always in the minority.

Jerry Richards: People would look out for one another. Someone came to our tent at one festival and said, 'I've got this Timothy Leary acid here,' and we said, 'Yeah, sure, sure you have mate.' But he said 'No, seriously, I'm a chemist and I've got the formula together and made this stuff up.' He got this blotter out that looked really professional, some sort of holographic paper and Steve Mills, the Tubilah Dog singer, and I, said we'd have some to try and it *was* really powerful stuff. Anyway, this guy at the same festival had tried it and was really off his head and going around hitting children because he was so far gone he said that they were 'like demons, small demons.' Of course, people spotted what was going on and grabbed hold of him, sat him down and tried to calm him, gave him a pipe and something to drink. But he was raving, and so someone put him on a flatbed truck and took him out of the festival site and into the nearest town and dropped him off. He wasn't abandoned, because he was somewhere he could get some help. He was just beyond *our* help.

Sheila Wynter: Afterwards we got some of the travellers and went up to the top fields and we had about twenty people in a line and we went over the whole lot in case there were any needles. I don't think we found anything. We had a few travellers who didn't leave at the end and that caused a lot of trouble. I think it was difficult for some of them to move on for one reason or another, they should have done but didn't. They all did go away eventually. One sinister lot had a big black hearse, there were about six of them and they weren't very popular. But it was a very difficult time for me; the farmer who'd lost a sheep came over and there was a terrible row in the kitchen. I had neighbours coming down and shouting at me, and that was very unpleasant. The village never forgave me, but then quite soon afterwards I had to sell the farm anyway – and they were very glad to get rid of me. I was one of the oldest inhabitants of the village by the time I left, but I'd say hello and people who I'd known for years, I was there for thirty-odd years, would just turn away from me in the street or shout at me. At one time I had a letter from Malvern Hills District Council saying that they were prosecuting me for making a noise after midnight for four nights running and they were charging me something like seven thousand pounds. Someone said to me 'What about this letter, this prosecution? What are you going to do about it?' Well, I didn't know what I was going to do about it because I didn't

Tractor lads watch The Hippy Slags (Sheila Wynter)

have seven thousand pounds so I said, 'Well, I suppose I'll have to go to prison.' I didn't realise it, but someone from the press was listening to this and they put it on Radio Gloucester, and Malvern Hills Council had farmers' wives from all over the place phoning up saying, 'What are you doing? You're going to put a farmer's wife in prison just because the children have been having a music festival!' They couldn't prosecute me because I didn't own the land, my husband did. I did take exception to [being prosecuted] though because we were [in those days] having planes coming zooming over the farm making a noise, but this was music... and noise and making music are very different things. It took about ten days to get everyone off the farm, and then we had to dispose of the abandoned cars. There was a scam with the AA, because they did a deal that guaranteed to get you from A to B if you broke down, no matter what condition your car was in. So a whole lot of cars arrived that were total wrecks – some were towed in because they didn't have any engines at all. The AA came in and took some of them to the next festival but others were just abandoned. Of course, the AA put that loophole right very quickly but the travellers caught this thing where they paid up at the beginning of the year and the AA towed them from festival to festival!

Hippy Slags at 88Aktivator (Collection of Bridget Wishart)

Treworgey Tree Fayre – 1989

There was dysentery; there were dead sheep in the water supply... It was like, 'Don't have anything to do with anyone who's been here more than a couple of days.'

Another example of something that started out as a 'pay' festival but through logistics (or, strictly speaking, lack of logistics) became akin to a free festival and is therefore associated with them, Treworgey Tree Fayre, in North Cornwall, began as something of a successor to the much-loved Elephant Fayre that ran in Cornwall during the mid-80s but gathered its own notoriety through the utter failure of the festival's infrastructure to cope with the mass of people and vehicles that descended on it. As such, it's another point in the history of the festivals that demonstrated both the good and the bad facets of the scene.

Dick Lucas: Treworgey was one of the best festivals ever. The main stage and the side stalls were much like Glastonbury, with the travellers' area taking up a third of the site and having its own much smaller stage. And, like the Travellers' Field at Glastonbury, there was an invisible border which some dared not traverse! It was comical to observe people watching the human zoo from some perceived 'safety zone' set up in their minds. Irritating as well... what's to be scared of? Apart from being blagged for change and cigarettes every thirty seconds and witnessing what alcohol can do to body and soul if worked on long enough! But there's nothing like being avoided to make you reclusive or belligerent.

David Stooke: My memory of the entire weekend is a total blur. There came a point on the Friday before the main weekend when you'd think, 'Holy shit, this is like Stonehenge.' It had started out as something completely different, a pay festival that we'd heard about up at Glastonbury that summer. We'd heard that vehicles were welcome, seen an advert for it that said 'Buses Welcome' and we thought, 'We're going!' But we didn't expect it to be that mind-blowing. There were a few bands, but those were never the interest for me – it was the art and the people that motivated me. I was there a couple of weeks before the main weekend and secured a fantastic spot, parked up by the trees. But did it grow… By the Wednesday before the start of the festival proper, we're thinking, 'The festival site is full and the tents haven't even turned up yet!'

Wayne Twining: We went in before it all kicked off, and we were in the backstage compound hidden away from the punters, away from everything. There was dysentery; there were dead sheep in the water supply… It was like, 'Don't have anything to do with anyone who's been here more than a couple of days.'

Kev Ellis: It's too easy to blame drugs and alcohol. Some people are just stupid. Or they're angry and pissed off and wanting others to feel like them. Treworgey sticks in the mind. Travellers running the gates and security, acting exactly like the asshole fascists they so despised. Power corrupts, I guess.

Breakfast at Treworgey (Dave Fawcett)

Craig Gregory: It was my first festival, a sixteen-year-old school-leaver without a clue what to expect. I was wearing my heavy metal attire of leather jacket and Iron Maiden t-shirt, white basketball boots and ripped jeans, thinking I'd appear different. Not that I stood out from the crowd or anything but when I arrived on site I realised there was a far more alternative culture out there than I'd seen before. My friend, Harry, and me were fans of Hawkwind and had our own band, Bionic Egg, in which we'd play covers of our favourite Hawks' tracks. When we heard of this festival away down in Cornwall we decided to get some cash together and go. We got to Liskeard after sundown and made our way down an unlit, high-hedged lane with the only lights being other festival-goers' torches, some of which were flames on sticks. It was eerie seeing faces suddenly appear from the darkness, and the noise from the festival site seemed dark and boomy. At the main gate we realised we didn't have enough money to get in. We decided to keep what we had for food and scoured the perimeter for a hole to sneak in through. Towards the back of the site we managed a quick climb into a tiny gap in the hedge only to be confronted by a guy with two German Shepherd dogs who were growling as their handler struggled to keep them from snapping at us. He was actually a very pleasant chap and let us in for a fiver between us. We stashed our gear and made a mental note of where we were, a bright kaleidoscopic flag on top of a bus being our beacon for when we came back.

David Stooke: On the drive up to get in there'd be God knows how many people lining up, tapping on the glass … 'Do you want to buy this, do you want to buy that,' offering 'it' to people going to the festival. But they were offering it to local people as well! Plumbers, electricians, people caught up in the crush. And then the toilets not arriving, it was a total catastrophe. There's a photo of the event, 'Fuck Everything, Let's Party.' That sums up Treworgey more than anything does; Friday I started partying with abandon. Saturday and Sunday went by in a daze! But the aftermath was serene and beautiful, seeing all these buses I'd never seen before, meeting all these people and it was like going to a vintage vehicle rally.

Craig Gregory: I remember feeling unnerved by all the activity, and the apparent sense that the population here wasn't quite right. A kid, who'd hardly been to any gigs, let alone a festival, had never seen anything like it. A few days here, though, and I soon learned who the real thinkers are. We spotted a chap who was slow-dancing to the sound of a burger van's generator. This was really comical and cheered me up no end. Loop were playing the main stage so we sat on the hill amidst the crowd. Harry had some resin on him and we quickly got into the spirit. That night we had silver plastic sheets to sleep under to keep us warm. I didn't know at the time it was best to sleep with them as close to your skin as possible, so I woke up shivering, fully clothed beneath a blanket that was as useful as a squash racquet for a paddle. Second night I found out how to use it properly! Rising from the tent quite early, I strolled around the site. The main stage had disappeared under a blanket of mist; looking down on it from the hill was one of the loveliest things I'd seen. You could see flags on their poles here and there, sticking up high into the air above the mist. There were a few stragglers still revelling and no doubt intoxicated, but the festival now didn't seem as scary and I knew then this was going to be a good time. That day turned out to be a scorcher, and everywhere dust was being kicked up and filling the air. The lack of toilets was becoming absurd and I heard a few stories of a JCB digging a huge hole for shit to be thrown into. I'm not sure it was true but I did see a JCB with a hole next to it and what looked like rubble piled up inside it.

David Stooke: It's widely said that there were no toilets, but they'd ordered them from some company who could deliver forty-foot long trailers that could be wheeled into position and dropped down and you'd have twenty cubicles on each side. Apparently there was a line of lorries outside with all these toilets on and in the front truck was the guy who owned the company. When he saw the festival, he just said, 'No way – I'm not leaving them' and just took them away again, and that was a big turning-point. Loads of people had got in for nothing, the water supply couldn't cope, and when the toilets got taken away… I think [the company supplying the toilets] thought it was going to be an agricultural thing, like a Young Farmers event!

Sarah Evans: The toilets were just unreal, piled two feet high with shit above the seat. How did people manage to go on that! They had to close the toilets down and we ended up going in the woods.

Craig Gregory: Climax Blues Band were the first band we saw that day, with a great 'tunnel' laser machine mid-front of their stage, followed by Gaye Bikers On Acid with their mental rockabilly getting the front of the crowd going. They were pogo-ing and slamming, kicking up loads of dust. Some said the slim and pretty girl who was going round with a kitchen tray full of White Lightning and weed was the girlfriend of GBOA's singer, but I think that was just urban legend belonging to the festival? My money had pretty much gone already and I was keeping my eyes peeled for friendly traders who had not managed to sell their stock by the evening. A few cheeky requests here and there, and I was brimming with ginger cake, buttered bread and some cans of pop. We went over to Wango Riley's stage to see Magic Mushroom Band followed by Ozric Tentacles and eventually Hawkwind! This was what I was really here for. On seeing two young lads who looked a little out of place, the fans around us were brilliant. They made us feel welcome and comfortable and shared with us all their banter and jokes. The sounds and the atmosphere were amazing and I soon learned what a *family* the traveller community really was. After Hawkwind we made it back to the tent tired but *buzzing*.

Bridget Wishart: The pole on the marquee cracked due to kids climbing and playing on the top of the tent. The Hippy Slags lost our slot to play while waiting for it to be checked by Health and Safety. The organiser told us we wouldn't be able to perform, but loads of people had turned up to watch us. I lost the plot and told the guy that everyone in the tent was there to see us, which might possibly have been a bit of an exaggeration, but there was no way we weren't playing! We'd come to the festival in the Slagmobile, Claire and Sarah's Bedford CA, and had brought bottles of Tequila, planning to recoup the petrol money by selling Tequila Slammers. I don't remember if we made any money, but the Slammers were great! There was a newssheet that we saw when we were at the festival, which declared the Slags weren't playing because we were all pregnant....as it turned out, two of us were. Nothing, however, stopped us playing the gig!

Joie Hinton: Treworgey? Bit scary that one! It was really dusty and I remember seeing a few weird instances there, couple of things I saw that weren't very good… a little kiddie got a syringe stuck in his heel, stuff like that. But the festival was great. The Ullulators gig was very good there. The Ozric gig was really mad, I remember the rhythm section was really out of it, Roly [Wynn] on bass and Merv [Pepler] who was so out of it I had to walk him back to the tent up the hill and he thought the whole hillside was made out of pigeons and that he was walking on these pigeons who were all cooing. Roly, who is deceased now, sadly, was a real character, a bit of a Sid Vicious type but a great bass player. He was obsessed culturally with what Hawkwind were, and also Jimi Hendrix, and he actually formed a band called Jimi Hawkwind and they played a few festivals. You know how people take bands and mix them all up – like Dread Zeppelin? This was Roly playing lead guitar on Hendrix songs but in a Hawkwind style; it was really funny. You'd get the punk types rolling around laughing watching that, it looked good on a blackboard outside of a café, 'Jimi Hawkwind' playing.

Craig Gregory: Treworgey's been labelled as a legendary festival, the last of its kind. It's something that has lived large with me ever since and I'll never get bored of telling tales of my adventure in the sun that year.

Treworgey (Bridget Wishart)

Roger's Story – Treworgey Tree Fayre

Here's Treworgey from the point of view of an American with little previous experience of the British free festival scene.

Roger Neville-Neil: This was one of many trips I took as an American living abroad; an excursion to experience a large festival and see a bit of Cornwall at the same time. I figured I might learn more about the culture, history... and the idiosyncrasies of crowd behaviour. Inadvertently, I would also come to learn something about the Cornish cops.

I journeyed with an intrepid, likeminded girlfriend. We left London by coach to Plymouth, where we experienced a modest layover before transferring to another coach that would take us to Liskeard. I had a good friend, Mic, living in a village near Bodmin, who'd offered to put us up for a few days before the festival to show us some of the local sites that he thought would particularly interest us. While visiting Mic, we managed to wander around stone circles and searched for springs and wells. We lurked in the remains of Tintagel, visited a witch museum in Boscastle. Rested in the ruins of St. Michael Chapel, a fifteenth-century hermitage perched on top of a granite outcrop known as Roche Rock, and teetered beneath the capstone of Trevethy Quoit, one of the portal dolmens littering the Cornish landscape.

Mic drove us back to Liskeard when it was time to head to the festival. I asked him what the locals thought of it. He told me that they were terrified of the travellers. They thought they were dangerous, and considered that the male travellers were hooligans and criminals whilst the female travellers carried razors in their bras!

We thanked Mic, got our backpacks out of his car and started our trek toward the festival. We'd a vague idea that it was a couple miles out of town. It was no problem to find. All you had to do was follow someone who was walking up the road wearing a backpack. I noticed a few signs in the shop windows that said 'NO TRAVELLERS.' A cop car was idling in a small parking zone set up at the side of the road, its occupant watching festival-goers trudge on by.

The locals had laid out their welcome mat. It was their version of a moat filled with sharks. Eventually our journey brought us to a long line of cars gathered at a side road. They were creeping along, bumper to bumper, like a rush hour traffic jam. We easily overtook them and continued down to the festival entrance and showed security our tickets. Yeah, we actually paid to attend this festival. Security allowed us to enter and join the crowd. There were more people out in the field than extras in a Cecil B. DeMille production. And it showed no signs of letting up.

I had a good time at Treworgey, particularly at night when the headlining bands played. During the day there were lulls in the music. And it was sunny and hot out there in the fields. You can get a little restless waiting for something to happen. We killed time by wandering about to keep ourselves occupied. Checked the stalls, eyed the food and drink supplied by enterprising individuals out to make a fast buck exploiting a captive clientele.

The loos were definitely places to avoid. The surrounding atmosphere was not meant for breathing, unless you had a gas mask or suffered from a severe head cold. Either way, you queued up and held your breath. To avoid these conditions, you'd have to pray for constipation. If divine intervention was not forthcoming, you could do the next best thing: hike out of the festival grounds and visit the local village. If you could get service, you'd find relief, and less expensive supplies.

The festival's sleeping conditions varied by your means and social status. The lowly festival foot soldiers kipped on the ground under the stars. The middle-class squires erected small tents, staking their claim to a piece of terra firma in makeshift communities that popped up like magic mushrooms. The lords simply slept in their cars and caravans. I found space inside a large festival tent. Sleeping like a disaster victim the first night. And down and dirty on the ground between parked cars on the second night. Wondering I'd wake up with tyre-tracks across my back.

Ozric Tentacles, Hawkwind, and The Climax Blues Band were the highlights of the festival, for me. During Hawkwind's set, I was watching drops of water dancing around overhead and captured by the strobes. I think it was a mist, but it added to the magic of their set. It was great to have the opportunity to see Hawkwind play at a large outdoor festival. I knew that Nik Turner was somewhere at the festival. I just didn't know where or when. So I didn't actually get to see his band play. But I did get to hear his Fantastic All Stars after we had left the festival to head back to London. We were walking along the road leading back to Liskeard, when we came to a road barrier with a cop standing guard at one end of it. It was while we were walking alongside it, that we recognised the music and could hear it loud and clear.

Daphne decided to listen to the music right there, and stopped at the middle of the barrier. Leaning against it like it was the front of a stage, staring off into the green countryside and listening intently. I glanced at the cop, sized up the situation and said, 'We better keep going.'

She frowned. 'Why? I can hear Nik perfectly here. It's a good spot.'

'No, it's not. It's his beat.' I jerked my head in the cop's direction to remind her of what was lurking close at hand. The cop was still patiently standing guard. I offered her a few words of wisdom, 'If this was America, he'd tell us to leave.'

'Well, this isn't America; I'm staying!'

'I glanced back over to the cop. He was now strolling casually our way. When he got to where we were standing he stopped and said, 'I'll have to ask you to move on.'

I nodded. 'Sure. It's easier to maintain security if you don't have people gathering at your post.'

He smiled. My girlfriend's mouth dropped. She muttered to herself and shook her head as we continued walking down the road. 'I don't believe it.'

'Welcome to America...'

We made it back to Liskeard earlier than we'd imagined. The coach to London wouldn't arrive for quite a while, so we meandered about the area. We came across a car park and noticed something rather peculiar. A small area of the car park turned out to be the perfect spot to listen to the music drifting from the festival. A shaft of sound touched down, as clear as a bell. Nik Turner's Fantastic All-Stars.

We sat down, ate a snack and listened to live, disembodied, music. It wasn't long before we had company. A cop car arrived and circled a few times around. Eventually, it came to a full stop and just sat there, idling, waiting for something to happen. The something arrived shortly. It took the form of a frantic, terrified couple. They dashed out from one of the buildings, ran over to the cop car and gushed in gratitude, 'Thank goodness you came.' Then they rushed over to a car, climbed in, fired up the engine and wasted no time in driving off. The cop car remained.

I had a funny feeling in my gut. I slowly stood up and walked over. The cop seemed surprised to see me stroll over for a chat. 'Hi. Do you need to talk with us?'

The cop screwed up his face. Then cut to the chase. 'Why are you here?'

'We're waiting to catch the coach back to London.'

'It doesn't leave from here. You need to catch it over on the main road.'

'Yeah, we know.'

He suddenly became more interested in me. Maybe it was my black paramilitary pants covered with silver zips and my steel-toed Navy boots. Not to mention my foreign accent. I thought I'd better just level with him. 'We noticed that you could hear the music from the festival really well, right here. So we decided to sit down and listen to it while we waited for the coach to arrive.' I glanced at my watch. 'The coach should be arriving any time now. We better go queue up.'

The cop nodded, watched us gather our things and walk over to the main road. Once we got to the designated coach stop, the cop car slowly drove off.

While we waited for our coach, more people turned up and joined us. This is when I noticed a large cop van arrive. The paddy wagon parked up the road a little ways. A very tall cop got out and surveyed the area. A few minutes later a cop car pulled up next to him. An impromptu discussion took place. It was brief, and the end result was a renewed interest in yours truly. The tall cop was glancing my way as he was briefed by his cohort. He started to make his move, in my direction. He crossed the road, and homed in on his target.

I turned and looked the other way. Behind me, I could hear the cop's footsteps clomping on the sidewalk like Frankenstein's monster; getting louder and louder, until finally he stopped dead in his tracks. There was a brief silence followed by a loud clearing of his throat.

I turned and looked up. Way up. This is when he actually uttered his first words. I'll never forget that voice. That distinctive Cornish accent delivered with a weird Hillbilly drawl.

'So, whadda ya doing here?'

'Waiting for a coach back to London.'

'Got a ticket?'

'Yeah.'

'Could I see it?'

I nodded and produced the ticket. He removed it from my hand and scrutinized it thoroughly. He was taking his time. I was just hoping that he didn't rip it up and then claim I never had a ticket. I interrupted his reverie. 'This is where I catch the coach, isn't it?'

He handed me back the ticket. 'Yes, you're at the right place.'

I glanced around a lot while answering his questions, keeping my eyes constantly on the move. Everywhere except where he wanted them. I wanted to see what he would do. Finally, I set my eyes in a fixed stare, directly into his. He seemed relieved, and visibly relaxed his posture, realising my pupils were perfectly fine. I wasn't strung out on drugs. And I was stone cold sober.

He moved onto another topic; one a little closer to home. 'I hear there's a band called Hawkhead that might turn up.'

'Hawkwind. Yeah, they turned up. And they were pretty good, too!'

He looked perplexed. Someone was saying something nice about Hawkwind. He seemed almost disappointed not to hear that they were out plundering the countryside and needed to be stopped before Cornwall crumbled under their relentless assault. We maintained our casual faux chat while I waited for the coach. He stood faithfully by my side. He was making sure that I made it swiftly and safely out of town; one less undesirable to deal with. When the coach rolled up to the kerb, he let me know. 'Here's your coach, best get on board. You wouldn't want to miss it.'

I frowned. 'What about the people who don't have tickets?'

He grinned. 'Oh, don't you worry about them. We'll see to it that they're taken care of.'

I climbed on board the coach, found a seat, and, as soon as the coach started to roll down the road, I looked out the window. And I wondered, what would happen to those people left to their own devices, after the paying witnesses were gone?

Member of the Hippy Slags and Hawkwind at Treworgey (Bridget Wishart)

Bristol band The Seers, main stage, Treworgey (Bridget Wishart)

Telscombe Cliffs – 1990

There wasn't so much 'peace and love'

Telscombe Cliffs, on the A259 between Brighton and Newhaven, has become a landmark in the decline of the free festival movement, partly because it was set against the backdrop of the hard drugs and brew that had come to dominate the scene, but particularly because at this grim and unforgiving 'festival', Hawkwind, for so many years seen as one of the linchpins of the whole free festival movement, were attacked on stage and ended up fleeing for their lives. Much has been said about this event, and Hawkwind even put it 'on record', literally, by recording and releasing a song about it, but the motivations for the attack become murkier the more the story is related, to the point that even the associating of the event with the 'Brew Crew' is questionable. Whatever the causes of the attack, it was totally symptomatic of the atmosphere then taking grip on the festivals, and the outcome is clear. Many long-time festival-goers retreated from the scene, some to Ireland, some to mainland Europe, others simply walking away from their involvement and assimilating themselves back into mainstream 9-5 society and so it's completely correct to identify this festival as a massive turning point after which the free festivals would never be the same again.

Sarah Evans: It became a bit trendy; a sort of a fashion, living on a bus or in a bender camp, and it did attract the wrong sort of person in the end. They didn't want the music there anyway; some festivals we'd turn up to play and people would just be telling us to shut up. We went to one site, a railway siding in Wales somewhere, to do a gig, it wasn't even really a festival, though they had a little stage set-up. We'd hired a van and there were two or three bands all crammed in together and people were throwing stones at the van whilst we were driving in. I just hated that festival, if I'd had a car I'd have driven home.

Dick Lucas: We once drove down to Camelford on the back of a phone call ('They've got a site and need some music!'), to find a muddy field and a non-working PA and a tarp to play under, and nobody 'in charge.' It seemed everyone was completely mashed already, so we helped sort it out with our knowledge of leads and plugs, and played, and managed to squeeze

£20 for petrol out of thin air. It was the luck of the draw, some gigs were more together than others, and the vibe was that drug or drink intake was setting the levels of togetherness. If nobody was taking time out from getting wasted, it was a pain in the ass having to more or less organise it ourselves.

Claire Grainger: [The festival scene had] got very violent. You had the Brew Crew, there wasn't so much 'peace and love', and lots more people were getting into heavy drugs and strong lagers and spoiling for fights. People came in to the scene who just wanted to be out of their heads and away from rules and the government, but without the fun that was in the festival scene. The organised chaos you could get in the festivals, where people would want to get things together, they didn't want to do that – it was more about *destroy*, unfortunately. When it gets to the point where people are smashing things up with baseball bats and being really heavy with dogs then you just want no part of it. It seemed to attract people who were up for a fight. You're frightened to get involved to split things up because you might get hurt. You had your hippies who would stand up for the cause because they believed in it, but you'd definitely have people there who were just intent on getting into confrontations with the police and once that had given the festival scene a bad name, it was really hard.

Clapham Common, 1990 (Janet Henbane)

Psilly Fayre, Last Festival of the Season circa 82/83 (Bridget Wishart)

Angel: Bottom line with everything as regards to drugs, drugs always ruined it, that's just how it is. That's what I've seen... The casualties, the corruption… I'll tell you what it's like, it's like you have the beautiful Tibetan Ukrainian Mountain Troupe, yeah? This leads in the Peace Convoy, which then turns into the Convoy, which were a much more hard-core lot. What I believe ruined that was the drug scene. I'm not talking about the Tibetans, but what went into the Convoy and became known as the New Age Traveller definitely had its casualties. The Peace Convoy was very different to what ended up being the Convoy. The Convoy were a lot more hard-core. Entering into their camp was an apocalyptic experience. It was how you imagined the end of the world and what would be left. They had a different kind of mentality. It's a shame, because I think it got corrupted. It was the downfall of those previous ideals and dreams. Don't get me wrong; there were positive elements to that more hard-core Convoy; Mutoid Waste with their astounding talent were decent guys, who worked really hard. There were people in it, some very positive elements, who still had a lot to offer and brought new things in that were very interesting. However, it's that classic thing of a rotten apple spoiling the barrel and unfortunately within life you can get a certain element that destroys what was initially there. It's gone to complete anarchy.

Jake Stratton-Kent: There were drug-dealers turning up who had a *posse* and *weapons* and were dealing in coke, which was kind of accepted but they became almost the new role models and the atmosphere changed. It became more about the drugs, more about the music as well but as a commercial thing. I can't say that wouldn't have happened if Wally Hope had still been around because big social things were happening as well. Unemployed youths were coming to the festivals, some of whom didn't have the hippie ethos. In a way, some of that was good, the punk rockers were bringing back some of the old values that we were losing anyway, but there was this rough element of very nasty people. I remember meeting a bunch of them in the street one day; I had an anarchist badge on, 'You've got no right to wear that badge.' Well, the fact that there's five of you and one of me makes you brave but when have you ever taken a site? Which I have… I've cut the locks off a gate to get people into a site, all these hippies milling around like headless chickens. There were two kinds of people who went to the festivals in the old days. The hippies and what I'd term the ravers or even hell raisers… a lot of the Wallies were ex-Merchant Navy, ex-bikers. Take the Wick Festival, there'd been a bit of trouble on site, the travellers had been chucked off but we still thought it was a good site to have a festival. We couldn't go to Stonehenge any more but there were alternative sites. This must have been 1988. A friend of mine had a car so we drove down and there were all these hippies hanging around in lay-bys waiting for this festival to happen. Nobody seemed to have any idea how we were going to get on site. The police were there circling around; so Trevor and I went down, found somewhere to park up, got onto the site on foot, built a fire but didn't light it, got back into the car and drove down to the gate and there were all these police coming up and this great long line of vehicles. So we skewed the car across the road so the police couldn't come back down again, got the bolt shears out of the car and cut the padlock off and started moving vehicles on. Then we went back up to the fire we'd built and lit it so all the hippies in the area could see the site had been taken. That was completely spontaneous. We took the site. The Brew Crew never took a site, and when the police came to beat us up the Brew Crew were nowhere to be seen. Much like Windsor, when things were going well the Hells Angels were all, 'We're your brothers, we'll look after you' but when the police actually turned up there wasn't an Angel in sight. That's the Brew Crew as well, tough guys, like to talk the talk but they can't walk the walk; people who were trying to protect innocent hippies at Windsor were peoples' dads… not Hells Angels, not tough guys. I saw one guy at Windsor, never saw him again, blood streaming down his face, saying: 'Don't fight them. Turn them on.' That was the ethos we had. Those were our warriors, ones who were prepared to make things happen. When thugs turned up to beat up the hippies, as frequently happened, there used to be this cry, 'Where are the warriors?' and we'd all pile out of our caravans and tents and were prepared to take a beating… but we didn't make trouble.

Richard Chadwick: There has to be a vanguard, actually going onto other peoples' property, or at least contestable as to who the land belongs to, common land or what have you; there's always that brave spearhead, advance guard [laughs] 'hats off', let's face it!

Claire Grainger: I think it was a lot of the heavier 'convoy' scene that started to spoil the festivals for us. If you didn't fit into their lifestyle, like if you turned up with a tent, then you weren't one of them, you were considered to be straight. Once you'd had that incident in Brighton where Hawkwind got attacked you thought, why waste time playing for these people, when they don't even really want us to?

Steve Bubble: Hawkwind arrived and parked up next to me with their new classic coach. During their performance the bass player, Alan [Davey], was apparently shot at by someone with an air rifle. I hadn't really been aware anything was amiss until I walked past the stage and all hell was breaking loose, people with steel bars lashing out at random passers-by and people with head injuries fleeing the area. I tried to get an ambulance onto the site to pick up wounded people, but the police said it was too dangerous for them – finally I persuaded one to drive up. The evening didn't get much better, with Hawkwind's coach being destroyed through the night, with dogs inside whining as the windows were put through. I never did get to the bottom of what happened that day, but the coach was destroyed and the festival fizzled out with people leaving the site as soon as they could.

Bridget Wishart: I have never felt more helpless than when I was dragged away from trying to stop those crazed idiots from beating up my friends. I'd called for help to the audience that remained by Wango's stage. They had come but remained spectators, frightened by what they saw. A few courageous individuals from bands, Chris from Amoebix for one, were challenging those mad bastards but were getting beaten for their bravery. Chris had his ankle broken. We needed to rush them… overwhelm them! I can still see them in my mind: two guys, silhouetted against the sky, crash helmets on, big sticks for weapons. They were off their heads. It was dark, it was out of control, and people were scared, I was scared… we were being hurt! Dave [Brock] and Alan [Davey] had disappeared. I didn't know if they were OK. I ran to the police and begged them to help, but they wouldn't come on site. I was just desperate to stop the violence. I thought that I might be able to draw them away, not that I know what I'd have done if they did decide to follow me, I had nowhere to take them. It was then that I was dragged away for my own safety. Alan survived a nightmare, trapped in his van with the vehicle being hit and attacked by a mob. I don't know how he managed to keep it together, to stay quiet and to escape when they finally left his van alone. We hid from the terrors of that crazy night and in the darkness with the headlights off we drove away. We didn't see who burned Dave's bus and terrified the dogs that sheltered there. We parked the Land Rover a few miles away, huddled for warmth under a car mat, and went back in the morning to face the night's destruction and to try and pick up the pieces of a shattered dream. We (Hawkwind) never played another free festival, though I tell you something for nothing, Telscombe was never a free festival.

Michael Dog: I didn't go to that festival but when I heard about it, for me that was the end. I don't remember going to a festival after that for many years. I've always liked Hawkwind's music though I was never a dyed-in-the-wool Hawkwind fan – so it wasn't so much, 'Oh My God! These people attacked Hawkwind ... have they no respect?' It was the fact that they'd attack *anyone*. They'd attacked a band playing on the stage and they had to be smuggled off the site in fear of their lives. But it was hugely disrespectful. Hawkwind had fled in fear of their lives and had hidden in people's caravans and vehicles because they were seriously afraid of being murdered.

Gary Bamford: I just think that people come into something, get excited and they love it. Then, all of a sudden, they aren't getting anything out of it, money wise, and two or three years down the line they're just normal people again trying to get a job or trying to kick a habit. They've either died, got a drug or an alcohol problem, or they're on the sick getting 'x' amount a week for being ill. It's all those different angles. I didn't see anything wrong with [the festival scene]. I was into the punk scene at the end of the 70s as a teenager and *that* was full-on because you're all of a sudden being chased around by skinheads, mods, rockers... everyone was out to kill us. Being on the streets, on a housing estate, was more frightening than being in a field full of nutty, savage travellers.

It seemed a bit easier than being stuck on those estates. Obviously people flip out a bit too easily, too many drugs, but then again there were a lot of families living on the scene then.

Then you had the Brew Crew, which was an excuse to bring it down. But that was a way of labelling people and putting them in a bracket and saying, 'Watch out for those people.' They became an excuse, like with us, if we were on a list of five bands on a bill and something went wrong or something went missing, then [blame] 2000 Dirty Squatters. I'm sure half the time we got booked *as* someone to put the blame on, and you'd be left going 'No, it was *them*.' You get labelled and if something goes off then it must be you – which is rubbish.

Dick Lucas: A lot of the negativity was caused by what became known as the 'Brew Crew', drunken 'crusties', who didn't care for anyone outside their own image, so took everyone outside it to be part of 'THEM' and therefore not worth a shit. This scared and pissed off a lot of people, gave all the travellers a bad name to anyone who didn't know any of them, and pissed off a lot of fellow travellers as well.

Fire Twirlling at Dragon Festival 1987 (Charles Herwin)

They gave an image of the traveller as drunk and exclusive, and put a lot of people off joining in. But the emphasis is on 'drunken', rather than smearing all crusties with the same brush. A large portion of Culture Shock's crowd were crusties and/or travellers, among them people who were then, or later became, a vital part of the festival scene. Like the tireless Wango Riley crew. They had the, imagination and planning skills to be the most likely and reliable stage at any festival, large or small, free or otherwise. Like Fleece and Sandra and their ever-expanding PA system, or Yatesy and Roz, who drove us around a few European tours. Or like Gary from 2000DS, who amassed such a dodgy reputation it's easy to overlook how much he got things happening. These people were driven and focussed, in a scene that was by its nature chaotic and spontaneous. Someone once wrote in a review that Culture Shock were to blame for the existence of crusties! News to us! Were WE crusty?

Jah Free: There was a mob of people that used to hang around with [the Wango Stage], we used to call them the Brew Crew... they used to do the tidying up afterwards and we paid them brew for whatever bags of rubbish they brought off-site. 'Here's all the black bags, collect all the rubbish, bring the bags back in your motor and when you get to the other end we'll pay you in brew.' That worked well, not of benefit all the time, but it utilised them in a way. They were controllable from our point of view, but they had their moves, they used to pick up people's rubbish bags off their doorsteps on the way through! So we had to start searching through, making sure it wasn't just household rubbish... 'Oh look, there's three bin bags over there, grab 'em, we'll take them and all.' Realistically you couldn't get rid of them, just sling them out and ban them, one way or another you'd get a problem either with the ethics of the thing, 'this is a free festival but you can't come,' or the thing that they'd get angry and start causing a problem. We found we could work with them in a reasonable way, couldn't police them all the time but there were limits. Nobody ever got stabbed, things like that as far as I know. The worst thing I did hear was that one of them got run over because he fell asleep in the middle of a field when a car went through.

Jake Stratton-Kent: The Brew Crew are still around, people call them crusties now and that name has got misused with as many nice hippies being labelled crusties as not so nice ones. But there are still plenty around who make life unpleasant for others and have a bad attitude to people they think aren't as hard-core as they are. They often don't know who those people really are; they're people who maybe helped start the festivals but are being given a hard time by Brew Crew types... 'Traces of soap have been found on your body... you're not one of us.'

Conspiracies & Consequences

For every commentator who sees conspiracies lurking at the heart of the festival movement's decline and collapse, there's another who views the troubled second half of the 1980s as being at least in part due to the problems being experienced internally, even if those problems where then further exploited by the authorities in its own very publicly avowed intent to break the festivals, The Convoy, and those who furthered the free festival ethos.

Simon Williams: The scene was always under attack. There was always a feeling of, 'We're going to do this despite the fact people in suits or in uniforms don't want these things to happen.' People didn't want it on their doorstep; they didn't understand it, as far as they could see it was a bunch of troublemakers, hippies. People these days would find it difficult to believe you could get a great line-up of bands together and it would be completely free. Now there's only one festival that I know of, that's the Burning Man, which costs a lot to get in but there's no trading once you're there and even the performers pay to get in.

Oz Hardwick: Somewhere on the outskirts of Oxford in 1987. Hardly anyone got through all the roadblocks, we were camping on tree roots, constantly aware of the police threat, and finally awoken by a helmeted head thrust into the tent about two hours after we'd got to sleep, telling us to clear off within the hour. Helicopters and full riot kit – they meant it. Just felt tired, beaten and very sad.

Jeremy Cunningham: I was living on buses until I moved off the travelling scene when the Criminal Justice Act came in and it got so hard… I'd done it to live a 'free' lifestyle but at the end you became less free living on the road than if you lived in a flat. You got so much grief, everywhere you went. The Levellers had got a lot bigger than we ever thought we would, and made that crossover, and I was getting just a bit too well-known on that scene. I didn't like that, I liked to be quite anonymous, so I left [the scene] in the end and just moved into a flat, though I still kept in touch with a lot of people. I still know people who are living in buses today, but not many. But I was living on the road from the mid-80s to the early 1990s.

Oz Hardwick: In the later years, say 1985 – 1989, there was always the dodging about to get to sites. Generally at small gatherings there wasn't much hassle once you were there, though after Stonehenge '85, which I've mixed feelings about having missed, there was always the threat of violence. At Oxford, for example, things looked like they might turn nasty, with the [police] shield wall and so on, but… I think most people had a sense that if it came to violence, the government-trained thugs were going to have the upper hand. A sense that face-to-face confrontation wasn't going to further any cause.

Dick Lucas: One night during the post-Henge time of high police paranoia, June '87 or '88, the local Warminster / Culture Shock crew, about fifteen of us, crammed into a large van at 5am and set off to find a gathering place that Tim Sebastian had located on a map showing the edge of the army territory that extends across Salisbury Plain. This was a hillside a few miles away. A helicopter buzzed over the van on the way there, and by the time the sun came up a dozen cops had come to join in. They let us stay there, tolerated our argument that this was common land and we had the right to assemble, and positioned themselves by the barbed wire at the top of the slope that marked the start of army territory. Behind them were some curious cows wondering what all the fuss was about, which made a great picture! A Channel 4 camera team didn't turn up, but Tim said they were interested in having someone talk about all this over the phone, and suggested I do it; later I called them, but as they were after a 'serious sun worshipper', it was all over before it began. Tim was older than us, full of intense passion about the Stones, a leading Druid by the time he died, and inspired a lot of people into action. RIP.

Boris, of Boris and his Bolshie Balalaika fame, reflects here on one aspect of the general anti-festival clampdown, the availability of access to the Stones during the solstice in the years immediately after the Beanfield.

Boris: We arrived at Stonehenge, 1987, on the afternoon of Thursday, June 18th. All was normal; tourists clicking their cameras at the roped-off Stones. A lone figure could be seen inside the circle; soon it was blessed with happy humans dancing thrice clockwise to invoke the Great Spirit. It was a peaceful protest and a small sign of things to come.

Our camp in Collingbourne was wet, muddy and miserable, but the people were joyful. We were taken into a bender, offered food and several joints, and tried to dry off. A band, Culture Shock, gamely battled with the elements to produce music from under several tarpaulins to the ankle-deep crowd. Vehicles had been kept off the site to comply with the Public Order Act. As soon as the 13th vehicle entered, the police moved in with an eviction deadline of 12.30pm Friday. That morning saw continuing rain, crowds of police and confusion. No-one seemed to know where to go. The car would not start, needing a long push to fire a reluctant damp engine. Slowly people drifted away towards the local village...

'Don't you people get fed up with all this?' asked a reporter. 'We love the rain, man! It's a part of nature,' our tongue-in-cheek reply. We moved away past the police lines to discover that our car was being followed by several others assuming we knew where to go. Asked in the village where people were heading. Someone mentioned 'Shipton Bellinger', found it on the map and headed off. We turned up a promising-looking track, drove half a mile and found a beautiful clearing - an ideal site. People piled out and began setting up camp. One car drove back towards the old site to tell people the news, while we covered our car with leafy branches from a fallen tree and hid from the helicopters. Three hours later we were invaded by two vans full of police, and two MOD Land Rovers. We were on army land and had to leave straight away. We were in no position to argue - half a dozen vehicles and maybe twenty people - so we left peacefully, having given the authorities a good run for our money. The infra-red scanner in the helicopter had given us away.

Drove into Shipton Bellinger to find the petrol station closed. A small convoy was forming so we joined it, heading towards the A303 into Hampshire. Slowly winding round country lanes we stopped, hopelessly lost, beside a row of houses in a small village. The curtains twitched, kids walked by on their way home from school to be whisked away by parents. 'Don't you DARE go near those 'ippies, Johnny.' Someone found some petrol, so we moved off again, winding our way back into Wiltshire, ending up near Salisbury.

Someone discovered that the site we should have been going to was in Shipton Bellinger all the time, we'd simply turned down the wrong track several hours, and half a tank of petrol, earlier. We found the site just as it was getting dark, setting up camp on dry ground, loads of wood about for a healthy fire. Had some food and went to watch the band.

A massive chalice was prepared from contributions all round. 'You'll have to walk half-a-mile to smoke it though...' We broke the Public Order Act by setting off through the woods up the track, then along a path with branches ready to blind the passing walker. 'Funny half-mile this!' said a dreadlocked companion. Across a stile, through a field of cows, over a barbed-wire fence. 'That wasn't in the script.' complained a girl wearing flip-flops! Through another field, over another barbed-wire fence, and up a steep hill to a large burial mound. We linked hands to form a large circle, prayed to our gods and goddesses and remembered those, like Wally Hope, who had not made it this far. Those injured and in prison. We vowed to reach the Stones for them. The chalice was lit and passed slowly, formally, around the circle. Each person paused to contemplate as the communion ritual was performed. Finally we linked arms and danced sun-wise three times around the tumulus, ending in a huge hug and cheer in the middle.

We woke the following afternoon to find the site filling up rapidly with 'weekenders' and drove into Amesbury for provisions. The village was full of festival-goers as if nothing had changed since 1984. Many headed straight for Stonehenge with the intention of staying out all night, others headed for the festival site. We were lucky; a copper had taken our number as we left the site so we were allowed back in. New vehicles were made to park in the village, and many people on foot were turned away, only to reach the site across fields.

On site rumours and counter-rumours were rife. People had been generally confident about reaching the Stones, but the police attitude had grown perceptibly more hostile. There was to be a police announcement at 8pm. Meanwhile, news of drug arrests at Glastonbury only served to frustrate campers more. There was a serious drug problem on site - no-one had any! People were resorting to drink, which didn't help the atmosphere.

Steve Bubble: Some three to four thousand of us actually gained access to the Stones and it felt like a victory, having walked through the night along the A303 from Shipton Bellinger, closely monitored by police, after watching bands play in the woods at the site.

Taking a break during the walk to Stonehenge, 1987 (Dave Fawcett)

Boris: We gathered together to hear the announcement: 'In view of the good behaviour of the travellers we had been prepared to allow people to walk to Stonehenge for the sunrise. However, in view of the increase in the number of travellers from 200 to 500, and the expressed intent on the part of some travellers to occupy the Stones, this will not now be permitted. Anyone approaching within 2 miles of Stonehenge will therefore be liable to arrest in order to prevent a breach of the peace.'

Chopper over Stonehenge, 1987 (Boris Atha)

If the police had been trying to provoke a confrontation they could not have done a better job. The mood turned ugly; some drunken individuals tried to attack the police and let down their tyres. There were some minor scuffles and the police withdrew. A site meeting was called. The louts who had tried to attack the police were soundly rebuked and denounced as '*agents-provocateurs.*' The mood was defiant but pragmatic. The question was not whether we would go, but how? Some favoured a single march by the direct route. Others favoured small groups travelling across the fields and through woodland to stretch police resources to the limit. Yet others pointed out that the astronomical solstice was at 11.11pm the following night so the true sunrise would be Monday morning when the police would expect no-one. The decision was left up to individuals after the arguments became circular. We started to pack, ready to leave the site, and make our own way to the Stones. There was a 2pm eviction deadline for the following afternoon; we were expecting to be arrested and didn't want our belongings trashed while we were in custody. We played music by the fire and prayed for a solution, waiting for the time to leave. Suddenly a whooping cheer spread up the site. The police had relented - we had won! We were going to march to Stonehenge with a police escort, vehicles would be allowed to leave the site and park in Amesbury, and we would be allowed to watch the sunrise from a position overlooking the Heel Stone.

At midnight, we marched out of the site led by torchbearers. Down a long lane the procession went, through deep mud and invisible puddles. We were greeted at the A303 by a long line of empty police vans all with lights flashing. Was it a trap? We reached the road safely and saw

Stonehenge 1987 - Sid Rawle Preaches (Boris Atha)

for the first time the size of the procession. There were thousands of us! We walked, and walked, and walked, entertained occasionally by a bright TV light as more footage was put 'in the can.' A 'No U-turn' sign was passed as if it were somehow symbolic. People were stopping exhausted by the road; food and drink were shared as the procession carried on its way. We finally arrived on the road beside Stonehenge at 2.30am, over 2 hours before sunrise. We were barred from the temple by a solid wall of police. Tired bodies demanded rest, so people lay down to await the dawn.

As the light grew, the ticket holders were allowed into the temple. Jeers and cries of 'SCAB' greeted those who had travelled in their luxury coaches laid on by English Heritage. The crowd of pilgrims grew restless and there was pushing and shoving at the police lines. More scuffles broke out, the TV lights came on for their shots of 'hippie violence', but it was over in an instant, the point having been made by both sides.

The 'Druids' emerged for their ceremony, in reality a 19th century 'revival' rather than a genuine ceremony, to be greeted with further jeers. They tried gamely to perform their ritual, perpetually harassed by the press photographers and the obtrusive helicopter. A cheer went up as a hang-glider appeared overhead, as if to land in the Stones, though the helicopter buzzed around him menacingly and he withdrew.

Druids at Stonehenge (Bridget Wishart)

The sky turned blue, then pink as the ritual drumbeats changed from conflict to joyful celebration. The orange sun slowly appeared above the low cloud as the pilgrims erupted into joy. Druids and police were forgotten for a while. Greetings were exchanged as Sid Rawle arrived from Glastonbury. The assembled pagans slowly formed a circle in the road, then two circles, and the ancient spiral dance was performed. A human chain spiralled in and out of a circle, lines of people winding inexorably between one another as a soft chant went up '*Tuate, kiwate, amane, Iano Iano Iano, Unite us - be one, Unite us - be as one.*'

As the dance ended, everyone came together in the middle of the road in a huge warm embrace. The police and press did not quite know what to expect next. Things got quiet and many people started to drift away, though most were determined not to leave until the Stones had been reclaimed. The police changed shifts and the druids went away. Eventually a party in fancy dress, including the cartoon characters Asterix and Getafix, came through the police lines, and Sid followed them back to negotiate. He returned with good news.

People were allowed past police lines in small groups, and then into the Sun Temple itself. Scenes of great emotion were evident as the pilgrims finally reached their Mecca. Sid Rawle, resplendent in multicoloured robes, brought order to the impending chaos by insisting the press and TV pull back so as not to interfere with the forthcoming ritual. Amazingly, they did so.

The pilgrims formed into a large circle, so large that not only were all of the Stones enclosed, but the entire bank and ditch. Sid told of the solstice ritual, when the ashes of Wally Hope were taken to the circle and spread among the faithful, of how much catching up there was to do, babies to be baptised, marriages to be blessed, bereavements to be remembered. He expressed the wish that the day might mark a new beginning, so the movement might start afresh, and that contacts between the pilgrims and the druids, who had refused to perform their ceremony unless all were permitted to attend, should grow. We concluded with ritual chanting, to raise the spirit and end the ceremony in joyous mood. We left well before the 2pm deadline, and returned home via the Rollright Stones, where we fell asleep in the middle of the circle beneath the midday sun, to the amusement of passing tourists.

We've moved on, the Stones are now open for public celebrations at the Solstices and Equinoxes, and the druids, previously aloof and regarded with suspicion by the hippie neo-pagans, have played a major role in the environmental movement and are now regarded as a respected part of the pagan family, rather than the fluffy re-enactment hobbyists they were widely regarded as at the time. Paganism is being increasingly recognised as a 'proper' religion, and many newer pagans take this for granted. Back in 1987 it was not cool to be pagan, there was a hostile press and public out there, and the battles for Stonehenge were the times the people fought back and stood up to be counted.

I remember Prince Andrew once being interviewed about his time in the Falklands saying that he had never felt more alive than when under enemy fire. After the experience of '87, I understood what he was talking about." [This account of my experience at Stonehenge in 1987 was written at the time. Extracts appeared in *Stonehenge - A Peoples' Pilgrimage*, Unique Publications, Glastonbury. (Boris, 2007)]

Steve Bubble: The following year we were not so lucky. Glastonbury wasn't held in 1988 and thousands decided to head for the Stones, this year people pitched up at Cholderton Woods where four thousand of us had a kind of festival in exile before, once again, heading out of the woods at midnight for the walk to Stonehenge. The authorities were ready for us, but allowed us to get within yards of the Stones, forced to stand on the other side of the fence with a senior police officer telling us to behave and stay calm and we'd get in shortly. As he was telling us this, reinforcements were lining up in boiler suits and helmets. When a handful decided to climb the Heel Stone and smoke a chillum a huge cheer went up. They raised a tattered black flag into the air, at which point it was too much for the police who decided to get them down. That set off scuffles, which quickly deteriorated when a small group started to throw the temporary barriers at the police. There were witnesses who reported seeing a number of those throwing stuff at the police show ID and cross police lines, as the mostly peaceful crowd were pushed and battened into the surrounding fields. People suffered head injuries, children were screaming and one nine-year-old had her arm broken. A number of people sat down in protest, believing the police wouldn't do anything in front of TV cameras, merely to be battered too. Thousands streamed across the fields heading back towards Cholderton in the early morning mist, still pushed and hit from behind.

Jerry Richards: You really did have to look out for the authorities because they were coming for people and infiltrating. Some of the stories of MI5 being part of the instigators are true. There was a guy from MI5 who tried to sell guns to 'The Convoy.' Now, who was the 'The Convoy', well, everybody and nobody, right? But he'd wormed his way in there, looked the part. Walked the walk and talked the talk, and tried to sell guns thinking we'd be paranoid and bloodthirsty enough to want to take his weapons to defend ourselves against the police. Absolute madness and he was chucked off site and exposed for what he was - an MI5 mole.

Michael Dog: There was a train of thought that suggested the Stonehenge Campaign itself had been infiltrated by *agents-provocateurs*, people who were associated with the government. It's not impossible, though you've got to beware of going on a paranoia trip with this sort of thing. In my view the post-1985 festival scene destroyed itself. I don't see that it was brought down by outside influence. I don't see that it died because the police made it hard to run festivals in certain parts of the country, because in other parts of the country, like Hampshire, they didn't give a hoot. That last Torpedo Town, the police didn't stop people going to the festival; the people themselves wrecked the festival. But it's hard not to wonder whether elements of straight-society, or people in Government, had decided the way to break this scene once and for all was from the inside. You can go one way and say, 'Oh that's just paranoid nonsense and it was actually just a bunch of irresponsible people who let this thing slip through their fingers.' Or you can see the other point of view, that there were people who were put into this situation and had pressure put on them, or maybe incentives were offered to them to wreck the movement from inside. The fact was that heroin use and dealing became a bigger and bigger aspect of the festival and traveller scene, seemingly unregulated and unstoppable... and un-stopped by the authorities. The establishment seemed happy to allow an element of the scene, basically travelling junkies, to just carry on what they were doing. On the Stonehenge Campaign there seemed to be individuals hell-bent on wrecking that movement on the inside, prominent individuals who spent more time creating dissent within than actually doing something useful.

Jerry Richards: I think there were a lot of political diversions. There'd just been the Falklands War and [the authorities] were looking for people to divert attention on to. The police that came at us were the ones that had been on the miners' strikes, at Orgreave, and they were tough people, I mean really tough. So the authorities used these people on the hippies, on the travellers. If you think about it, this could have been one of the reasons why Thatcher was deposed, because things had to change. The police were under a spotlight where they had to answer to things in the press, people asking difficult questions. But they also had to look at themselves and decide whether they were going to be used by *whichever* political party to be their political assault force and do the party's bidding. Now, the police may be whatever the police are, and I'm not anti-police, but they don't want to find themselves used as political pawns, because they're going to get a bad rep. The police are there to stop people ripping you off or attacking you, that's what they're there for, not to protect property but to protect us. But they find themselves at the end of some politician's tryst up in London, who wants to make office again next time the election comes and who'll use any diversion available. They'd use the miners' strike, Falklands War... Thatcher had been elected three times, John Major after her, and we were a happy distraction whilst they did whatever they did – like selling off the nation's assets. So the Americans own the Royal Train – how do you figure that one out? The French, the Spanish and Germans own our gas... then there's the telecommunications, so they'd flogged off the silverware. And this was the legacy from the Second World War, that sense of social conscience that tackled Beveridge's 'Five Giants' [want, disease, squalor, ignorance, idleness] which is where we got the National Health Service from. The people who'd fought the war had rebuilt the country's infrastructure. In some sense, all of us festival crew were children of that sensibility, we'd grown up with all of that. We might have rejected part of it in wanting to live the alternative lifestyle but the values were there, that you helped your fellow people. Now it's all about 'me' and 'I want it now and I want it faster' and if you make your own stuff it's kind of looked down on, seen as a bit naff. Now, for me growing up, if you wanted embroidered jeans, you embroidered them yourself, you didn't go to GAP or Prada! You did it yourself and that was what was cool about it. People would say, 'Bloody hell, man, where did you get that?' Well you went down the shops and got some needle and thread. Stitch one, purl one! That sort of sensibility where you made your own stuff has a thrill to it. So, if you were a *fashionista* at the festivals, hey, get real! You'd see all of these wonderful, colourful shirts all dyed, and special fatigues, and be aware of the amount of creative energy in these art students, or former art students, potters (as I was) – all these talents.

Michael Dog: My personal conspiracy theory is that if you accept that there were elements within the Thatcher government that set out to change the face of society, then they got what they set out to achieve. If you study the history of society, then the key to effecting a transition to any kind of totalitarian regime is to create a generational break. Suddenly there's a huge gap between an older generation that knows how it used to be and a younger generation that have no idea how it used to be. That's what we've come to now. For the people who came of age between 1990 and 2000, and even really to the present day, there isn't an alternative culture any more. There's nothing for them to slot into. I feel very fortunate; I came of age at a time when that culture still existed and I just fell into it. There were lots of festivals, underground publications, bands and all the political movements were there. I just found them and went, 'that's me' and I joined the club. For people coming of age in the 90s, that club wasn't there any more for them to find some sense of purpose or belonging. And now, that whole culture is a thing of the past. It shouldn't be, but for young people now, there's nothing for them to slot into.

Nigel Mazlyn Jones: I've been travelling around Britain and Europe since 1975 and I've been in a good position to compare things and I'm completely outraged about the way the country is and its [lack] of rights and freedoms. The counterculture movement, complementary medicine, alternative thinking, has always been there, it's never gone away. A lot of what it espoused has now become both mainstream and very corporate: Body Shop, Centre for Alternative Technology as advisors to ICI, ethical investments, the huge graphic industry that is employed by Greenpeace and Friends of the Earth, the massive administration structure right the way up through the qualified people who are on immense salaries *for* Greenpeace and Friends of the Earth. It's a huge corporate structure turning over millions, or billions, of pounds. A constantly moving volcano that's being fed from underneath and lots of elements of it are bubbling and difficult and not accepted by society. But out of the top of it eventually comes the heat and steam that creates your Greenpeace or your Friends of the Earth that has an impact to the viewer. You can't see what's going on in the volcano but you can see the point at the top. I think that's how the counterculture does feed how we move forward as a society, that's how we are still vaguely a democracy; people are forced to debate issues because everybody's got so much knowledge on-board. I go back to Harry Hart, who started Green Deserts, and I was twenty-eight years of age and I came across all this information. I saw all the slides he'd taken, and I'd made a point of going to find the core people and listen to them sitting around the campfires, what was being debated, what they were going to do, and I was deeply inspired by the core issue. Yes it was an entertaining cross-cultural event with tepees over there and Romany caravans over there – but for that melting pot of humanity, think of all the youngsters who learned stuff. Move forward to the rave culture and you will have pockets... the early *Whirl-Y-Gig* raves were set up by humanists. Those humanists booked me to do the Parachute Chill-out Tent in the 1990s; I first met them at Rougham Tree Fayre in the 70s, sitting playing under the trees. Those humanists became very impressive social workers, dealing with drug addiction in the heavy parts of London. They didn't start *Whirl-Y-Gig* to make money; they started as a like-minded group of adults, and all from that counterculture, who'd got older and recognised there was a huge youth problem. They thought, 'Let's not have thump, thump, thump, mechanical auto-robot music, let's use world roots music. It's wonderfully educational, it's a lovely vibe, it's great to dance to, and you can get the same rhythms as the thumping auto-music.' So, wonderfully successful *Whirl-Y-Gig* raves, running at Hammersmith Town Hall, all the festivals, all the mainstream things like Peter Gabriel's WOMAD, mainstream acceptance. They got through their doors at their raves over a million people, I'd have thought. Now, I remember being at events with *Whirl-Y-Gig* and being there before my gig, which wasn't going to be until three o'clock in the morning because I was doing the chill-out, and listening to youngsters of all backgrounds and they'd be chilling-out drinking flavoured mineral water, because there was no alcohol. They'd be in the café or in the chill-out rooms and they'd be discussing stuff and it would be absolutely mind-blowing to hear their intelligent terms, talking about different issues that they were active on, like green activities or raising money for some socially-aware event that wasn't being funded.

Michael Dog: [Unemployment] galvanised people into either feeling pissed-off about the situation they were in or wanting to react against the yuppie ideal, whereas now the yuppie ideal has become the norm. The Thatcherites forced the bulk of British society to go and get a job because they had to pay rent and it became almost impossible to claim benefit and to lead that alternative lifestyle, which requires you *not* to be doing a nine-to-five job. I debate this with my son, who grew up very much involved in the things I was involved in. He went to festivals from when he was two and, for his peer-group, has a fairly privileged upbringing in that he just about remembers what it was like and is very frustrated with the apathy of his own generation. But he understands that as they left school and went into life they were immediately obliged to get jobs and settle into a nine-to-five. It takes up so much of their time and brain-space that they don't have the time or energy to do very much else. He figures it's completely down to that. He's forever ranting and railing that anybody he knows who is involved in art of any sort be it music, video or fine art feels so obliged to produce art that will sell that they see it as pointless to produce art for art's sake. That if it isn't going to sell, there's no point in producing it at all. So the Thatcherites got want they wanted.

Jeremy Cunningham: I got a lot of hassle [on the road], everybody did, but I learned early on to play the game with the police. The police were quite happy, as long as you'd go along with them. When I first started getting pulled over on the roadside, which used to happen all the time, the immediate reaction was to lean out the window and start shouting obscenities but I remember doing that once and this copper started to look around the front of the vehicle and he said, 'If you carry on shouting at me like that, I can think of a hundred and twenty violations for this vehicle' and pulled out this long sheet of paper. I thought, 'Maybe this isn't the right way of going about it' so after that, when I got stopped, I'd be going 'Oh, how are you, officer? Everything alright?' We called it 'playing the game', as long as you showed that they had some kind of authority and were nice to them, they usually moved on to the next guy, who was pissed and wanted to fight with them! They used to let us go, most of the time. We did have trouble but it was usually only when you'd get a lot of vehicles all together, before the days of mobile phones when we were all trying to find a festival site or a rave. You'd have fifty buses going up the road one way, then coming down the other and you'd see the ones coming down the road, 'Oh, they must know the way.' Eventually pagers came in and we could find the sites straight away! I'd usually travel with a group of about six or seven vehicles, not a big group. When we'd go to a festival it might end up as a big group, the Peace Convoy and all that, but I didn't live with a big group.

Bridget Wishart: I think there was the thing of people taking over the Convoy and moving in and the Brew Crew becoming an ever-bigger element. Other people who had been part of the scene and had put up with a certain amount of anarchy and drug-dealing just moved away, moved to Spain… 'This isn't why I moved onto the road or moved into a vehicle.'

Martin: I went to the last Elephant Fayre, in '85 or '86 and the reason [the organiser] never had another one was that the Peace Convoy turned up there. It definitely wasn't a hippie, 'Save the Earth' kind of thing. My memory of it was a very kind of punk, 'I'm in it for what I can get, fuck the lot of you.' But then, if you take a group of people who are very alienated in the first place, and then herd them around with a heavy police presence then you may well push them in that direction. Now, that was definitely my experience, having said that, and I visited quite a few sites that my brother was at, and there *were* family people there. I'd say the common factor that linked everybody was drugs, was a lifestyle, but there were family people there, I wouldn't say nobody there was looking after their kids. There was a *mix* of people, but most of the places I visited were places that had been found for people to park up. I think at the time, the strategy was to try and break up this huge entity and try and make life difficult for them. In Longwell Green, in Bristol, a piece of wasteland that's now a big industrial estate, there were a lot of vehicles there for a very long period of time and it was just Smack Central, it was a really bad place. So it went from that Haight-Ashbury idyll of '*If you're going to San Francisco / Be sure to wear flowers in your hair*' to just a really degraded, everybody washed out, drugged out sort of place, really.

Hippie Van Man: Winter '91-'92, I bought and converted a Bedford Vega 31 Coach and moved in full-time, with the intention of spending 1992 on the road. I got the job of taking a load of jugglers down to Glastonbury. We had the vehicle pass and were told to pick up the people passes when we got there. When we got there we had to wait in line outside, oddly enough the TK behind me in the queue was owned and lived in by a girl who lived opposite me when I was a kid. Neither of us knew about each other living on the road! After fourteen hours of queuing we were eventually let in, just to be booted out again after three hours for selling cider… I never really wanted to be there anyway. On the upside, we found our way to the free alternative, which was at the old airfield near Smeathorpe. There were loads of folk there and a few very loud raves. I moved the bus after a few hours because the sound system near us was so loud and always seemed to be turned up to number 11 even when there was nobody dancing; it seemed the owners or folk who ran these systems didn't give a toss about other festival-goers. We went into the village for some bits and bobs and in the grocer's shop we got talking to a few locals. They were disgusted at how much money must have been spent on policing the site; the police helicopter was causing a greater disturbance to them than the noise from the festival. I'd become disillusioned with the whole thing. Raves seemed to have taken over and I was sick of the sight of police helicopters. In early '93 we were staying in a lay-by on the A34 and a mate turned up in his Hedingham bus on his way down to the Avon Free Festival; this ended in fiasco in a service station on the M5. We were eventually forced onto the motorway and pushed north, the police kept overtaking the convoy and blocked off the exits, again and again. When folk ran out of fuel they were arrested… what a load of bollocks. This marked the end of the festivals for me, I sold the bus and moved into a Commer Walkthru [Van], then in late '94 I moved onto the canal and finally in 2004 we moved to Orkney. I thought I'd happened upon a way of living in the UK that was kind of Utopian, and sometimes it was, but I'd discovered it too late. For me, the raves killed off the real free festivals. I'm just glad I saw a few old style festivals before they disappeared. To quote [Radical Dance Faction] '*I caught a glimpse.*' The whole experience of the festivals and living on the road has had a lasting effect on me. I still keep a living van and I'm proud to say have never stayed on a campsite. After nearly twenty years I still have dreams where I'm at free festivals… maybe subconsciously I'm still longing for those days… I've absolutely no regrets.

Simon Williams: A lot of us all went out to Europe after Thatcher started attacking our scene, went to festivals in Italy and Germany and Holland. They were fun and comparatively new and it was a good scene to be a part of. But it was different in that it wasn't so linked to the Pagan calendar and the hippie vibe that was prevalent in Britain. In Italy, because they have such a right-wing government at times, to have parties or festivals, the organisers will actually identify themselves as being very left-wing. The reason for that is because if it's seen as hippies with no specific agenda it's easy to shut it down. If they say, 'You are suppressing our human rights because we're left-wing people,' then that's a political card they can play. They'd have two-thousand-capacity venues with their own radio station and their own printing press and do everything themselves. It was comparable from that point of view, but probably better organised! The British way was to say, date, place and everything else would just happen, provided everyone turned up.

Gary Bamford: After the clampdown in 1990 we ended up living in Berlin for a few years. It was as close as you could get to that free festival thing. Berlin was something else. We'd gone there about a month before the Wall came down, with something like ten vehicles, and did one show in the East one night, and then one show in the West. We ended up moving onto a site on no-man's-land in an area of Berlin called Kreitzberg which was like a white Brixton. If you went to West Berlin, you didn't have to join the German army, so all the freaks and people who wanted to drop out went there. There were lots of squats, lots of bombed-out streets, and a massive punk scene. It was like a free festival just being in that city, hundreds of vehicles parked on no-man's-land. Lots of squatted streets in the East, the place was in chaos. Six months later they were demolishing streets with people in them. There'd be helicopters overhead, and you'd hear sirens going off all the time. There weren't many bands, no site bands, but people were living in bowvans, big trailers that get pulled into construction areas for workmen to have their breaks in. You'd find a couple of fields and there'd be twenty, thirty bowvans all quite tidy and organised; we'd turn up with that British mentality of madness, and people falling out of vans and heaving beer cans around. So we'd look out of place, not up-to-date or tidy enough, because we were still used to being evicted once a week whereas they'd stayed still for a while and got quite organised.

Jeremy Cunningham: We all lived in Amsterdam for a while, on a big travellers' site there. When it started to get bad in the late 80s we thought, 'Just fuck it, we'll go abroad', because we'd heard there was this site in Amsterdam and the laws there were a lot more liberal than they were in Britain, so we lived over there for six months until it got bulldozed. When you went to a squat in Amsterdam, it was nicer than most people's flats... I couldn't believe it. Whereas squats in the UK were pretty rough and ready affairs, people over there, because they had been living in them for ten or fifteen years, they were much more together about everything. There was a big free festival there, called the Last Bus Shelter which was the name of the travellers' site in the East Docks and was the last stop on the bus route; now it's a big housing estate. 2000DS were over there with us as well, I knew Gary very well. They had this huge old Greenpeace coach that they lived in, a massive great thing, towing a trailer on the back of it with a recording studio in it. When they turned up it was always guaranteed chaos! When we were in Amsterdam, Gary and the DS of the day, because they frequently changed line-ups, went off to live in Berlin... probably because they found living in Amsterdam too easy, not confrontational enough, so they went to live in Berlin! Everyone else was just looking for a peaceful life!

Oz Hardwick: I was affected on a very deep, personal level. I felt a profound despair. For a long time, I lost the belief that one could make a difference. It took a very long time to regain a sense of purpose.

Michael Dog: I think the scene imploded on itself by becoming too cocky. I don't think becoming too big was the problem. I don't believe it attracted lots and lots of nasty people. My memories are that on the whole, people were there for all the right reasons and very respectful. It's only the later festivals, post 1985, that slowly but surely attracted people who weren't there for *any* of the right reasons. But people had taken it for granted that you could do these things and cock a snoot at the authorities and in retrospect I saw that *that* had brought about the demise. People didn't realise how brutal the Thatcher regime was, *until* it was. We were blessed in the 60s and 70s with relatively benign governments and nobody was prepared for how brutal and how hard-line the Thatcherite regime would be.

I've always wondered whether there was some Tory think-tank at the time that realised there was this quite large and relatively influential alternative scene based around squatting, the underground press and free festivals and other aspects of that scene, that wasn't exactly a threat to them but couldn't be allowed. The mid-80s were really the darkest days of Thatcherism and I guess it pulled people to either being a part of that or not being a part of it at all. Stonehenge being a victim of its own success, with more people hearing about it and wanting to go, and the hardening of the political atmosphere, probably forced people to decide which camp they were in. Of course, after 1984 fewer and fewer people went to the festivals. I personally feel the government set out to fragment that movement and they were very successful at doing so. It was no accident that they made squatting illegal – it wasn't really about protecting the rights of property owners, that wasn't their prime motivation, they realised that squatting was a key element of the alternative scene. When I was a kid, or a teenager, when you finished school you could leave home and go and live in a squat and live on very little money and pursue the lifestyle that you wanted to pursue. If you wanted to do music, or arts, or politics, or whatever, on a cheap budget, you could squat. By taking away squatting, it falls to people to have to earn a living and get a job. And by forcing people into having to get a job, they couldn't devote time to these other things unless they had money from other sources. It was a quite deliberate policy. Of course, what happened after 1985 was that they used more and more Draconian powers to break up the festival movement. But sadly, from my own point of view, I think the festival movement destroyed itself.

The words on the poster are so ironically true; 'the peace and tranquillity....will be totally ruined' ...the site was a mess! It became a dust bowl... too many people, too few facilities...

Laurence and his axes, A44 layby site (Dave Fawcett)

Danny's Story

Danny is the editor of the fanzine back2front and reflects here on the festival scene in Ireland alongside his recollections of the aftermath of the Beanfield.

Danny: In 1985 two travellers found their vehicle smashed up by police at the infamous Beanfield debacle in which Margaret Thatcher enforced social control and the neo-conservative agenda on people travelling to Stonehenge for the People's Free Festival. Those two travellers eventually made their way to Belfast, after continuing harassment by the State, aided and abetted by the one-dimensional tabloid media witch hunt that passed for news. New Age Refugee was one term in use at the time. We spotted one of them busking on the streets, said hello and before you could say *anarcho-syndicalism* they were sharing our squat, telling us of the police harassment and the free festival scene which had emerged out of the heady days of the 1960s.

Being from Belfast we could identify with State harassment and police abuse, but as anarchists we could see the beauty in the free festival idea and were keen to find out more. Because of the ongoing paramilitary and security presence, new ideas didn't easily take root in Northern Ireland and yet Ireland itself has a long history, one of the longest in Europe, of a free festival tradition probably centred on the old pagan wheel of the year, from solstice to equinox and the cross-quarter days in between. In 1988, keen to find out more, a few of us packed our ruck-sacks and headed off in the general direction of Stonehenge. It's a long story as to how we eventually got to the A303 in early June, including rather innocently asking a friendly bobby directions from Bath. As a reputable ambassador of the State he kindly pointed us in the opposite direction! A bus stopped for us and we ended up at the Silchester Free Festival where we joined with the London Walk group who were making their way across country towards the summer solstice festival, hopefully at Stonehenge. Silchester, set among old Roman ruins, was a real eye-opener. It was such a positive experience seeing all these people gathered peacefully enjoying the sun, the music and the freedom. There was a good punk band on the little stage and Hawkwind (as Hawkdog, I think) headlined. It was a running joke that they would headline every festival.

There was one bit of trouble. A gang of Brew Crew, bent on hassling anyone for money, drink, and food. They actually drove over the tents of people who refused them. I was taken aback that nobody would do anything about this, and that's sometimes where non-violence falls down. A few of us did confront them and they were eventually driven off.

After Silchester, we moved off. A hired minibus would carry everyone's tat, whilst each morning we agreed a place to meet. We went cross-country, probably thirty to forty of us at the start, taking in some of the wilder parts still left in the countryside, camping by night and sharing vegan food. Richard led us. He lived in Australia, taxied in Germany and came back to England for the summer festivals. He was a kind, considerate and very welcoming character who made you feel at ease with his confidence and experience. There was also a homeopath whose name I forget who helped anyone feeling unwell. The others were a real eclectic mix of travellers, anarcho-punks, old hippies and ne'er-do-wells but everyone was accommodating. We had all sorts of discussions *en route* about how the festival scene had changed over the years – we spoke of Belfast and we all agreed that Mrs Thatcher wouldn't be invited to our collective future.

We eventually reached Cholderton Woods, about seven miles or so from Stonehenge, but due to police activity in the general area we couldn't get any further. By that stage our numbers had dwindled but what was fascinating for me was that we were the first at the woods and waking next morning we watched as a few others began to arrive and set up camp, then a few more and the whole thing began to unfold organically. Soon there were naked men and women on horseback, campfires and food, music and festivity and all the while the din of Harrier Jump Jets, helicopters and police loudspeaker warnings in what had been one of the biggest police operations since the Miners' Strike only a few years before. On the whole the experience was amazing, thousands of people gathered and the only trouble was a few misinformed souls trying to burn live wood or dismantling fencing. Others would explain, spades were offered for going to the loo. It remains an example that people can come and work together to celebrate without the use of money or heavy-handed control measures.

On the night of the solstice a few bands played, with the mighty Culture Shock playing a blinder and rallying everyone towards marching towards the Stones. It was all very surreal. We packed our sacks intending to head onwards the next day – but first joined the march to the Stones. As we got closer more and more police began to appear, until the Stones appeared in the distance and it was like something from a movie. Inside the barbed-wire fence, a line of riot police stood while helicopters with search beams filled the air. We were right at the front and with a surge the crowd pushed over the fence. A few people climbed the Heel Stone, which encouraged the crowd further, but there was a standoff and we were pushed back. In the background Ken Barlow [William Roache] and the druids were doing their thing.

[**Dick Lucas:** There was a lot of respect. The druids weren't all dressed up for the ceremonies, just like average people walking round the site so you wouldn't know which one was a druid and which one wasn't, there were no tattoos or anything! [Laughs] They did their thing, it was something that ultimately we didn't know about but there was a cautious interest and respect for what they were doing because it was very old. I don't like religions but it wasn't *really* religious, it was worshipping things you can see, like the sun, and the stones and the grass and the sky… nature… so it kind of makes sense.]

We went to the back of the crowd. It was about 4.30am and we were tired. I got out a sleeping bag and decided to have a rest, telling my mate to wake me for sunrise. He did. Only he was pulling me along in the sleeping bag in one hand with both rucksacks slung over his shoulder as riot cops used truncheon and boot indiscriminately. And that was Stonehenge Free Festival 1988. We left and headed on, sticking our thumbs out at a roundabout not far from Woodhenge, but two squaddies were circling the roundabout in a jeep and each time they passed they were shooting ball-bearings from a duck-caddy. My mate got hit, and went down. There was nowhere to shelter. This was the way travellers were treated in the UK for the crime of celebration. Luckily a car stopped and took us to Marlborough. They gave my friend a balm for his wound which worked very quickly. As they put the balm back in the car and said farewell, we noticed the druidic robes folded neatly in the boot.

Later that year we also made our way to Chanctonbury Ring, a rather curious place, and destination of a free festival after the Cissbury Ring event had been cancelled. We arrived and there was one truck, but by nightfall a few hundred people had gathered and we sold sweeties to them, to help pay for our food and transport. There was no police presence, which made this a very relaxing and inspiring event. After a stint squatting in Wales we ended up in a squat in Brighton, formerly occupied by the band Gong. The folk who lived there were the same ones who had climbed the Heel Stone at Stonehenge earlier that year. There are many tales of coincidence to tell, including how a friend of ours had been arrested for the grand crime of "violent disorder (while running away from a police officer)" at Stonehenge a few weeks before the solstice. Deciding that the charge was ridiculous he headed off to Holland for some work he had lined up, but on returning he was arrested at Harwich for non-attendance at court over the charge and was whisked off to Wiltshire. Ironically when he did go to court two certain squaddies were up before him, charged with firing ball-bearings and causing a vehicle to go off the road shortly after the event at Stonehenge!

Eventually we came back to Ireland, inspired by what we had seen. Now there were events going on in different parts of Ireland, but compared to England, these were small scale affairs. There had been a big event outside Dublin, against nuclear proliferation, in 1985. In the early 80s a gathering around the solstice at Fleskwater, in the north-east, had become a regular event, and by the late 1980s this was a regular free festival attracting hundreds of people. In 1989 there was an attempt to hold a festival just outside Belfast at Giant's Ring, an ancient circular embankment with central dolmen. Quite a few showed up but the lack of PA spelt the end of that event. As Fleskwater continued, there was also a regular free event called Frankie's Hooley with quite a few bands playing every year. With the advent of rave, these events became smaller and eventually fizzled out, though other small-scale events continued to go on.

In hindsight the free festival concept was a continuation of the carnival spirit that is present in every tribal and village culture throughout the world, when everyone worked together, bringing along the best of harvest and craft to celebrate life. The festival movement which was reborn at Windsor following the free happenings of the Freaks of the 60s, was an affirmation that society was drifting hazardously away from the natural world and towards a conceited and self-serving State which placed the profits of a few at the expense of all. The festivals were not highly politicised in nature, however, being generally peaceful events but towards the end of the 80s there was a surge in anarcho-punk involvement with Crass, The Mob and Chumbawamba and others playing at these events, which brought social concern and direct action centre stage. Festivals began to coincide with anti-nukes or animal rights protests. It began to be seen as a threat. The Stop the City marches in London in 1983/84 cost the city millions of pounds and so the clampdown began.

Rave On

Though the festivals had been an ever-evolving entity that took their identities from the geographical landscape and sense of history as much as they did from the political and social landscapes of their day, until the mid 80s they could at least be seen as a part of one continuous thread. What we discovered as we talked through the development of the Rave culture, towards the end of the free festival movement, was that many 'traditional' free festival-goers saw the Rave scene as an unwelcome interloper that had little in common with the tone of the gatherings they were used to.

Jake Stratton-Kent: Raves were condensed festivals. You couldn't go and camp up on Stonehenge for a month or six weeks, you had to cram it all into an evening with an illegal rave and the drugs got stronger for that reason. You've got to cram that whole experience into one night. It had a similar ethos in some ways; there are lots of crossovers, making your own fun in a society that hasn't given you much. One blurred fairly seamlessly into the other and you don't notice the changes starting until you are a bit further down the road.

Michael Dog: Ecstasy becoming widely available was the catalyst for change, because many hippie types resisted dance music and for a couple of years the two scenes were mutually exclusive. So there were people who only went to see space-rock stuff and there were people who only went to dance music events. And then there was a crossover point where I guess it reached critical mass. If you were a hard-line hippie who only listened to guitar music you might have had these friends around you going 'Oh, I just took this drug and I went to one of these raves and it's really good, I really enjoyed it.' I think there's something innocent about those first few times of taking Ecstasy and going to a rave, you never look back... like the first time you took acid and life was never the same afterwards. So the passing of the space-rock musical form was just down to that and people moved on.

Angel: I went to India in 1981/82 and I was on top of a hill in Anjuna, in Goa, and I remember hearing this rave and thinking, 'What is *that*?' It was music, but it was music that I'd never heard before. 'What *is* that sound?' The lights flashing, that certain dance, the way people were moving their bodies was completely different to anything I'd ever seen before, with these incredible colourful clothes which were obviously a part of it, the whole regalia, you know; wild, funky, crazy, colourful rave clothes. It was the light, the sound, the dance… and of course it hadn't hit the whole London scene yet, hadn't come here at all. That was where I first saw it... the whole festival rave scene was there. When that hit our scene, at first there was a wonderful infusion, such as at Treworgey in 1989 when the raves were happening alongside the festival. Again it's the same like-minded thing. It's very anti-society and very anarchistic. The original concept was about light and sound elevating the brain to a certain level where you could then step into another realm within your head. Drugs entered into that equation along the way but the initial concept was about light and sound on brain activity. Different ones complemented different times and different things. That was the very nature of it.

Morton Lighthouse Free Party July 1991 (Dave Fawcett)

Hippie Van Man: In '91 we went to Wales. 'Happy Daze' in Bala (Gwynedd) was my most memorable one that year; we met up with some mates who were spending the summer in a bender. It was here that we first encountered a *rave*. It was odd to see so many straight folk on a free festival site, but the sound system itself didn't seem to be too imposing and the festival was still very much a traditional kind of affair. On the Sunday morning you could see ravers walking around looking bemused at all the weird trucks and buses and crustie types. There was a Reliant Robin there on the Friday morning being driven around, then on Saturday it was being pushed around and had lost its windows. Then on the Sunday it went up in flames, a great black cloud of smoke billowing up into the summer sky. This was followed by a nasty fistfight between two blokes. Parked just by us was a fellow who had turned the back of his truck into a kind of shack with a veranda, like those shacks you see in the Deep South of America. He was sitting in his rocking-chair shouting, 'Tequila Slammers makes your head go fizzy, wizzy, pop' all day long. Then come Sunday morning he'd be shouting 'Lucozade, Lucozade' ... well sussed! I think a lot changed that year...

Gary Bamford: It's just money and availability and business, isn't it? People get addicted easily, and bored easily, and compete with each other on drugs. They can't do music without drugs and they can't do drugs without music, one feeds the other and it's all just business at the end. What pissed me off, people would turn up with a marquee to put on a performance – artists and bands and stuff – and the next year the same people would turn up and they wouldn't put a band on, it was just a rave so that they could sell Ecstasy. How can you turn your back on something that you've been part of all your life just to make some money out of that shit? I departed from so many people because they just weren't in the same scene anymore; over one summer! They weren't keeping their roots or doing anything that was tribal, they were just jumping on the back of something. 1987, we were *selling* our big squats so they could have parties in them, at the end. Ravers would just come up, we'd have three days left, 'Yeah, you can have the last two days. Give us a grand, see you later.' They started their big parties in London at places we'd had, and that got into the festival scene because people found it so much easier to turn up with a PA, a marquee and a DJ. 'Here's an E, there you go, turn the lights on.' Why didn't it all mix properly? Why didn't they get that side going, and that side, and do the whole thing full-on, because you'd have had double the amount of people, double the amount of *energy* - rather than DJs going 'Oh, we've had enough of watching all those posing bands that go on for ages.' That was great, because I didn't like them either, but let's find a compromise and keep the whole thing going because we need everybody. You can go 'They're musicians, they've come to entertain people for free, walking across fields with their instruments... let them play somewhere.' Don't just say 'We don't put bands on any more, we're having a rave.' But that's what happened.

Mark Wright: For some time after this new phenomenon started, there was the 'live music versus sound system' debate. Many felt that the sound systems were a bit of an invasion, but over time people were won over as they did bring in the punters. The first Es appeared, and at fifteen pounds each to the punters they weren't cheap, but they were fantastic, not like the rubbish quid-a-go shit available today. On site they were about a tenner, so there was easy money to be made. This had its up sides and its down. It's good for people to make some money but how many egg butties or veg curries does someone have to sell to make the same as selling one pill? In my opinion this was the beginning of the end. We'd had some fantastic years, but Pandora's Box had been opened. After a while people were doing so many pills that they were searching for something to help with the comedowns at the end of the festivals, and heroin got in by the back door. At first it was done quite quietly but over time it took hold of entire sites. Also the 'Party, Party' at almost all costs was all well and good for those who went back to their squat sites in the city, but for the rest of us we had to deal with the fallout all year round. You have to remember that a lot of travellers kept themselves to themselves but what was happening on the party scene affected everyone. People stopped working together. They would stand back when trouble started, when in the past we would all stand together.

Gary Bamford: The punk thing, the music was full-on, but the scene was a bit drab because of the venues and the problems you'd get with bouncers. Then the travellers' scene, the venues were great and there was no hassle with bouncers or anything like that, but the music was a bit more tranquil because of it. Then you'd have bands like Chaos UK or Disorder coming in and doing their bit, so you did have that punk element. But that went a long time ago and we were the last of it. But you know, the punks called us travellers and the travellers thought we were punks. The punks couldn't handle us because we lived on the sites, but the travellers *could* handle us being punks. Look, put three bands on after each other in a pub and they're all going to be the same in the way they act or put their gig over. Put three bands in a field and you'd hope they'd loosen up a bit, have a few chillums with people in the crowd and have a laugh. But everybody wants to be structured. Go and nick some music equipment from school and put a band together; *that's* punk rock. The kids now in the same situation are all MCs and DJs, so the bad boys are all DJ'd up and MC'd when in the past people like that would become musicians. People would be adding different bits but a DJ is just that *thing*, you know? Someone's got a sound system and some records of *somebody else* and it's so strange. And it's drugs again, because there's no way they'd have sold Ecstasy… imagine what it was like for us as people in 1987 crawling around in the mud, jumping up and down to 'Scrap the Church' and all these mad songs that we had and smoking chillums and whatever. And a couple of years later it becomes 'I can't watch your band on Ecstasy, man.' Well, fucking don't then. There's no way Techno would have come through without the mass sales of Ecstasy. People couldn't go out and dance to Techno unless they'd done an E.

Sim Simmer: Spiral Tribe came together around about 1989, 1990; people from all walks of life going to squat parties, hanging out in London. We started putting on parties towards the end of 1990, just quite innocently really; we had a squat in North London, a school house, and our first parties were put on there and that was where we forged our friendship, a general theme of everybody coming together to make things happen. I was working in a PA hire shop, there were graphic artists doing backdrops... the energy was there. There'd been the whole 1988 acid house thing, but a lot of us were quite poor and couldn't go to clubs. It was a force of us making it happen without having to go to big M25 parties, although we all did go to those sort of things at certain points. We'd put on our own parties and after that the core were really committed to taking it a bit further and putting on regular things, so we got together a sound system and started finding venues and putting on more parties. We got a bit of a following, everyone was taking part, and there was a real mixture of music, a real mix of people.

Mark Wright: One year, after the usual messing about trying to get to Stonehenge we ended up at Longstock. It was well named as it was in an old drove. The site itself was about half a mile long. This was the first festival with a rave sound system. Also it was when meat came back onto site in a big way with someone selling 'Murder Burgers'. Soon after pulling up we were approached by some punter type wanting a generator to run their sound system. I was a little suspicious, I'd never seen this guy before, but after taking a deposit at least equal in value to the generator off he went with my genny. As it happened, the sound system was Spiral Tribe. We had had some traveller sound systems before but this was possibly the first time real outsiders had set up on site, and they didn't get off to a good start. In those days setting up your sound system outside peoples' trucks and trailers, and blasting out 24 hours a day did not make you popular. I've read a bit about Spiral Tribe in *Altered State* by Matthew Collin [but] Spiral Tribe were not organisers or co-ordinators at the free festivals… maybe at their raves. Reading the section on Spiral Tribe you'd think they were our saviours. I don't think anybody followed the ST fashion style, in fact quite the reverse. For a more altruistic, 'we are one' thing, DIY and The Free Party People would be a better place to look. DIY were from Nottingham. Freaky Phil was still carrying around the pyramid tent (loaned or given by Hawkwind I believe).

Sim Simmer: We all took a weekend off and went down to the Avon Free Festival and that was wicked. We didn't have our sound system with us but it really inspired us to bring it out of London and find out when the next festival was. Back in town, we organised a 'Leaving London' party, packed up everything on our truck and headed off to Longstock, which was like a displaced Stonehenge Festival for 1991. Some of us had a bit more knowledge of it all, but for me, I'd been to Glastonbury the year before and that had blown me away. I'd been quite sheltered and didn't know things like that existed. It all unfolded for us once we'd got to Longstock and set up our rig; a bunch of squatters from London turning up not really knowing what to expect. It was amazing. It blew us all away, being outside under the night sky, seeing the sun rise in the morning, dancing; it just worked amazingly. That was it for us, we had to move forwards like that. The following week we gravitated to the next place, which was Stoney Cross. As this happened and you got talking to people, some would talk about the Beanfield and how crushed and political the whole travelling scene had become. We were all communicating with each other sharing stories, but it seemed disheartened at the time. There were a lot of unhappy people, if you like, who were perhaps a bit nervous about the music because that was quite different, it wasn't like a band stage, a different concept. That's quite normal, a new thing comes along and it takes a bit of communication to understand that you all come from the same place essentially. Things around you have changed but the concept of being free, in your mind, making things happen and living autonomously is pretty much the same; it's just a different look. Nothing was planned, there was no great conspiracy to come along and bring the travelling festival scene on top and for it to never happen again, that was never... no one had that plan, it just unfolded and took its course and evolved. Looking back, it's a bit of a cloud as things were happening so fast, so furious... like a whirlwind. Some had a problem with us but the majority didn't. It became our life, we lived it, breathed it, every day. There was no possible way... we'd come so far there was no way [of going back], we were on a mission and it was working. Things were connecting, we'd somehow miraculously get from one festival to the next, people would help, people would take part, it would have been insane to somehow go, 'Okay, we've got to go back...,' that wasn't an option. A lot of people who came out to the events were holding it down and going back to work, but the mental shift in everyone was pretty unanimous. I look back now, and it's almost taken twenty years to talk about it, I think a lot of people feel like that; we're reconnecting now with people on Facebook or Myspace, it has been a massive shift in people's consciousness, they're still on that dance floor.

1991 was an incredible summer. We did Camelford, which went on for two weeks; you do a festival for three or four days, you get in a mindset but extending that for two weeks, the music continuing non-stop, the sun rises, the sun sets, the night sky, is a really intense experience. At the end of that, if your brain hasn't shifted a bit then you're probably... well, there's no way, it couldn't happen! Then we were getting towards the end of the summer, the evenings were getting darker, the nights getting colder, and soon after we headed back into London and carried on doing parties. We'd gone from being a bunch of squatters in London to nine months later being absolutely huge with a hard-core travelling posse, we'd really come a long away."

Castlemorton Common - 1992

Held in the beautiful and definitively English surroundings of the Malvern Hills, Castlemorton Common Festival was at one and the same time the largest free festival gathering since the glory days of Stonehenge in 1984 and the death knell of the whole festival movement. It sparked front page headlines across the daily newspapers, cost the taxpayer millions in legal fees and led to the passing of the Criminal Justice and Public Order Act of 1994. No other festival has a backdrop and a story that exposes the hypocrisy of the authorities and the media in the way that Castlemorton (after all, at 25,000 attendees, dwarfed by the zenith of Stonehenge) delineates the total lack of ability on the part of authority to have a consistent and measured response to free festival events. In fact, it grew out of 'Operation Nomad', a well-titled Avon and Somerset Police initiative that pushed revellers making their way to the Avon Free Festival out of their jurisdiction and into the idyllic surroundings of 'Elgar Country.' At what point, one might wonder, could effective use of constabulary resources be represented by one police authority delivering their problems onwards to neighbouring forces? Yet this was the scenario that played out every summer, with local constabularies metaphorically battling each other to move their problems across county boundaries whilst they attempted to alleviate the congestion problems associated with the massed ranks of the Convoy by the self-defeating tactic of forcing them to keep driving. It's hard to imagine clearer delineation of a lack of a joined-up response than the one that drove the Avon Free Festival into Greater Malvern and spawned the Castlemorton Common Festival. Carol Midgley, writing for The Daily Mail, somewhere that was never going to harbour any sympathy for the travellers, reported from Chipping Sodbury, then a part of the county of Avon, on the residents invoking ancient bye-laws as part of the master plan to prevent the Avon festival from proceeding in 1992. Midgley reported on the residents watching in 'horror' the events in Malvern, quoting a Chipping Sodbury parish councillor's sorrow for the Malvern residents. 'We know exactly what they are going through,' he commented.

Margaret Thatcher had gone, her career and her premiership assassinated from within, but her replacement, John Major, as legendary circus owner Gerry Cottle would comment to The Independent in 1993, appeared to be 'going nowhere... [running] off at angles, banning bull-

dogs and New Age Travellers.' Major himself, never the most inspired or inspiring of political leaders, would, soon after Castlemorton, tell the Tory Party conference, 'New Age Travellers? Not in this age! Not in any age!' Words of comfort to the blue-rinsed heartlands of Middle England, no doubt, but a government focused on such 'issues' reflected an administration that had run out of steam and which was casting around for scapegoats that would be easy targets and for which targeting they could reap the kudos of their loyal supporters without fear of alienating voters who might be persuaded to sign up for another parliament of Conservative persuasion.

Castlemorton was, then, the epitome of everything the Major administration loathed about the festival scene. The media too, still relishing the sniff of an opportunity to whip up frenzy, focused itself on this gathering with the ironic juxtaposition that the more coverage they fed the situation, the greater in number the crowds attracted to the festival grew. 'Let others speak for the New Age Travellers,' asserted Major that following autumn. 'We will speak for their victims.' In the aftermath of Castlemorton, the lines between who were the beneficiaries and who were the victims became ever more blurred until in the ultimate irony, and by the same token the ultimate vindication of the British justice system, the taxpayers were obliged to put their hands in their pockets to both prosecute and defend Castlemorton's protagonists.

Sim Simmer (Spiral Tribe): We got into 1992, there was a big party in Kings Cross in a massive warehouse that really stands out, and then there was Acton Lane for the Easter weekend that was really *on top*, we got completely battered by the police that weekend. By this time we'd got a bit of a name and though we weren't the only people doing things, I think because our graphics were so catchy and the name Spiral Tribe was resonating around everywhere, we became scapegoats really. The movement itself... free festivals had got so big in the summer, and parties were getting bigger and bigger, we became a threat and they just made their presence felt that weekend; they were violent. Unprovoked violence, for playing music; that was the response. My personal opinion, it was the coming together of people from all walks of life, being united by the music. There was no segregation, no door policy, no money... no taxes being paid; it was happening at such a rapid rate that it put fear into [the establishment], they've got to divide and rule. It's like complete youth unity, which was a bit scary for them. I think times have changed now, but I think something is brewing. I look at my kids now and I see that the world has changed massively. They've got everything at their fingertips... those parties we pulled together in 1991, which isn't that long ago, we had no phones... If Spiral Tribe were to put on a party now, it would just be too big, it would be too massive because the publicity... it's just not a feasible option now. But it doesn't need to be, we know now that the massive events lose the magic of the small gatherings which everyone is capable of creating. A couple of weeks before Castlemorton there was Lechlade, that was massive as well, and that all went off fine. A few sound systems, etc. Then everyone was heading to the Avon Free Festival, but because of the build-up, I think the police were like, 'No fucking way is this happening around here.' They were digging trenches around potential sites and redirecting people. Moving them on into the next county, and somehow everyone was turning up at Castlemorton. I left a message in London on an answer machine, a phone number everyone had for the party, telling everyone to go to Castlemorton. By the time I'd arrived it was heaving; loads of sound systems: Bedlam, Circus Warp, Adrenaline, us... I mean, half our rig was actually broken but we set up in a circle and it all looked great, and it was a great weekend. But we knew something was stirring, the police were waving people onto the site, you had the noise of helicopters buzzing around and it was incredible but at the same time it was a bit disturbing. You could kind of envisage something might happen.

Spiral Tribe at Castlemorton, 1992 (Stephen McCarthy)

Paul Bagley: Castlemorton Common Festival was my very last 'free' one, although I've been to some small parties and smaller paid festivals that I suppose could be classed in that category for the 'vibe.' It was a local site for me and I was overjoyed when the word spread around my home town of Malvern like wildfire that a festival was on my doorstep. Aware that the police blockades had already been set up I, and most, if not all, of the people involved on the underground scene in the town, took a three-mile hike to get there. That part was wonderful, as people marched in a line over the hills like pilgrims on a common cause. Sadly that was the last positive memory. It was not so much a festival but a mass rave. Over twenty thousand people had crammed onto the common and sound systems blared out from every corner. As I walked around the site I naturally got separated from my group. In the past this was a natural event, but on this occasion the atmosphere was very different.

Everywhere there was strewn rubbish, excrement, used needles, and discarded beer cans. Large groups were taking down trees, garden fences… anything they could grab to make a fire. It was an atmosphere of fear and resentment far removed from the festivals of old. I made my way back across the hills and was actually relieved to be home. I regret missing bands like AOS3 and Back to the Planet who apparently played there, but the general anarchy and 'Brew Crew' mentality was the nail in the coffin for me and free festivals at the time. The fun and laughter of sitting chilled-out in a field with a 'good vibe' had gone and been replaced by a type of anarchy based on a lack of respect for others, the site and the world. I did hear of some later festivals that thankfully I didn't attend where people had been beaten up when the two groups came into conflict. Tales of drug dealers at one in Kent who took it upon themselves to track down and hound out the 'hippie' types who were just there to have a peaceful time, beating up folk, stealing cars, burning tents down and generally creating havoc and mayhem.

Sim Simmer (Spiral Tribe): I think we stayed there until the Wednesday or Thursday, everyone was clearing up the site, leaving it spotless, and then as we were driving off, we all got arrested. Everything was taken off us, vehicles impounded; money taken off us, everything but the clothes on our backs and that was it, charged with conspiring to cause a public nuisance. We just camped out on the steps of the police station for two weeks, just alerting people as to what had been going on. It wasn't the first time we'd had attention from the police, but it was the first time they'd taken it that far. We'd had parties stopped, and been questioned, stuff like that, but this one... everything was impounded as evidence.

One of us had a little place in London and that was raided, they took every bit of paper, every phone number off the wall, they went to town, it was a big operation. The chief investigator was actually quite cool and whispered to Mark [Stormcore] one day on the steps of the police station, 'Look, this is a stitch up, it's nothing to do with us,' but we kind of knew that, really. We didn't have a lot of options, we had nothing, but people were very generous, someone gave us a truck, people were giving us things and the decision was made to move out of England and across the Channel to France. By this time our profile had been raised, we were starting to make music, so we cashed in on that to get a record deal with Big Life which enabled us to buy a mobile recording studio. So once we'd regrouped we decided to move out of England.

Tofu Love Frogs, Castlemorton, 1992 (Geri Winter)

Steve Bubble: This was, actually, the last proper free festival in the UK, no-one wanted to do the list of summer festivals anymore, the risks to personal freedom were too great. The police were watching everyone. I'd ended up with three appeals at the High Court in London with 'Rubbish' Martin who got arrested and injuncted regarding Torpedo Town despite having little involvement. He used to do the festival lists and ran a phone-line providing up-to-the-minute festival info. Initially our injunctions were overturned with the judge telling the council that they couldn't expect to have injunctions on people that lasted a lifetime, which was our point exactly! Our defence quoted part of the Magna Carta, the part that states that no free man shall be shackled unless judged by his peers, or something along those lines, and we hadn't been able to argue or defend ourselves against the accusations made by the council. But we won. We were amazed it had been so quick and easy. The decision though, was soon overturned following the council's own appeal, and the injunctions were reinstated as before. There were three business judges on this one, who were used to dealing with long-lasting injunctions in business, apparently. We appealed against this decision, of course, but when our date came up, rather conveniently, I'd been arrested whilst Otterbourne and Romsey were being invaded... obviously I was guilty as I was under arrest, so we lost that appeal. The fol-

Castlemorton, 1992 (Stephen McCarthy)

lowing year, our case was to go to the House of Lords as this was an untested point of law, regarding perpetual and everlasting injunctions without trial. At this point our legal aid was withdrawn; I think the authorities were determined that this wasn't going to go any further, and we ended up in court undefended and without a barrister, and losing, with costs of a quarter of a million quid awarded against us, though I'm pleased to say this was never claimed. I think they knew they'd pushed the moral and legal limits, though I still have the injunctions against me to this day.

Sim Simmer(Spiral Tribe): A year and a half after the festival, the Castlemorton thing got to court; the trial lasted eight weeks, it cost the taxpayer four million quid and everyone got found not guilty. The very stuff they tried to incriminate us with backfired, like leaving the message on the answer machine. They'd publicised the thing on the *Six O'Clock News* on the Friday and Saturday nights, saying there was a massive illegal festival going on at Castlemorton Common.

From the helicopters that were buzzing around, keeping an eye on everybody, they had video footage into the next week which showed people going around picking up cigarette butts, and leaving the site spotless and it defeated their argument that people were creating a public nuisance. We were coming back at them, saying, 'Actually, look, we care very much, we're environmentalists, we care about the planet, we care about what's happening.' And the jury found us all not guilty. But everything they'd tried to come at us with was so ridiculous and was turned around so simply; we were just completely honest with what we were doing, said that there was no big conspiracy. I think the whole court case enlightened most people really.

Steve Bubble: The scene had grown exponentially and the loud sound systems meant that residents in the local area, and for miles around, had no escape from the techno, often banging 24/7. It got too big to be sustainable… going from a few thousand people listening to bands in a field to fifty thousand with an untold number of sound systems running non-stop for days on end – it had to be stopped, and was. I mean, up to 1989, public reaction was often okay. There were exceptions when an event was too near a village or town, but until the loud sound systems came along, people would come out of their houses and wave as a convoy went past. I remember Cissbury Ring in '88 or '89 when some little old ladies sitting on a bench on the path up from the National Trust car park we'd borrowed for the weekend chatted to festival-goers, saying they were glad to see us when we came!

Sim Simmer: With Castlemorton, we'd been riding this great big wave, surfing it, and at Castlemorton the wave came crashing down onto the shore... the rave wave. It was too big, it had to happen; it was natural progression... this seed that grew into a plant and at Castlemorton it died and yet got reseeded in many different places. The roots were still there and spread, it hadn't damaged anything. You had the Criminal Justice Bill but did that stop anyone? Not really. It stopped great massive gatherings like that, but different things mean different things at different times.

Steve Bubble: Like quite a few people, I was even more politicised by the downfall of the free festival scene – on 9th October, 1994 the Criminal Justice Act became law and I'd headed to London for the demo, an amazing day of defiance as sound systems surrounded by dancing people managed to get into Hyde Park despite two thousand police who were determined not to let this happen. Thirty police on horseback were galloping around whacking people with batons and causing innocent picnickers to flee in panic until they were forced out by five thousand or so people who'd had enough and fought back. The police, some of whom had been pulled from their horses, were humiliated and pushed back out of the park. The crowd then watched and pelted the police with rocks whenever they approached the fence – this went on for hours, completely mental! 'Reclaim the Streets' took off, there were large demonstrations, road protests, animal rights demos, it was really going off in the 90s, I was having a good time, despite having no festivals to go to because there were so many smaller parties going on, the whole thing just got driven underground, or out onto the streets, fantastic times.

A letter to The Independent, published on 12th October 1994 and signed by, amongst others, left-wing Labour MPs Jeremy Corbyn and Tony Benn, took issue with a previous article in the paper that quoted a police statement suggesting that anarchists turned the previously peaceful Hyde Park demonstration into a riot. 'People attempting to leave the Park peacefully were attacked by riot police on horses,' they claimed, before assigning blame to an 'incompetent and aggressive policing' by the Metropolitan Police Force. Tony Benn, in his published diary entry of 9th October, 1994 seemed rather more ambivalent about the cause of the rioting, which spread through Oxford Street and down onto Tottenham Court Road. 'Maybe a few anarchists did engage in a battle... maybe they were agents provocateurs... or maybe it was all caused by the police,' he wrote, before conceding (whilst admitting it was not something he, as an elected representative should have said), 'historically riot has played a role.' [Free at Last – Diaries 1991 – 2001, (Hutchinson, 2002)]

Bridget's Story – Coming Back

The effect of the festival scene varied according to the experiences of the attendees and, whilst we look at how our contributors reflect on the influence that their involvement in the festivals has had on their lives after leaving the scene, here's one very personal recollection.

Bridget Wishart: Many of my memories of free festivals, and the adventures that I had there,

Bridget with Steve Stoat and Rob Stoat (Jocelyn, 1982)

include drug taking … this was mainly cannabis but sometimes LSD or magic mushrooms. Once I realised the dangers of being caught smoking, the criminal record, the fines, and the fear that my home would be broken into in the middle of the night, these fears pervaded my days and there was an underlying paranoia to a lot of my activities that was very unpleasant and unsettling to experience. I don't regret taking drugs, though I do regret continuing to do so when it was clear there was no benefit to my health or lifestyle. At free festivals there was the risk you might be searched on entering and leaving and the police also observed the crowds by helicopter or by infiltrating, usually the very obvious 'undercover' drug squad. You were generally left alone on site, though some of the more well-known festival characters were subject to snatch squads. Myself and everyone else I knew who went to the festivals enjoyed and relished the paranoia-free zone. I do wonder sometimes if the laws about consuming drugs hadn't been so stringent and harsh and the penalties so severe, would the hedonistic, single-minded consumption of large quantities of drugs at festivals have occurred the in the way that it did? In the 80s it was the case that mental health wards in hospitals in the South West were swollen by people suffering drug induced mental health problems after Glastonbury Festival. I don't know, now the festival is policed, if this is still the case.

The majority of people who smoke cannabis do so with no ill effects. This can lead people to believe that smoking is harmless, safe and non-addictive. Sadly this isn't true. Smoking may not be physically addictive but psychologically it is. If you have ever come across a grumpy, stressed out hippie, ten-to-one they haven't had a smoke that day… In some individuals the drug can induce feelings of paranoia, an inability to communicate clearly, and for a few, these feelings never go away. Smoking cannabis, skunk in particular, can induce paranoid schizophrenia which can be recurring and hard to treat. Schizophrenia and other mental illnesses sometimes do not appear instantly and so can lull an individual into a state of confidence in their ability to live the rock 'n' roll lifestyle, but breakdowns and mental traumas can also occur with continued or more frequent drug use.

Ecstasy has been a cause of mental illness in some users; particularly clinical depression. I think this is because of the nature of ecstasy, it stimulates the production of serotonin, our body's natural happy juice, and once the gland gets over-stimulated it is unable to produce it naturally, sending the individual spiralling into a depression.

This is what happened to me.

In the mid-90s I was working up to eighteen-hour days designing, painting and hanging décor for big raves and festivals. I needed to stay awake, to be able to work long hours and I was fast running out of steam. During my second summer working I was introduced to Ecstasy and it seemed to be the perfect answer. I felt great; I could do the work, party all night and still be

Bridget Wishart, Womad 1996 (Anna Tolson)

clear headed and able to take the décor down afterwards and be confident and safe on the ladders. It was only after the festival season was over that I became more withdrawn and quiet. I stopped going out, I found it hard to talk to people, to go shopping... and telephones were out of the question. Every time I smoked I felt ten times worse and was angry with myself that I felt so bad. I lost all confidence. I thought I was a crap person and went into a dark space that, as far as I was concerned, had no end. Eventually it got so bad that I went to the doctor and after filling in a form he diagnosed depression, which I hadn't even considered, though looking back now it seems so obvious. He recommended counselling and medication. I grew up thinking that depression was an excuse and an indication of a weak personality and that taking medication would be a waste of time and an admission of defeat so I refused. However, I did agree to counselling though I wished I hadn't as the woman I saw was no help to me and used her influence on my vulnerable state of mind to ensure I kept seeing her. By this time I had cut myself off from all my friends and couldn't cook or create or do anything. I was only able to sleep four hours a day and was constantly confused and exhausted. A neighbour started to visit, taking both me and her dog out for walks every day, and my best mate Claire refused to give up on me. She persuaded me to go back to the doctors and to try taking anti-depressants. Sadly the tablets I took disagreed with me and made me feel like I was walking through a thick invisible fog. (This can happen, but I didn't know about it). I despaired of life ever getting better and retreated further into the darkness. After another month or so Claire managed to persuade me to go back to the doctor and I tried a different anti-depressant which, after a while, started to work. (Anti-depressants usually need to be taken for at least three weeks for any benefit to be felt).

Slowly I felt my life was turning round but it was a lengthy process. Depression seems to shut the brain down, a self-preserving mechanism perhaps, but it made life quite challenging when I got some temporary work in a hippie shop in town. I couldn't remember numbers or prices… I had to look at them, write them down, then walk the few feet to the till and read the numbers off the paper. Gradually my memory improved and I started eating more than muesli and banana which had been the only foods I had eaten for five months. I started going out again, and in fact I felt better than I ever had. A few of my friends noticed and were a bit concerned that I was so flamboyant and confident.

One morning I woke up full of the joys of life. It was a summer's day; I was going to work. I was now in charge of opening and closing the shop, I was keen and enthusiastic, I was going out partying and I clearly remember thinking, 'I don't want to be any happier than this.' The next morning I had gone beyond happy, I had gone manic and had lost all insight into my health and behaviour.

A few weeks later I went to WOMAD 97 as a guest of Temple Décor having resigned as their

Artistic Director. I ended up dancing with Mega Dog and sorting out a posse to go to the Lizard Festival, in Cornwall, with passes for everyone, and hanging out with a whole new bunch of 'friends'. I was started to spend money more freely and easily upped my credit on my card to £3,000 with one phone call. My most bizarre spending spree was when I went into the Pound Shop in Bath to buy a joss stick holder to take to the Lizard Festival, which they didn't have, and ended up spending £400. It seemed like everything I saw had a use. I filled five baskets full of 'useful' crap! The guy serving wouldn't accept my credit card so I went to the bank and drew the money out. I'm sure he thought he wouldn't see me again and was really surprised when I came back with the cash. I then had a car full of stuff to lose or give away at the festival!

On returning from the Lizard, I was acting more and more strangely. I stopped using the door to my flat preferring the window instead. Charlie waltzed into my life and at first he accepted my madness as eccentricity but when we flew to J4J, the juggling festival in Italy, it became very obvious I was seriously ill - to everyone but me!

I took all my costumes from when I was in Hawkwind and created a character named Princess Freya. I then annoyed the hell out of a lot of people by being where they thought I shouldn't be. I sat in corners and painted small plastic flies orange and gave them to children. I did interviews with the Italian Press that I had no cause to as I wasn't technically 'on the bill'. I wore one shoe on and one shoe off so I could touch Mother Earth. I became obsessive about my place in the landscape. I had to sit where my position harmonised with my surroundings, even if it meant being far away from the people I was with. I stopped sleeping and rarely ate.

Things came to a head on the flight back to the UK. I became caught up in following the luggage lines painted on the floors of the airport and followed them right into the X-ray machine… which, they said, luckily they had immediately turned off as the dose is way too strong for a person. I had problems getting out of bathrooms as all the noises of the water sounded like dragons communicating and I wanted to hear what they were saying. We had to pick up a connecting flight in France and when I saw some purple and pink chairs I knew that's where I was supposed to be, where the rockets heading for Mars left from, where royalty sat, where Princess Freya needed to be.

I persuaded Charlie and Haggis I needed a cigarette and promised to catch them up. I didn't. I followed the luggage lines again. They took me to a baggage chute; I lifted the flaps and slid down the chute. It really was just like a helter-skelter! I popped out on the tarmac and startled the hell out of two guys getting the plane ready for take-off. I saw the luggage hold was open and hopped in there, 'off to Mars'. The hatch was shut behind me and the straps on the hatch formed an X. Well, X always marks the spot on a treasure map, so that's where I attached myself. It did make things a bit awkward when someone tried to open the hatch and get me out. Back out on the tarmac, I didn't see the Land Rover full of armed cops. I just saw a little guy walk up to me with a big mop of hair and say, 'Hi my name's Ziggy', which convinced me I would still get to Mars (Ziggy Stardust & the Spiders from Mars) so I happily went with him, into the Black Maria and on to the Police Station. Charlie joined me and persuaded them not to section me there and then by promising to take me to my parents, who would take me to get help. The journey to my parents was most interesting as I watched the M4 go from horizontal to vertical and take me to the moon. I never saw my costumes again. I think they must have got blown up by the police in France or at Heathrow, if they got that far, or dumped in a bin somewhere.

I spent four months in hospital. I was sectioned on a number of occasions and had to take anti-psychotics, tranquilizers and other medications in order to get well. Then it was another six months before I felt properly recovered. The side effects and withdrawals from some of the tablets were very uncomfortable indeed but I had the support of a fantastic team of psychiatrists and nurses. When I left hospital I still wanted to continue to smoke dope, it had been part of my way of life for so long and I still hadn't seen my addiction to it. And, as everyone says... 'It's harmless isn't it?!' I smoked it a few times but it made me feel so vulnerable, paranoid and out of control that it just seemed stupid to keep doing it.

That was many years ago now, and I don't regret my decision to stop smoking. I don't have to avoid making friends with 'straight' people. I can go shopping when I want, I answer the door to my home without fear and I have written more songs in the last four years than I did in the last twenty. Everyone has their own opinions about the risks and gains of taking illegal drugs, their place at the free festivals, and in society as a whole. People place different risks on particular drugs, there are myths mixed with truth about what drugs are dangerous and what drugs aren't and confusingly, kudos and coolness are also included in the bag. All I know is what happened to me can happen to anyone. Looking back I needn't have let peer pressure and a desire to be 'one of the boys' influence my decisions, but having said that it's easily done and sadly, not so easy to undo.

All Our Yesterdays

In the years since Castlemorton, the festival scene has fragmented and dissolved. In large part this has to be seen in the context of the increasing pressures from myriad laws and by-laws that were forced through to prevent large scale events from taking place outside of organised society. Not all of this is sinister in motive, however much conspiracy theorists want to examine the background and the motives behind it; events such as the tragedy at Hillsborough football ground and the increasingly litigious nature of the public in respect of accidents and personal safety have played their part. Even though individuals bemoan the 'Nanny State' and look back to a perceived 'Golden Age' where the restrictive practices laid down under the twin banners of Health and Safety were not all-intrusive, the cold reality is that in the end, society gets what society wants, and enough of mainstream society wants to wrap its activities in cotton-wool that it's hard to see just how the legal infrastructure of the current day could possibly accommodate another Windsor Free Festival, or a Stonehenge, and certainly not another Castlemorton.

That doesn't necessarily mean that the free festival has disappeared altogether; as contributors note quite clearly, they do still occur under the radar and labelled in different ways – but they most definitely are not eighty-thousand-strong gatherings. Nonetheless, the overarching philosophy imbedded in the concept of the free festivals continues to permeate through many strands of our culture and much of what drove activists into the scene has quietly become part of mainstream thinking.

The festivals have had a lasting impact on British culture, and their legacy continues in the environmental movement, in animal rights, in the way that vegetarianism has become a normal choice rather than a cranky ideology, in Green politics. Via the Internet, that whole concept of providing a platform through which 'creators of content' can distribute and disseminate their artistic endeavours 'for free', the free festival's en-masse attendance numbers have been dwarfed by the way in which like-minded individuals can now come together. That's on a mass level, but equally interesting is the way in which the life experiences gained through the festivals have affected the scene's attendees and supporters in such deep ways that those experiences still resonate through them decades later.

Castlemorton, 1992 (Melinda Poole)

Sheila Wynter: Young people getting together, sitting around fires and talking is terribly helpful to society, and it's awful that it has been clamped down on. They did their best to contain the more difficult members of society, they're out in the open for everyone to see, but there are plenty of difficult people hidden behind closed doors. A lot of them were trying to live off the state, but a lot of them *weren't*; some were professional people who'd spend a couple of years travelling and then they'd go back and work at their professions. Others were wonderful sign-writers or mechanics who could look after their own vehicles and they'd trade with each other. I don't know enough about the ethics but I think society should accept them as *part of* society, but it doesn't. Maggie Thatcher did the country terrible harm by forcing these people abroad. They've had to go away because not many could cope with it which is terribly sad.

Dick Lucas: Recently, The Subhumans played at a two-day punk festival in North Wales, where a small field was set aside for tents, and after the gig the night was spent smoking and drinking and talking nonsensical logic with semi-strangers sat around fires, and it was excellent. It cannot be over-estimated how superb a fireside gathering is, it's socially adhesive, a leveller of status and presumptions. If you could build a good fire you got respect, warmth, and a cooker! This is primordial stuff, really. Fires at festivals are the street lights of the de-civilised.

Nigel Mazlyn Jones: It was an educational establishment, and there is a kind of tribal feeling because it's a young person's thing, to be able to camp out under canvas for days on end. Survive it, enjoy it; there does become camaraderie with your mates because you help each other out and maybe they're smoking their dope or whatever, because the drugs are a lot stronger these days, so there are probably more edges of mayhem. But the core issue is to help your friends out, have a good time and really, the music, the theatre, the visuals, they're there for the entertainment, but there is a bonding.

Sim Simmer: It has shaped the person I am. That short period of time has taken me a long time to digest but at this point in my life I completely appreciate the magic of what happened. I understand it a lot more than I did then, I was very young... things reveal themselves to me every day but I think the greatest thing I learned was that you can make things happen. If you have an idea, or even a spark, and its intentions are good then generally speaking it *will* unfold and become something. We did our thing with no money, we passed the hat around for diesel, sure, but you didn't have to have pockets full of money to make things happen.

Jeremy Cunningham: A lot of the people who work at *Beautiful Days* are from the free festivals. Gary from 2000DS works there, does one of the kids' music workshops… The girl who runs the whole kids' area is Helen Hat, who was at the Beanfield and is the girl in the song ['Battle of the Beanfield', The Levellers], who was pulled out through the front windshield of her bus when she was pregnant. Dave Farrow, who is our agent, we met on the travelling scene in Amsterdam… everyone who works with us, we met on that scene. We had RDF play there a couple of years ago, though I didn't get to speak to Chris… I was looking straight at him but had my hood up and I don't think he recognised me! We still try and have that vibe with our festival, even though it's not free, that's the vibe we go for. It's not just about the bands playing; it's about seeing weird alternative lifestyles, meeting interesting people and seeing different ways of doing things. It was a pleasure and a privilege to be part of that scene.

Chris Hewitt: We had a Deeply Vale anniversary in 1996, just an exhibition and a collection of photographs. We came up with the idea of perhaps looking for more photographs and video footage and sound recordings and generally just recording the event. I went to ITV with the idea of making a programme and they said 'No, we're not interested'. So I pursued doing it myself and eight years later we'd put out a little bit of Deeply Vale bonus footage; we put out a Tractor DVD and we put a small section about Deeply Vale on the end and the next day after ITV had received a copy of it they rang me up, eight years after they said they weren't interested in making a programme, and said 'We'd love to make a programme about Deeply Vale', so I did the deal with them that they could have access to my archives as long as I could have the rights to the programme and extend it for DVD afterwards. It's the first time ITV have ever done a deal like that. But we managed to push it through and then after we'd done the Deeply Vale DVD we decided to do the Bickershaw DVD and we did the John Peel DVD and we've just carried on in that direction so we're doing I suppose hippie-related rock DVDs more on the counter-culture side of things. Even within the counter-culture there is this certain Stonehenge/Glastonbury almost elitist pre-festival hierarchy and I think one of the things that we did with the crew at Deeply Vale was perhaps broke the mould of that and we certainly broke the mould in terms of tolerance of punk bands and perhaps tolerance of the fact that you didn't have to be some sort of person who came from Ladbroke Grove and then had some sort of cool album out to actually get on the stage and perform.

Nigel Mazlyn Jones: At Rougham Tree Fayre I first heard the phrase, from an old Romany gypsy, 'Life without a festival is a road without an Inn.' We have this rather bland, socially engineered, paranoid, fearful, disapproving and overblown society that can't do this and can't do that, but yet it can allow our youngsters to go out and 'export our democratic model' at the point of a gun in Iraq and Afghanistan. In the 70s, two hundred and fifty thousand people on a march could create huge debate across the whole social and media board about the nuclear issue; I move forward thirty years and one million people can't create a debate about Iraq. So I reflect, 'Life without a festival is a road without an Inn.'

Mark Wright: People's politics changed. Do people do *anything* anymore? Has the 'spirit' died? An ideal way of killing the festivals was by allowing loads of paying festivals for the student and townies to pretend they're festival types. You can buy the uniform from your local hippie chic boutique. For God's sake, they've even opened up Stonehenge for the solstice; I've bumped into one or two people from the past but who the fuck are *all* these people? There weren't that many of us that did the Stonehenge run each year, certainly less than a hundred vehicles, perhaps less than fifty. We used to work together at that time of year and put ourselves on the line for each other, most of us had bounced a police car out to get someone on site. Yes, sour grapes, but I've certain resentment towards most of those who are there, all the years of battling, and then the whole thing gets packaged and sold.

Angel: Hawkwind were very deep in the psyches of people and Stonehenge was a wonderful vehicle - that's how it was. You could go there and you could listen to them, you could talk to them. You were part of it. We were all part of that same thing. I feel very sad, I did try going there in recent years, when they allowed people back to the Stones for the summer solstice and, to me, it was like sacrilege. To have false lighting in a situation where you're waiting for the dawn, so all the naturalness of the earth and the light and everything is taken away with these clinical, horrendous, bright lights and an intense police atmosphere. In the old days all the ceremonies would go on, the rituals within the Stones, it wasn't just druids, everyone was having their own individual rituals and then they were a part of the whole, great ritual that was happening there, that was respected and allowed. There would be the odd policeman scattered around but at a distance; they just used to watch. People were literally doing whatever they wanted and they were just a watchful eye and a presence. Whereas now, one of the last times I went to Stonehenge I looked up and there was one of my children being dragged out of the middle of the Stones by four policemen, two on each arm, *completely* unfounded. There was a guy that actually took pictures of it because his job was to record any kind of brutality or over the top behaviour from authority, when all people are about really is peace and love, respecting nature and honouring a time that has past, that should still be recognised now.

Nigel Mazlyn Jones: It has become the rock proms. Younger people have to have their own tribal thing, something to react to and separate themselves from the older generation. The free rave movement, you could say it was children of children of the very early festivals who'd set that precedent of diggers and levellers. Now, who knew about the history of diggers and the levellers? I've got stuff that I've been trawling through, I've got box files of stuff I've squirreled away over the years because I'd be at a festival and wandering around the stalls, having fun and enjoying the wonderful inspiration of everything and I'd pick up stuff that I'd be interested in. And here I am thirty years later, looking at anti-nuclear stuff, and I think, 'Good Lord, we aren't having a public debate about the ten new power stations we are going to have.' I picked up an envelope that an activist from Germany sent me in 1977, at the time a banned document that he'd smuggled out of the German civil service. It just reminded me, wading through all this stuff, that it has had a huge impact. It's a powerful reminder that no matter how you socially engineer the democratic structure, you will not crush a core bunch of people who will explore everything in sight.

David Stooke: I left the scene in 1992, '93 and I really had had the best of it. I'd met great people and been at really good festivals. After that, when things like Castlemorton had come to an end, there were no more raves and we were in the hands of oppression. The people who really mattered to me started disappearing. Decker Mick moved from Salisbury down to Cornwall, a couple went abroad, some went to Southern Ireland and in the end the people who were so amazing were gone. The people who took their places weren't the same; with no offence to them, there wasn't the same stimulation. The ultimate was Green Lane because it was full of jewellery-makers, craftsmen, thinkers, philosophers and I was so attracted to it. Being an artist I felt I had a really powerful thing to contribute. By the end, '92, nobody had any interest in my paintings; they were just into brew and it was a different scene.

Jah Free: I've been working over the last five or six years with Southend Mencap, I go into schools, working with kids with learning difficulties who are in transition from school to college; my experiences from the festivals comes into that. Talking and encouraging, telling them to do what *they* want to do, individualism, and all that. It may be a strange analogy, but I have to talk to them about where they're going to live next, sooner or later someone has to let them know that one day, their mum and dad are going to die. That can be taken in different ways; there was one particular student I talked to about it, and it really shocked him, the first awakening that such a thing might ever happen. But it's also the ease of talking to people, because I have to go to council meetings and talk to officials about what I do; because of the Wango's experience it doesn't faze me. I'm me, I dress like I dress, I wear my little hat, I'm not your normal... I'm still waving the freak flag high! I'm not scared of who I am, I'm proud.

Dolores Dina: When I look at photographs, I can imagine myself right back there, with no effort; I can *smell* that field. It's really quite emotional. Today's gigs don't have the same flavour. Festivals don't have the same atmosphere. If you don't make a gig you just go on the Internet [and download a copy]. In my day, it was such a big thrill to go to a gig, and young people are missing that because it's not special any more. The problem is that they have everything today, and they don't realise the value of what they've got. Every teenager I meet has an iPod, a computer, recording equipment, a guitar and amps - and they don't understand the value of it. I went to see the White Stripes at the Wireless festival and people were leaving *during* the *headlining* act, whether to get their train back or whatever. In my day, you never did that, you went and got the 4am train home because it was such a special event to see one of your favourite bands; now they just watch a webcam or a podcast or whatever they do. That's why Glastonbury is having problems now, it's over commercialised, there's no sense of community; everything is branded.

Swordfish: Kids today are into one particular genre or thing. Plus, even though everyone's doing drugs, nobody's getting out of it; there are no psychedelics any more so there's no Magical Mystery Tour with it. Everyone's using drugs for the wrong reason, just for escapism whereas what was going on was the enhancement of the whole trip. People don't do drugs for that reason now. We play a lot of these dance festivals but it's self-limiting, the whole psychedelic trance scene was self-limiting. They kind of know they need to go in other directions, but it's like they can't. Who says that everybody has to be put 'there' or 'in there', everybody should be a Hawkwind. Everybody should be a Pink Floyd. We find ourselves in this constant situation... to give it a simile, we're in this little village and there's a lane that we take out but wherever we go in this journey, it leads back to the same village. It isn't a bad thing, but you want events just to be a bit more eclectic, a bit different.

David Stooke: The thing that appealed most… if you drive through town you see endless rows of houses all the same – then people tried to express their individuality by having different net curtains, different front doors. Now everyone's got UPVC front doors, you haven't even got *that* and towns just seem drab and uniform and crap. Well, vintage buses with chimneys sticking out and curtains with suns and moons on them… We were looking at these buses and you could see through the windows and catch little glimpses of things like kettles or there's a telly on or music coming out and we thought, 'Wow, imagine being at a festival in a bus.' It was all about having a chance to express your individuality. It was a chance not to be in some horrendous rabbit hutch, the same as all the other rabbit hutches – it was just brilliant.

Trailer Life (Mark Wright)

Mick Moss: It was something I did when I was young. It was never a way of life, just a *part* of a way of life. Things change. I think the rave scene sort of took over the good vibe. The old anarchist/hippie/traveller thing just got boring and sad. My only regret is that the dream – if ever there was one – turned out to be a fake. But you grow up. You learn. You understand that to be naïve in youth is OK, but not when you become an adult. To live outside the law you have to be rich. I wish I was still naïve!

Keith Bailey: At the outset, music was the main force of cultural change… I don't see that now. What you get now is a kind of lunatic fringe, musically. You've got these Death Metal or Goths who go around and are nihilists. I believe that anarchy is about accepting responsibility for your own actions. That was the concept of floating anarchy, which Here & Now promoted. These days there's a bunch of people who are still very radical and totally anti-government but in a nihilist way rather than a personally responsible way. They're just destroy, destroy, destroy; I think Punk started that and the Death Metal guys are an extension of that Punk ethos. So everything has become more polarised as time has gone on and the extremes are more extreme whilst the middle-way is that much blander. But with the birth of the Internet, the electronic communication age, people are slowly ... you know, there's a whole world out there, billions of people, but it takes years and years for an idea to infiltrate. People are waking up to the way the Internet can be used politically and as a result of that politics is becoming less polarised - even though society is becoming more polarised. I very much see the Internet as the new free festival. Alright, there are lots of negatives to Myspace, and the fact that Rupert Murdoch has taken it over, but I see a whole bunch of people who are joined to the Here & Now site that are really radical. It empowers independently-minded artists because we can now communicate directly and work with people who are genuine fans and sell direct to the fan-base and therefore survive.

Simon Williams: I'm actually of the opinion that there are a lot of little free festivals still, but they don't call them that any more, they're private parties. They're on some farmer's land or you actually hire a bit of land. Things change. The dance scene had a really big effect on the festival scene; I don't see it as a negative thing that stopped something great from carrying on. I see it as an evolution with new, fresh, electronica coming into the scene. That was the whole point of it, there had to be fresh influences coming in, whether that's world music or the techno-scene of electronica and technology coming in there's a place for it. I think dance music moved things on a bit though there was something of a clash at some point. But whatever anyone says, that whole scene has survived. I mean, maybe it's morphed into the scene we see today with the very organised corporate, Virgin Festivals or whatever, but they thought 'Wow, what a great idea,' and now in a Thatcherite way they're making money out of it. It's like you can't have it unless someone is making money out of it, then you *can* have it.

Jerry Richards: The paying festivals ... you turn up at the gate at a certain time, you go in, buy your merchandise, see the bands, they stop playing and you're ushered out by security, you get on your bus and go home. At free festivals you could come and go and do whatever you liked and talk to as many people as you wanted to. The police, or someone in authority, could come around and say, 'who's in charge here' and you'd go 'nobody – there aren't any leaders here, mate'. There's a magic to it, a karma and people aren't just coming together to see a gig, they're coming together for all sorts of different reasons. We've had this huge tradition for hundreds of years, people living on the roads, travelling; we haven't always lived in cities. Then, since we've got clocks, people have had to know what time it is to be able to go to work at someone's cotton mill ... that's where it comes from. It's the post war social sensibility, it's that modern British-ness that means you know you should do the right thing whatever situation you find yourself in and it's about taking responsibility for your own actions. That's the kind of vibe that was prevalent. Now, free festivals are springing up again, small little encampments out of the way enough for the authorities not to really bother. They know there's a party going on and someone's just keeping an eye on things but it's no big trip and people just generally get on with it.

Dick Lucas: Where did all the old-style travellers and the Brew Crew go? I don't know, although I can have a fairly rational guess. A lot of people went to Ireland. They got totally sick of it all and just left the country, especially with the Criminal Justice Act coming in. As freedom of movement and speech became more or less illegal a lot of people went to Ireland, a lot went to mainland Europe, especially Holland, Belgium, France, Germany, Spain. A lot of people just travelled and carried on travelling out of the country and didn't really come back much. A few people sobered up and did the same thing but on a larger scale, like the Wango Riley stage moved itself out of the fields and into the gig circuit. So some people just carried on what they were doing but on a more, shall we say, socially acceptable level. They just made use of their talents without sinking into a depression because it was all over. A lot of people probably went back to relatively stable lifestyles – a lot of travellers had stable lifestyles, they were summer travellers, they were out for the festivals and then back to work. Others just joined in with the rave scene that was coming soon afterwards, and the rave festivals and the paying festivals. It's not like all the festivals disappeared, it's not like all the Brew Crew disappeared but they were less visible but quite a few people just became casualties and actually died. Not a lot, but more than a few.

Sim Simmer: The continental scene was very different. They took it on board amazingly. The French were very receptive but there wasn't anything like a travelling scene in France in any case, it was completely new for them. Everything had been in clubs, prior to us arriving, but it spread quickly; even today we're huge in France, compared to England. People in England vaguely remember us, but everybody in France know who Spiral Tribe are, it's incredible. They still have *teknivals* here, which is kind of what we introduced, not a festival but a *teknival* and they are massive, and actually *allowed* to happen, there's four or five days a year when you can have a *teknival* in France, which is completely different to what happened in England. That's great; they are lacking the diversity of musical styles, at the moment, but that's starting to change... France, Germany, Austria, Czech, I mean, twenty years ago it was so different to how it is now; there are parties every weekend and the music has really infiltrated and it has really changed.

Swordfish: I still have what you might call a false hope in society, that if you treat everybody properly and with respect then they'll respect you. We still play at places where that happens and they exist virtually without any security. It's still done. That's what came across at Stonehenge in '82, it was total anarchy, chaos, but it was held together.

Michael Dog: There is a whole generation of people, in their late twenties or early thirties now, who have no inkling of what went on before because there's nothing out there to tell them. It's kind of like the book *1984* where the main character's job is going through archives deleting things so there is no memory of what went on before. That's how I see it with the festival scene, the squatting culture, and the scene of *International Times* – there's no memory of it. If you go through archives of even the music press, the only references you'll find to the [free] festival scene are taking the piss out of it, making it seem uncool. They had as active a role in stamping on it as everyone else did. And yet, it was a movement that was so important to tens of thousands of people and their personal development. One of the good things that came out of it is that there is a general trend towards liberalism in this country that has a lot to do with that movement. People who were active between the 70s and the 90s - and though they might now be middle-aged and remembering it fondly and living fairly conservative lives and having houses and cars - the fact that they experienced it is colouring and influencing how they live. And that can only be for the good and has played its role in stopping Britain becoming more right-wing than it might have. We've had war in the Middle East, and lots of other places, but they don't have the popular support that the Falklands War did; people don't want to know – the government might have gone ahead and done it but people didn't want it. I think that owes a lot to the movements of the 70s and 80s. For any of us involved in that culture, it has made a difference.

Trading at Castlemorton, 1992 (Melinda Poole)

What does it all mean?

So, what does it all mean? We've had so many people, who've now moved into all walks of life, expressing their own thoughts on the free festivals. But were they just a place to get off your head, or were they in some way a spiritual haven?

We think they were both, and more. The idea of the younger generation getting themselves outside of mainstream society and finding a way to grow up, educated in a whole new way, was for its time, a unique opportunity. That included negatives alongside the positives; but the interesting juxtaposition is that it brought in new values whilst as Jerry Richards points out, actually incorporating some of the ethos of the generation that fought the Second World War and established the Welfare State as a result of their experiences. That generation might not recognise its values in the free festivals, indeed it might be horrified to find such an analogy applied. But that sense of mutual dependency and support for the disaffected and the disadvantaged is so clearly laid out in what the best of the festivals had to offer.

That's because people at free festivals need each other to make things happen. Food, electricity, warmth, theatre, music, these things didn't put themselves on, they required a concerted effort on the part of the committed to make these things happen. We asked of our interviewees, 'Does the interdependency of that culture mean that there could be no onlookers?' In essence, we think it's a rhetorical question in many ways. To be there, meant to be involved. Everyone had something to offer; their time, their hash, their teapot, their strength, their love, their madness, their soul, their pain, it was all there. What we're talking about is a huge pool of human resource that enabled incredible things to happen.

Now, let's not look back on that with rose-tinted glasses only. The festival scene had its share of tragedies. Some were brought upon it by external forces, but few of our contributors thought that the pressures from outside of the scene were the sole reason for its problems. Drug overdoses, accidents, violence, arson, thievery, animal cruelty, abuse, bullying, mental health problems, and tribal in-fighting were all factors that the festival scene itself had to face up to as being issues driven from the inside, just as it had to confront and react to the outside pressures from the mainstream.

Wherever people congregate, there's an opportunity for money to be made. Nothing is ever truly 'free', or to qualify that, nothing ever remains truly 'free'. There's always someone with an eye for a scheme to enrich themselves, not always in a detrimental way, but the fact remains that for all the goodwill and anti-materialistic intent, someone will come and make a fast buck. Wherever there is money to be made, or power to be gained, there will be individuals who want a bigger part of it, who live by different rules and who are prepared to be violent or manipulative in its pursuit. But that shouldn't ever, not once, deter those whose reason for being involved with something is to enhance the experiences of others or to freely express their own creativity for others' benefit.

So the counterpoint is that wherever people congregate, wherever there is an opportunity for something special, there will be attracted to it people who want what's best for everyone, who want to share what they have and pass around some of their own happiness.

We are complex individuals, full of contradictory needs, desires and emotions. If we accept that the free festivals were the sum of the people who made them happen, how could they have been any less contradictory than ourselves?

Further Reading

Abrahams, Ian. *Hawkwind – Sonic Assassins* (SAF Publishing)
Allen, Daevid. *Gong Dreaming – Volumes 1 & 2* (SAF Publishing)
Berger, George. *The Story of Crass* (Omnibus Publishing)
Berger, George. *Dance Before the Storm: Official Story of the Levellers* (Virgin)
Clerk, Carol. *The Saga of Hawkwind* (Omnibus Press)
Collin, Matthew. *Altered State – The Story of Ecstasty Culture and Acid House* (Serpent's Tail)
Deakin, Rich. *Keep It Together! Cosmic Boogie with the Deviants and the Pink Fairies* (HeadPress)
Dearling, Alan. *Travelling Daze* (Enabler)
Farren, Mick. *Give the Anarchist a Cigarette* (Pimlico)
Fawcett, Traveller Dave. *Traveller Homes* (Amberley Publishing)
Green, Jonathon. *Days in the Life: Voices from the English Underground* (Pimlico)
Lake, Steve. *Zounds Demystified: Lyrics & Notes* (Active Distribution)
McKell, Iain. *The New Gypsies* (Prestel)
Masters, Garry 'Moonboot'. *Mushrooms & Moonboots – An Autobiography* (Self-released)
Neville, Richard. *Hippie Hippie Shake: The Dreams, the Trips, the Trials, the Love-ins, the Screw-Ups... the Sixties* (Bloomsbury)
Reynolds, Simon. Energy Flash: *A Journey Through Rave Music and Dance Culture* (Faber & Faber)
Rimbaud, Penny. *Shibboleth – My Revolting Life* (AK Press)
Sandford, Jeremy. *Tomorrow's People* (Jerome)
Salewicz, Chris. *Redemption Song – The Definitive Biography of Joe Strummer*
Stone, C.J. *The Last of the Hippies (Faber & Faber)*
Tait, Kris. *This is Hawkwind, Do Not Panic* (Hawkwind Merchandising)
Worthington, Andy. *The Battle of the Beanfield* (Enabler)
Worthington, Andy. *Stonehenge – Celebration and Subversion* (Alternative Albion)

Further Listening

Various Artists:

The Deeply Vale Boxset (A4 Book + 6 x CD, Ozit Morpheus)

The sound of Deeply Vale… rough and ready but dynamic and evocative

The Last Daze of the Underground (3 x CD, Esoteric Records)
Delerium Records compilation and the sound of the 1980s free festivals: Treatment, Mandragora, Omnia Opera, Boris and his Bolshie Balalaika and much more.

Travellers Aid Trust (CD, Anagram)
Bands of the 1980s free festivals, curated by Dave Brock and Marc 'Frenchy' Gloder. 2000DS, Hippy Slags, Ozric Tentacles, Culture Shock, Tubilah Dog, Hawkwind, Nik Turner…

Stonehenge EP (Bluurg Records).
Benefit EP released in 1987 by Culture Shock and also featuring Rhythmites, Military Surplus, and Hippy Slags.

A Psychedelic Psauna (Delerium Records)
Compilation album put together by Richard Allen and featuring, among others, Magic Mushroom Band, Sun Dial, Poisoned Electrick Head, Mandragora, Dr Brown, Ozric Tentacles, Treatment, and Porcupine Tree.

Ozit Morpheus Records Deeply Vale Archive Releases
The Fall *Live At Deeply Vale Festival 1978*
Steve Hillage *Live At Deeply Vale Festival '78*
The Ruts *Live At Deeply Vale Festival, Late 1970s*
Nik Turner *Live At Deeply Vale Free Festival 1978*

Boris & His Bolshie Balalaika:
Psychic Revolution (Delerium Records)

Culture Shock:
Everything (3CD set: all their albums plus demos and extras)

Hawkwind:
This Is Your Captain Speaking... Your Captain Is Dead (11 x CD, EMI/Parlophone)
Spirit Of The Age 1976 – 1984 (3 x CD, Atomhenge)
The Dream Goes On 1984 – 1997 (3 x CD, Atomhenge)
All the early albums, and two thorough anthologies.

Here & Now:
Give And Take and *All Over The Show* (Their early albums, reissued by Atomhenge)
Coaxed Out From Oxford (Terrific live show, released by 4Zero)

Inner City Unit:
The President's Tapes (Flicknife Records)
Now part of a Gonzo ICU reissue sequence. 'Stonehenge, Who Knows'.

The Levellers:
Levelling The Land (Edsel, expanded edition)
Their second album, includes 'Battle Of The Beanfield'.

Magic Mushroom Band:
The Politics Of Ecstasy (The first MMB album, long out of print but pending reissue)
Feed Your Head (Cassette only live album, later reissued on CD by Voiceprint)
For MMB and Astralasia keep an eye on www.magickeye.com

Omnia Opera:
Omnia Opera / Red Shift (2-CD compilation of their Delerium recordings, Atomhenge)

Ozric Tentacles:
Vitamin Enhanced (6 x CD, Snapper Records – the festival days of the Ozrics)
Jurassic Shift (Snapper Records – their mainstream breakthrough)

Smartpils:
No Good No Evil (Bluurg Records)

Spirits Burning with Bridget Wishart
Earth Born (CD, Voiceprint)

Treatment:
Treatment (Live at 'Club Dog', Number! Records)

Zounds:
Can't Cheat Karma (7" Single, Crass)
The Curse of Zounds, *The Redemption of Zounds* (New albums, 2001 and 2011)

Further Viewing

A Curious Life – The Story of the Levellers (Dir. Dunstan Bruce, On The Fiddle)
Bickershaw Festival: Volumes 1 & 2 (Dir. Various, Ozit Morpheus)
Deeply Vale Festivals (Dir. Various, Ozit Morpheus)
Glastonbury (Dir. Julian Temple, 20th Century Fox)
Glastonbury Fayre 1971 (Dir. Nic Roeg, Odeon Entertainment)
Message to Love – Isle of Wight Festival 1970 (Dir. Murray Lerner, Sanctuary)
Stonehenge 1984: A Midsummer Night Rock Show (Al Stokes, Floating World)

Jim and his mare, Barnstone Railway Site, Notts (Dave Fawcett)
Raffle ticket courtesy Kev

PYRAMID ARTS..

STONEHENGE GRAND RAFFLE 50p
Help support our festival.
All money raised will go to pay and contribute to the main stage, Festival Aid, Convoy Mag, Polytantric, St Johns hospital, Youth CND, site newsletter etc
DAILY DRAWS AT 11.00pm NIGHTLY

Where Are They Now?

ANGEL FLAME brings her dance and performance skills to Space Ritual and The Crazy World of Arthur Brown, among others.

BORIS ATHA is now self-employed, providing services to the legal profession. He reached the 2010 World Finals for Table Football, and also runs a small Table Football operations and hire business. Married to the punk performance poet 'Briggsy', he still performs occasionally with his legendary Bolshie Balalaika.

PAUL BAGLEY continues to perform with the classic festival band Omnia Opera.

KEITH BAILEY still performs and records with different versions of Here & Now. He contributed to a BBC 4 television documentary on the free festival scene.

GARY BAMFORD continued to perform with various 2000DS line-ups. He died in 2011 after a tragic road accident in Jamaica.

ADRIAN BELL is a writer whose work includes the highly regarded football book *Fever Hitch* about his beloved Sheffield United.

ANGIE BELL describes herself as "a ceramic artist, living on Earth, and an occasional stick twiddler."

STEVE BEMAND makes music as one half of The Timelords and with Hawkwind members as T.O.S.H. and as The Elves Of Silbury Hill. He's also made available on-line recordings from his various Bath band associations.

STEVE BUBBLE releases music under his own name and as Bubbledub Soundsystem.

RICHARD CHADWICK has drummed for Hawkwind since 1988, becoming their second-longest serving member in their entire history.

JEREMY CUNNINGHAM records and performs with The Levellers.

CHARLIE DANCEY tells us he was a disillusioned and bomb-traumatised middle-class hippy in 1977, when the tale he told in this book took place. Since then he's worked variously as a designer, writer, illustrator, computer guru, street entertainer, and comedian. He's subsequently run his own engineering company in Glastonbury, building electric bicycle trailers.

MICHAEL DOG has run Planet Dog Records and works as a DJ and musician; along with Steve Rowlands he recorded albums under the name Pushmipulyu.

KEV ELLIS still performs in various musical situations and has most recently released solo albums under the collective title *Space Cadet* – volumes one and two are available for download.

SARAH EVANS has been a member of bands such as Heated Rollers and Jo And The Strummers, and now works in a haberdashery.

KLIVE FARHEAD plays bass with The Mighty Dub Generators.

MICK FARREN continued to perform music and worked as a lyricist, columnist, music critic, science fiction writer and chronicler of the counterculture scene. He died in July 2013 after collapsing on stage at a gig with The Deviants at London's Borderline venue.

CLAIRE GRAINGER now works as a gardener, though her musical exploits since being a member of Smartpils and Hippy Slags have included Heated Rollers and Jo And The Strummers.

OZ HARDWICK teaches, writes and recites poetry and continues to generously make available his extensive archive of rock music and festival photography, contributing images to books, magazine features and sleeve notes. He writes on an eclectic range of music for *R2* magazine.

CHRIS HEWITT keeps alive the spirit and legacy of Bickershaw and Deeply Vale festivals through his Ozit-Morpheus record label and publishing business, releasing live recordings, documentary DVDs and other documents of the festivals.

JOIE HINTON has been a member of many bands associated with the free festivals including Ozric Tentacles, Eat Static and Here & Now as well as recording several albums with Deborah Knights under the name Inverse Gravity Vehicle.

STEVE LAKE reformed Zounds in 2001 and continues to play and record under that name; their most recent album was 2011's *The Redemption of Zounds*.

PETER LOVEDAY works as an artist, counting festival posters, greetings cards, album covers, and book illustrations, among his myriad productions.

DICK LUCAS records and performs as Culture Shock, Subhumans, and Citizen Fish.

NIGEL MAZLYN JONES continues to record as a singer-songwriter. His classic albums, *Sentinel* and *Ship To Shore*, are regularly reissued and in 2014 he released his most recent work, *Raft*.

MICK MOSS writes, teaches, and makes music.

ROGER NEVILLE-NEIL returned to America, where he photographs bands and writes reviews. His 'Tales of the Action Man' noir gig reviewing styling is a regular feature of the website *Aural Innovations*.

JOHN PERRY continued to play in a reformed The Only Ones and most recently has been performing under his own name.

GLENDA PESCADO records and performs with Kraut/Spacerock band Sendelica.

PETER PRACOWNIK has become a renowned fantasy artist with his work gracing the covers of records by Astralasia and Hawkwind among others. He owns a shop in North Cornwall and records music with Astralasia.

JERRY RICHARDS after a stint playing with Nik Turner in Space Ritual, was a driving force behind the 21st Century reimaging of Hawklords and also works as a composer of film and television soundtracks.

DAVE ROBERTS has worked as a tour manager and merchandiser with Hawklords and other psychedelic and spacerock bands.

ADRIAN SHAW has recorded albums under his own name, and with bands such as Bevis Frond and the reimagined 21st Century version of Hawklords. He continues to perform live with Bevis Frond and released his latest solo album in September 2015.

DAVID STOOKE has painted vistas and characters of the free festival scene, his work appearing on-line and in books such as *Travelling Daze*.

JAKE STRATTON-KENT is a practicing magician and is a respected writer on the subject.

SWORDFISH has, aside from his on-going membership of trance rock band Astralasia, worked as a musician, producer and songwriter with many notable musicians, including an acclaimed album with Judy Dyble. In 2015 he invoked the legacy of the Magic Mushroom Band with a new album, The Mushroom Project.

NIK TURNER continues to perform and record with a multitude of bands and musicians, including versions of Nik Turner's Fantastic All-Stars, Space Ritual and Inner City Unit and has also most recently released albums under his own name.

WAYNE TWINING is a member of Astralasia and The Mushroom Project.

BOB WHITFIELD lives in Bath and works as a photographer.

SIMON WILLIAMS specialises in web, audio and video design.

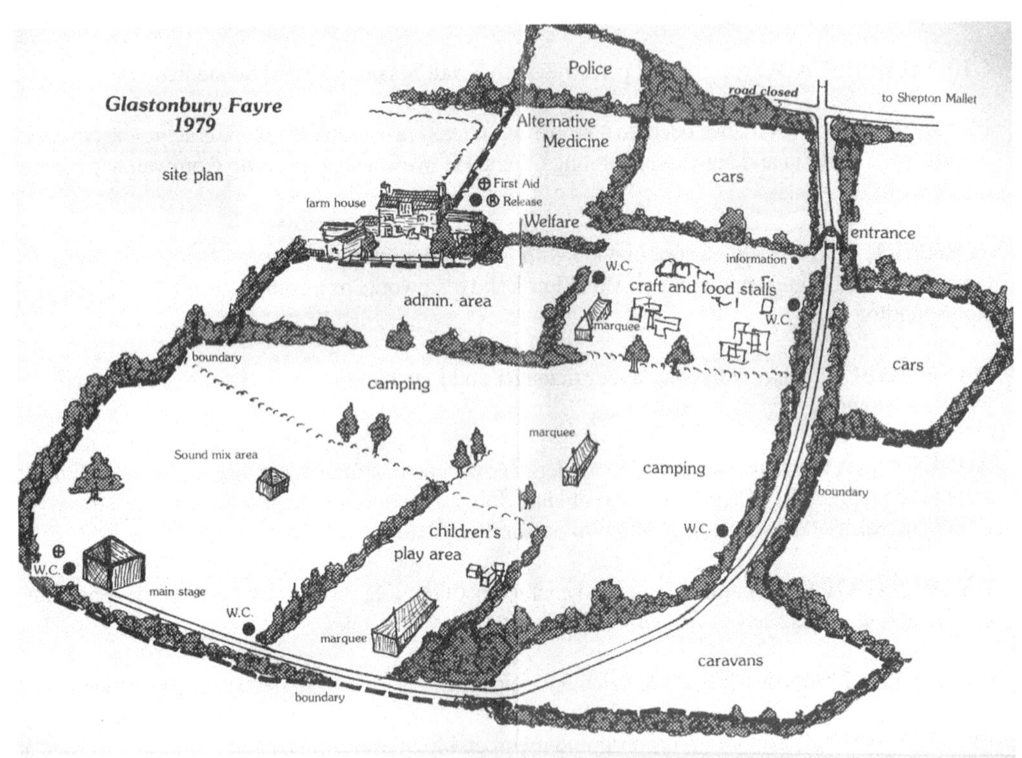

Scan courtesy of Ben Lovegrove

About the Authors:

Ian Abrahams is the author of *Hawkwind: Sonic Assassins*, *Strange Boat – Mike Scott & The Waterboys* and, with Bridget Wishart, *Festivalized: Music, Politics & The Alternative Culture*. He has also written for *Record Collector, R2, Shindig!, Vive Le Rock, The Guardian, The Independent* and others. He lives in Cornwall and has two retired greyhounds which have never been to a muddy festival, tied on the end of a string.

Connect with Ian:

Follow Ian on Twitter: http://twitter.com/Abrahams_Ian
Find Ian on Facebook: http://facebook.com/ianabrahams.musicjournalist
Read Ian's Blog: http://spacerockreviews.blogspot.com

Bridget Wishart performed with many notable festival bands during the 1980s and early 90s, including Hawkwind, Hippy Slags, The Demented Stoats, and Next Year's Big Thing. Retiring from music in the mid-90s she moved on to contribute dance and choreography with Techno Pagan and then, in 1995, along with Tim Carroll, formed the UV design company Temple Décor, who, among their credits, provided backdrops for the WOMAD festival. In 2002 she was lured out of musical retirement by American composer and musician Don Falcone to work with his spacerock collective, Spirits Burning. Since then she's also joined experimental outfit Omenopus, co-created the Arabic-toned Djinn with Hawkwind bandmate

Alan Davey, and guested with psych and spacerock bands such as Spaceseed, Mooch, Hola One and Automo Tone. Alongside her husband, Martin Plumley, she is one-half of Chumley Warner Bros, mixing Bridget's vocals and EWI with Martin's guitar and co-vocals.

Connect with Bridget:

Find Bridget on Facebook: http://facebook.com/bridget.wishart
Bridget on Soundawesome: http://bridget.wishart.soundawesome.com
Bridget with Spirits Burning: http://spiritsburning.com
Bridget with Omenopus: http://omenopus.com

Robert Newton Calvert: Born 9 March 1945, Died 14 August 1988 after suffering a heart attack. Contributed poetry, lyrics and vocals to legendary space rock band Hawkwind intermittently on five of their most critically acclaimed albums, including Space Ritual (1973), Quark, Strangeness & Charm (1977) and Hawklords (1978). He also recorded a number of solo albums in the mid 1970s. CENTIGRADE 232 was Robert Calvert's first collection of poems.

Hype 'And now, for all you speeding street smarties out there, the one you've all been waiting for, the one that'll pierce your laid back ears, decoke your sinuses, cut clean thru the schlock rock, MOR/crossover, techno flash mind mush. It's the new Number One with a bullet … with a bullet … It's Tom, Supernova, Mahler with a pan galactic biggie …' And the Hype goes on. And on. Hype, an amphetamine hit of a story by Hawkwind collaborator Robert Calvert. Who's been there and made it back again. The debriefing session starts here.

Rick Wakeman is the world's most unusual rock star, a genius who has pushed back the barriers of electronic rock. He has had some of the world's top orchestras perform his music, has owned eight Rolls Royces at one time, and has broken all the rules of composing and horrified his tutors at the Royal College of Music. Yet he has delighted his millions of fans. This frank book, authorised by Wakeman himself, tells the moving tale of his larger than life career.

There are nine Henrys, pur ported to be the world's first cloned cartoon charac ter. They live in a strange lo fi domestic surrealist world peopled by talking rock buns and elephants on wobbly stilts.

They mooch around in their minimalist universe suffer ing from an existential crisis with some genetically modified humour thrown in.

Marty Wilde on Terry Dene: "Whatever happened to Terry becomes a great deal more comprehensible as you read of the callous way in which he was treated by people who should have known better many of whom, frankly, will never know better   of the sad little shadows of the past who eased themselves into Terry's life, took everything they could get and, when it seemed that all was lost, quietly left him ... Dan Wood ing's book tells it all."

Rick Wakeman: "There have always been certain 'careers' that have fascinated the public, newspapers, and the media in general. Such include musicians, actors, sportsmen, police, and not surprisingly, the people who give the police their employ ment: The criminal. For the man in the street, all these careers have one thing in common: they are seemingly beyond both his reach and, in many cases, understanding and as such, his only associ ation can be through the media of newspapers or tele vision. The police, however, will always require the ser vices of the grass, the squealer, the snitch, (call him what you will), in order to assist in their investiga tions and arrests; and amaz ingly, this is the area that seldom gets written about."

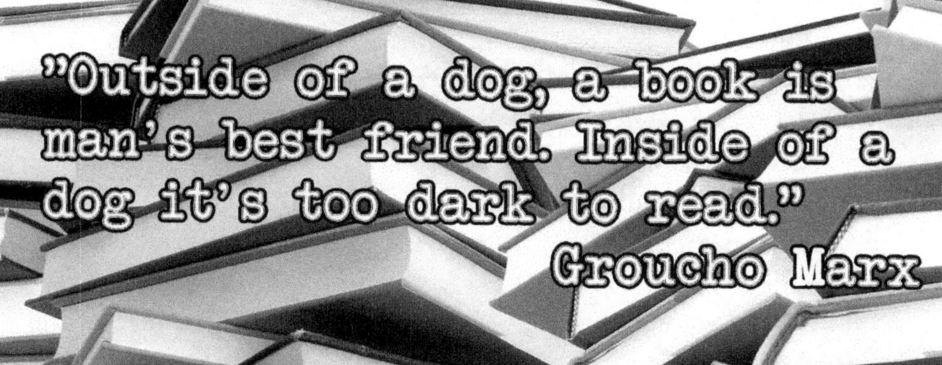

Bill Harkleroad joined Captain Beefheart's Magic Band at a time when they were changing from a straight ahead blues band into something completely different. Through the vision of Don Van Vliet (Captain Beefheart) they created a new form of music which many at the time considered atonal and difficult, but which over the years has continued to exert a powerful influence. Beefheart rechristened Harkleroad as Zoot Horn Rollo, and they embarked on recording one of the classic rock albums of all time Trout Mask Replica - a work of unequalled daring and inventiveness.

Politics, paganism and .... Vlad the Impaler. Selected stories from CJ Stone from 2003 to the present. Meet Ivor Coles, a British Tommy killed in action in September 1915, lost, and then found again. Visit Mothers Club in Erdington, the best psychedelic music club in the UK in the '60s. Celebrate Robin Hood's Day and find out what a huckleduckle is. Travel to Stonehenge at the Summer Solstice and carouse with the hippies. Find out what a Ranter is, and why CJ Stone thinks that he's one. Take LSD with Dr Lilly, the psychedelic scientist. Meet a headless soldier or the ghost of Elvis Presley in Gabalfa, Cardiff. Journey to Whitstable, to New York, to Malta and to Transylvania, and to many other places, real and imagined, political and spiritual, transcendent and mundane. As The Independent says, Chris is "The best guide to the underground since Charon ferried dead souls across the Styx."

This is is the first in the highly acclaimed vampire novels of the late Mick Farren. Victor Renquist, a surprisingly urbane and likable leader of a colony of vampires which has existed for centuries in New York is faced with both administrative and emotional problems. And when you are a vampire, administration is not a thing which one takes lightly.

"The person, be it gentleman or lady, who has not pleasure in a good novel, must be intolerably stupid."

Jane Austen

Los Angeles City of Angels, city of dreams. But sometimes the dreams become nightmares. Having fled New York, Victor Renquist and his small group of Nosferatu are striving to re establish their colony. They have become a deeper, darker part of the city's nightlife. And Hollywood's glitterati are hot on the scent of a new thrill, one that outshines all others immortality. But someone, somewhere, is med dling with even darker powers, powers that even the Nosferatu fear. Someone is attempting to summon the entity of ancient evil known as Cthulhu. And Ren quist must overcome dissent in his own colony, solve the riddle of the Darklost (a being brought part way along the Nosferatu path and then abandoned) and combat powerful enemies to save the world of humans!

Canadian born Corky Laing is probably best known as the drummer with Mountain. Corky joined the band shortly after Mountain played at the famous Woodstock Festival, although he did receive a gold disc for sales of the soundtrack album after over dubbing drums on Ten Years After's performance. Whilst with Mountain Corky Laing recorded three studio albums with them before the band split. Follow ing the split Corky, along with Mountain gui tarist Leslie West, formed a rock three piece with former Cream bassist Jack Bruce. West, Bruce and Laing recorded two studio albums and a live album before West and Laing re formed Mountain, along with Felix Pappalardi. Since 1974 Corky and Leslie have led Mountain through various line ups and recordings, and continue to record and perform today at numer ous concerts across the world. In addition to his work with Mountain, Corky Laing has recorded one solo album and formed the band Cork with former Spin Doctors guitarist Eric Shenkman, and recorded a further two studio albums with the band, which has also featured former Jimi Hendrix bassist Noel Redding. The stories are told in an incredibly frank, engaging and amusing manner, and will appeal also to those people who may not necessarily be fans of

To me there's no difference between Mike Scott and The Waterboys; they both mean the same thing. They mean myself and whoever are my current travel ling musical companions." Mike Scott Strange Boat charts the twisting and meandering journey of Mike Scott, describing the literary and spiritual references that inform his songwriting and explor ing the multitude of locations and cultures in which The Waterboys have assembled and reflected in their recordings. From his early forays into the music scene in Scotland at the end of the 1970s, to his creation of a 'Big Music' that peaked with the hit single 'The Whole of the Moon' and onto the Irish adventure which spawned the classic Fisher man's Blues, his constantly restless creativity has led him through a myriad of changes. With his revolving cast of troubadours at his side, he's created some of the most era defining records of the 1980s, reeled and jigged across the Celtic heartlands, reinvented himself as an electric rocker in New York, and sought out personal renewal in the spiritual calm of Findhorn's Scot tish highland retreat. Mike Scott's life has been a tale of continual musical exploration entwined with an ever evolving spirituality. "An intriguing portrait of a modern musician" (Record Collector).

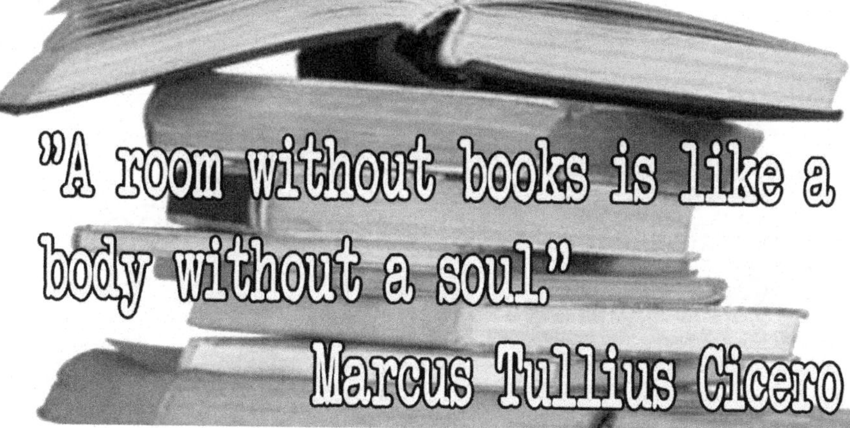

The OZ trial was the longest obscenity trial in history. It was also one of the worst reported. With minor exceptions, the Press chose to rewrite what had occurred, presumably to fit in with what seemed to them the acceptable prejudices of the times. Perhaps this was inevitable. The proceedings dragged on for nearly six weeks in the hot summer of 1971 when there were, no doubt, a great many other events more worthy of attention. Against the background of murder in Ulster, for example, the OZ affair probably fades into its proper insignifi cance. Even so, after the trial, when some newspapers realised that maybe something important had hap pened, it became more and more apparent that what was essential was for anyone who wished to be able to read what had actually been said. Trial and judgment by a badly informed press became the order of the day. This 40th Anniversary edition includes new material by all three of the original defendants, the prosecuting barrister, one of the OZ schoolkids, and even the daughters of the judge. There are also many illustrations including unseen material from Feliz Dennis' own collection...

Merrell Fankhauser has led one of the most diverse and interesting careers in music. He was born in Louisville, Kentucky, and moved to California when he was 13 years old. Merrell went on to become one of the innovators of surf music and psychedelic folk rock. His travels from Hollywood to his 15 year jungle experience on the island of Maui have been documented in numerous music books and magazines in the United States and Europe. Merrell has gained legendary international status throughout the field of rock music; his credits include over 250 songs published and released. He is a multi talented singer/songwriter and unique guitar player whose sound has delighted listeners for over 35 years. This extraordi nary book tells a unique story of one of the founding fathers of surf rock, who went on to play in a succession of progressive and psychedelic bands and to meet some of the greatest names in the business, including Captain Beefheart, Randy California, The Beach Boys, Jan and Dean... and there is even a run in with the notorious Manson family.

On September 19, 1985, Frank Zappa testified before the United States Senate Commerce, Technology, and Transportation committee, attacking the Parents Music Resource Center or PMRC, a music organization co founded by Tipper Gore, wife of then senator Al Gore. The PMRC consisted of many wives of politi cians, including the wives of five members of the committee, and was founded to address the issue of song lyrics with sexual or satanic content. Zappa saw their activities as on a path towards censor ship,and called their proposal for voluntary labelling of records with explicit content "extor tion" of the music industry. This is what happened.

"Good friends, good books, and a sleepy conscience: this is the ideal life."

Mark Twain